THOMAS HOCCLEVE'S
COMPLAINT AND DIALOGUE

EARLY ENGLISH TEXT SOCIETY
No. 313
1999

And [...] so noble a prince muweth
So excellent [...] and honurable
Shal haue needith good auise soothly,
þt it may be plesant and delitable
To his noblesse it is nat couenable
To write to a prince so famous
But it be good mateer and vertuous

Thogh craft wel who shal an hous edifie
Looth nat thee to withoute auisement
If he be wys for to his mental ye
Craft is it seen purposed cast & ment
How it shal wrought been / elles al is shent
Certes for the defaute of good forsighte
Mis tiden thinges þt wel tyde mighte

This may been seyn to thee in thy makynge
I good inwey- thogh [...] nat hangte J trolle
Seyn to thy penne / and thee [...] werke heedfully
Or thow auysed be wel and wel knowe
What thow shalt write o Thomas many a throwe
Smerteth the fool / for lak of good auys
But no wight hath it smerted þt is wys

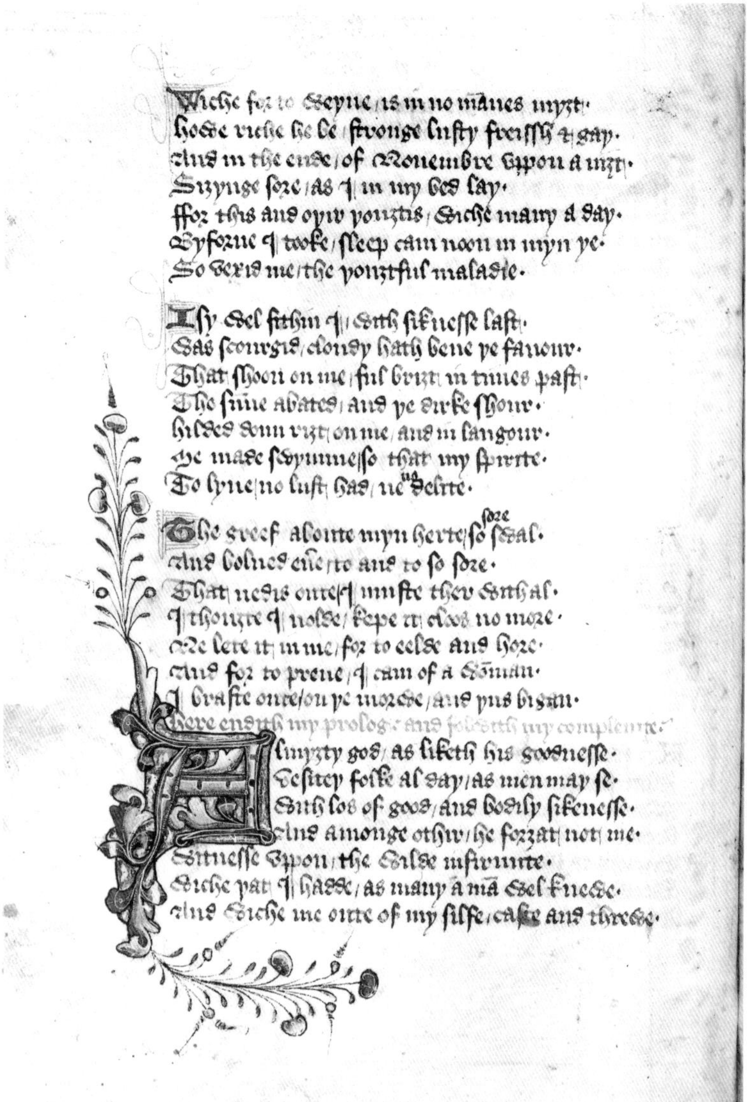

Which for to weyve is in no mannes myght
Howe riche he be stronge lusty freissh & gay
And in the ende of Novembre upon a nyght
Sighynge sore as I in my bed lay
ffor this and othir thoughtis which many a day
Byforne I tooke sleep cam noon in myn ye
So vexid me the thoughtful maladie

I sy wel sithin I with siknesse last
Was scourgid cloudy hath bene ye favour
That shoon on me ful bright in times past
The sunne abated and ye dirke shour
Hilded doun right on me and in langour
Me made swymme so that my spirite
To lyve no lust had ne delite

The greef aboute myn herte so sore swal
And bolned evere to and to so sore
That nedis oute I muste therwith al
I thoughte I nolde kepe it cloos no more
Ne lete it in me for to eelde and hore
And for to preve I cam of a womman
I braste oute on ye morwe and thus bigan

Here endith my prologe and folwith my compleinte

Almyghty god as liketh his goodnesse
Visitep folke al day as men may se
With los of good and bodily sikenesse
And amonge othir he forgat not me
Witnesse upon the wilde infirmite
Which pat I hadde as many a man wel knewe
And which me oute of my silfe caste and threwe

Oxford, Bodleian Library, MS Selden Supra 53, f. 76v

THOMAS HOCCLEVE'S COMPLAINT AND DIALOGUE

EDITED BY

J. A. BURROW

Published for
THE EARLY ENGLISH TEXT SOCIETY
by the
OXFORD UNIVERSITY PRESS
1999

OXFORD

UNIVERSITY PRESS

Great Clarendon Street, Oxford OX2 6DP

Oxford University Press is a department of the University of Oxford
and furthers the University's aim of excellence in research, scholarship,
and education by publishing worldwide in

Oxford New York

Athens Auckland Bangkok Bogotá Bombay Buenos Aires Calcutta
Cape Town Chennai Dar es Salaam Delhi Florence Hong Kong Istanbul
Karachi Kuala Lumpur Madras Melbourne Mexico City Mumbai
Nairobi Paris São Paulo Singapore Taipei Tokyo Toronto Warsaw

and associated companies in Berlin Ibadan

Oxford is a registered trade mark of Oxford University Press

Published in the United States
by Oxford University Press Inc., New York

British Library Cataloguing in Publication Data

Data available

Library of Congress Cataloging in Publication Data

Data applied for

ISBN 0-19-722317-6

1 3 5 7 9 10 8 6 4 2

Typeset by Joshua Associates Ltd., Oxford
Printed in Great Britain
on acid-free paper by
Print Wright Ltd., Ipswich

PREFACE

I am glad to acknowledge permission to print texts, and include plates, from manuscripts in Durham University Library and the Bodleian Library, Oxford. I am grateful to those libraries for their help, and also to the Coventry City Record Office and the Beinecke Library, Yale University. Traugott Lawler kindly transcribed for me the glosses in the Yale manuscript. Charles Blyth with great generosity made available the concordance of Hoccleve's holograph writings prepared for his forth-coming edition of the *Regiment of Princes*. Without it my own work would hardly have been possible. Ian Doyle, Judith Jefferson, and Thorlac Turville-Petre have given me valuable advice; and I am also variously indebted to Colin Burrow, Malcolm Godden, Richard Higgins, Anne Hudson, Nick Mayhew, and Michael Seymour. The Council of the Early English Text Society is also to be thanked for accepting an edition in which normalisation plays some part, contrary to their general policy.

CONTENTS

INTRODUCTION

The *Complaint* and *Dialogue* are the first two poems in the sequence of
linked writings by Thomas Hoccleve now known as his *Series*. They are
followed by *Jereslaus' Wife*, with its prose moralisation; then *Learn to
Die*, concluding with a prose passage on the joys of heaven, and *Jonathas
and Fellicula*, again with a prose moralisation. This concludes the work,
although the Durham MS, a copy made by Hoccleve himself, adds an
envoy stanza. The *Series* was first edited by F. J. Furnivall, from the
Durham copy, in his EETS volume of 1892, and subsequently, from the
same source, by Ruth Pryor in a 1968 doctoral dissertation.[1]

The present edition confines itself to the *Complaint* and *Dialogue*
because its prime concern is with restoration of the text. The need for
such restoration arises, in those two items only, from the state of the
Durham MS. For the latter and greater part of the *Series* this careful
holograph copy provides an authoritative text, challengeable only on the
rare occasions where Hoccleve miswrites; and that text can be read in
the revised Furnivall edition, where it is reproduced with sufficient
accuracy. However, Hoccleve's copy of the whole *Complaint* and the
Dialogue up to line 252 was lost when someone extracted the first two
quires from the Durham MS, leaving a gap which the Tudor antiquary
John Stow filled with his own transcript from some other source. Both
Furnivall and Pryor give Stow's text; but an original text can be restored
with considerable confidence, from two sources: the other five scribal
copies, one of which (Selden) is distinctly superior to Stow, together
with the Hoccleve holograph corpus, which extends to some 7000 lines
of verse (the rest of the Durham *Series* and the contents of the two

---

[1] *Hoccleve's Works: I The Minor Poems*, ed. F. J. Furnivall, EETS, ES 61 (1892),
subsequently revised by J. Mitchell and A. I. Doyle and reissued in 1970 in one volume
together with I. Gollancz's edition of the other minor poems; Mary Ruth Pryor, 'Thomas
Hoccleve's Series: An Edition of MS Durham Cosin V iii 9', Ph.D. Thesis (University of
California, Los Angeles, 1968). Editions of portions of the *Series* may be found in the
following: E. P. Hammond, *English Verse between Chaucer and Surrey* (Durham, NC,
1927), the later part of the *Dialogue*; J. A. Burrow, *English Verse 1300–1500* (London,
1977), the earlier part of the *Complaint*; M. C. Seymour, *Selections from Hoccleve* (Oxford,
1981), the whole *Complaint*, extracts from the *Dialogue*, the earlier part of *Jonathas and
Fellicula*; B. O'Donoghue, *Thomas Hoccleve: Selected Poems* (Manchester, 1982), the whole
Complaint, extracts from the *Dialogue*. It was Hammond who first proposed *Series* as an
overall title: *English Verse*, p. 69.

Huntington holographs). This extensive corpus displays the poet's linguistic, orthographic, and metrical practice with remarkable consistency; so it serves to establish norms by which the scribal tradition can be judged and corrected—an editorial opportunity unparalleled elsewhere in Middle English verse.[2]

This edition, accordingly, sets out to restore the texts of the *Complaint* and lines 1–252 of the *Dialogue*, following them with the holograph text of the rest of the *Dialogue* (ll. 253–826). At the same time, the opportunity has been taken to explicate, annotate, and gloss the two poems in more detail than was possible for previous editors.

MANUSCRIPTS

Durham, University Library MS Cosin V. iii. 9

A fair copy of the *Series* made by Hoccleve himself, probably in the latter part of the period 1421–26, in his 'accomplished secretary hand'.[3] A final envoy stanza, not present in other copies, directs the volume to Joan, Countess of Westmorland (d. 1440). The book had lost its first two quires of eight (containing 95 stanzas, up to *Dialogue* 252) by the time it came into the possession of the Tudor antiquary John Stow (1525?–1605). Stow supplied the missing matter on ten paper leaves, probably some time between 1561 and 1598.[4] The manuscript later passed into the possession of the poet William Browne of Tavistock (1591?-1643?), who inscribed his name on ff. 3^r and 14^r.[5] A note 'Geo. Davenport.

---

[2] Hoccleve's other major writing, the *Regiment of Princes*, survives only in scribal copies. A new edition, with the text restored according to similar principles, is in preparation by Charles R. Blyth. I am particularly grateful to those concerned with that edition for making available to me their complete concordance of the Hoccleve holographs. Without its help, the present edition would hardly have been possible.

[3] From A. I. Doyle's forthcoming catalogue of Durham MSS, in which a fuller account will be found. I am grateful to Dr. Doyle for making his entry available to me. The Durham MS was identified as an authorial copy by H. C. Schulz, 'Thomas Hoccleve, Scribe', *Speculum*, 12 (1937), 71–81. Furnivall anticipated him, *Minor Poems*, pp. xliv-xlv, but retracted, p. xlix there.

[4] The hand was identified as Stow's by Furnivall, *Minor Poems*, p. xliv. Stow's 1561 *Chaucer* included the *Letter of Cupid* without comment; but the ascription of that poem to Hoccleve in the Arguments to Speght's 1598 *Chaucer* was probably due to Stow, who wrote 'Epistle of Cupid' on f. 24^v of the Durham MS, opposite *Dialogue* 754. Stow advised Speght: see Anne Hudson, 'John Stow', in *Editing Chaucer: The Great Tradition*, ed. P. G. Ruggiers (Norman, OK, 1984), pp. 53–70; p. 56.

[5] Browne published a modernised version of *Jonathas* from the Durham MS in his *Shepherd's Pipe* (1614). He projected an edition of Hoccleve's poems: see A. S. G. Edwards,

1664.' locates the manuscript at that time in Durham, where it has remained ever since.[6]

1. f. 3^r Prologue to *Complaint*.
2. ff. 3^v–8^v *Complaint*.
3. ff. 9^r–26^v *Dialogue*.
4. ff. 26^v–49^r *Jereslaus' Wife*.
5. f. 49^{r-v} Prologue to Moralisation.
6. ff. 50^r–52^v Moralisation of *Jereslaus' Wife*.
7. ff. 52^v–74^r *Learn to Die*.
8. f. 74^v Prologue to a Lesson on All Saints' Day.
9. ff. 75^r–77^r A Lesson on All Saints' Day.
10. ff. 77^r–79^r Prologue to *Jonathas*.
11. ff. 79^v–93^r *Jonathas*.
12. ff. 93^v–95^r Moralisation of *Jonathas*.
13. f. 95^r Envoy to the Countess of Westmorland.

Paper ff. 1–2 s. xvii, ff. 3–12 s. xvi; parchment ff. 13–95. ii + 93 leaves. ff. 3–12 about 225mm by 165mm; ff. 13–95 232mm by 170mm. Collation of parchment section: III–XII^8, XIII^4 (lacks 4, blank?). Catchwords by Hoccleve.

Stow's copy has 5 stanzas to a page, reducing to 4 (ff. 11^v, 12^r) and 3 (f. 12^v). Stanzas spaced. No decoration, though 3–line spaces are left for large capitals, unsupplied, at *Complaint* 1 and 36, and *Dialogue* 1. Hoccleve's copy has 3 stanzas to a page, spaced and separated by horizontal lines. Gold initials, on blue and red with sprays, 3- or 2-line (as indicated in Furnivall), mark major text divisions. Blue or gold paraphs, generally alternating, mark changes of speaker and other notabilia. Headings in larger script; glosses in margin, with paraphs.

Oxford, Bodleian Library MS Selden Supra 53 (SC 3441)

A copy of the *Series* preceded by Hoccleve's *Regiment of Princes* (as in the Coventry MS) and followed by Lydgate's *Dance Macabre* (*IMEV* 2591, as in Coventry and MSS Bodley, Laud, and Yale). Later hands

'Medieval Manuscripts Owned by William Browne of Tavistock', in *Books and Collectors 1200–1700: Essays Presented to Andrew Watson*, ed. J. P. Carley and C. G. C. Tite (London, 1997), pp. 441–49.
[6] Davenport wrote 'Perlegi. 1666' at the end of the MS. He also supplied two paper sheets at the beginning, with an entry on Hoccleve on f. 2^r, taken from a standard biographical source, the *Relationes Historicae de Rebus Anglicis* of John Pits (Paris, 1619).

add two supplementary stanzas from the B Text of Lydgate's *Dance* (*IMEV* 1867), a French moral quatrain, and a text of *Earth upon Earth* (*IMEV* 704). The main hand, of early in the second quarter of the fifteenth century, writes a good anglicana formata. The same hand copied Bodleian Library MS Digby 230.[7]

1. ff. 1^r–76^r Hoccleve, *Regiment of Princes* (imperfect).
2. f. 76^{r-v} Prologue to *Complaint*.
3. ff. 76^v–83^v *Complaint*.
4. ff. 83^v–98^r *Dialogue*.
5. ff. 98^v–115^r *Jereslaus' Wife*.
6. f. 115^v Prologue to Moralisation.
7. f. 116^{r-v} Moralisation of *Jereslaus' Wife* (imperfect).
8. ff. 117^r–133^r *Learn to Die* (imperfect).
9. f. 133^r Prologue to a Lesson on All Saints' Day.
10. ff. 133^v–134^v A Lesson on All Saints' Day.
11. ff. 134^v–136^r Prologue to *Jonathas*.
12. ff. 136^r–146^v *Jonathas*.
13. ff. 146^v–148^r Moralisation of *Jonathas*.
14. ff. 148^r–158^v Lydgate, *Dance Macabre*, Text A.
15. f. 158^v Lydgate, *Dance Macabre*, Text B, ll. 65–80.
16. f. 158^v Four rhyming French lines.
17. f. 159^v *Earth upon Earth*.

Parchment. ii + 159 + ii leaves; 250mm by 185mm. Collation: two quires of eight missing before f. 1, with loss of *Regiment* 1–896; I–II⁸, III⁸ (lacks 7, with loss of *Regiment* 2129–84), IV⁸ (lacks 3–6, 8, with loss of *Regiment* 2367–590, 2647–702), V–XV⁸, XVI⁸ (lacks 3, with loss from *Jereslaus* moralisation and *Learn to Die* 1–21), XVII–XX⁸, XXI⁸ (lacks 7, 8, no loss of text). Catchwords; quire and leaf signatures.

4 stanzas to a page (as commonly in *Regiment* manuscripts). Stanzas spaced; stanza initials blue on red. Blue 2–line initials with red decoration and 4–line initials of gold with blue and red decoration mark minor and major text divisions. Headings and marginal glosses red, with blue or red paraphs. On f. 118^r a picture showing Death, a dying man, and (probably) the disciple (cf. *Learn to Die* 85–6).

---

[7] So Doyle, *PMLA*, 83 (1968), 25.

Coventry, City Record Office MS Acc. 325/1

A copy of the *Series* preceded by Hoccleve's *Regiment of Princes* (as in Selden) and followed by Lydgate's *Dance Macabre* (*IMEV* 2591, as in Selden and MSS Bodley, Laud, and Yale). The same hand, mid fifteenth-century anglicana formata, follows with six of Chaucer's minor poems and the metrical version of *Mandeville's Travels* (*IMEV* 248.5).[8] Another hand, from f. 98ʳ, copies two siege poems, *Titus and Vespasian* (*IMEV* 1881) and Lydgate's *Siege of Thebes* (*IMEV* 3928), followed in a hand of *c.* 1500 by some moralising verses (*IMEV* 502.5).

1. ff. 1ʳ–40ʳ Hoccleve, *Regiment of Princes*.
2. f. 40ʳ⁻ᵛ Prologue to *Complaint*.
3. ff. 40ᵛ–43ʳ *Complaint*.
4. ff. 43ᵛ–49ʳ *Dialogue*.
5. ff. 49ʳ–56ʳ *Jereslaus' Wife*.
6. f. 56ʳ Prologue to Moralisation.
7. ff. 56ʳ–57ʳ Moralisation of *Jereslaus' Wife*.
8. ff. 57ʳ–63ᵛ *Learn to Die*.
9. ff. 63ᵛ–64ʳ Prologue to a Lesson on All Saints' Day.
10. f. 64ʳ⁻ᵛ A Lesson on All Saints' Day.
11. ff. 64ᵛ–65ʳ Prologue to *Jonathas*.
12. ff. 65ʳ–69ᵛ *Jonathas*.
13. ff. 69ᵛ–70ʳ Moralisation of *Jonathas*.
14. ff. 70ʳ–74ᵛ Lydgate, *Dance Macabre*, Text A.
15. ff. 75ʳ–76ʳ Chaucer, *ABC of the Virgin*.
16. ff. 76ʳ–77ʳ Chaucer, five balades (*Bukton, Purse, Gentilesse, Stedfastnesse, Truth*).
17. ff. 77ᵛ–95ᵛ *Mandeville's Travels* (imperfect).
18. ff. 96ʳ–97ᵛ blank.
19. ff. 98ʳ–129ᵛ *Titus and Vespasian* (imperfect).
20. ff. 130ʳ–136ᵛ blank.
21. ff. 137ʳ–167ʳ Lydgate, *Siege of Thebes*.
22. ff. 167ᵛ–168ʳ Moralising verses.

[8] The Chaucer texts are printed and the whole manuscript described and discussed by A. I. Doyle and G. B. Pace, 'A New Chaucer Manuscript', *PMLA*, 83 (1968), 22–34. Doyle there describes the first hand as 'an upright, bold but somewhat ungainly *cursiva (anglicana) formata*', dating it to the middle or third quarter of the fifteenth century. The same hand wrote Bodleian MS Douce 372: 'They may be products of the professional book-trade, though not of the highest quality in writing, and semiprofessional copyists are not out of the question' (p. 23). See also the description by N. R. Ker, *Medieval Manuscripts in British Libraries*, Vol. II, *Abbotsford-Keele* (Oxford, 1977), pp. 410–12.

Parchment. ii + 168 + 1 leaves; 320mm by 250mm. Collation: I^8 (lacks 5–8, no loss of text), II^8 (lacks 1–3, no loss of text), III–XII^8, XIII^8 (lacks 1, 3–6, 8, with loss from *Mandeville* after ll. 2001, 2161, 2321), XIV^8 (lacks 6, 7, no loss of text), XV–XVIII^8, XIX^8 (lacks 2, with loss of *Titus* 5145 to end), XX–XXIII^8. Catchwords; quire and leaf signatures, suggesting that some 180 leaves were detached before the present f. i (Ker, pp. 410, 412).

Two columns to a page, generally five stanzas to a column. Stanzas spaced. 4- or 5-line initials of gold with blue and red decoration mark text divisions. Headings red with blue paraphs; glosses red with blue paraphs, incorporated in the text column. On f. 1 a picture of a man in white gown and round cap (Aristotle?) standing in front of green hills.

Oxford, Bodleian Library MS Bodley 221 (SC 27627)

A copy of the *Series* followed by Lydgate's *Dance Macabre* (*IMEV* 2591) and Hoccleve's *Regiment of Princes*, in a mid fifteenth-century secretary hand. The order of contents is the same as in MSS Laud and Yale, to which Bodley 221 is related textually, sharing with LY some Midland and Northern forms, relicts derived from or through their common ancestor β. It has more Northern features than LY, however: e.g. *thof* for *thogh*, -*s* endings for 3rd pers. sg. pres. indic. of verbs, and pronouns *there* and *them* for *hire* and *hem*.

1. f. 1^r Prologue to *Complaint*.
2. ff. 1^v–6^v *Complaint*.
3. ff. 6^v–15^v *Dialogue* (imperfect).
4. ff. 15^v–28^r *Jereslaus' Wife*.
5. f. 28^{r-v} Prologue to *Moralisation*.
6. ff. 28^v–30^r *Moralisation of Jereslaus' Wife*.
7. ff. 30^r–42^v *Learn to Die*.
8. f. 42^v Prologue to a Lesson on All Saints' Day.
9. ff. 42^v–44^r A Lesson on All Saints' Day.
10. ff. 44^r–45^r Prologue to *Jonathas*.
11. ff. 45^r–52^v *Jonathas*.
12. ff. 52^v–53^v *Moralisation of Jonathas*.
13. ff. 53^v–62^r Lydgate, *Dance Macabre*, Text A.
14. ff. 62^v–130^v Hoccleve, *Regiment of Princes* (imperfect).

Paper, with parchment inner and outer bifolia in each quire. i + 130 + i leaves; 292mm by 215mm; ff. 57–8 and 60–70 torn. Collation: I^{20} (lacks

12, with loss of *Dialogue* 400–551, i.e. the content of two leaves), II–III²⁶, IV–V²², VI²² (lacks 2, 17–22, with loss of *Regiment* 4106–181 and 5271 to end). Catchwords; quire and leaf signatures.

Between 5 and 6 stanzas to a page. Unspaced stanzas, separated by horizontal red lines (sometimes misplaced). Rhymes bracketed in red. Alternating red and blue paraphs mark stanzas. Blue initials, 4– to 2– line, for major text divisions, with red decoration. Headings red; marginal glosses red.

Oxford, Bodleian Library MS Laud misc. 735 (SC 1504)

A copy of the *Series* followed by Lydgate's *Dance Macabre* (*IMEV* 2591) and Hoccleve's *Regiment of Princes*, made in the third quarter of the fifteenth century by the same scribe who copied the Yale MS, in an anglicana script with secretary forms. The two copies were evidently taken from the same exemplar. The same contents, in the same order, are set out in the same way on the page.⁹ Their texts are very close; and Laud shares with Yale, as well as the closely related Bodley MS, some Midland and Northern forms derived from or through their common ancestor β: e.g. *mich* for Hoccleve's *moche* or *mochel*, *luffe* for *loue*.

1. f. 1ʳ Prologue to *Complaint*.
2. ff. 1ᵛ–5ʳ *Complaint* (imperfect).
3. ff. 5ᵛ–15ᵛ *Dialogue*.
4. ff. 15ᵛ–27ᵛ *Jereslaus' Wife*.
5. ff. 27ᵛ–28ʳ Prologue to Moralisation.
6. ff. 28ʳ–29ʳ Moralisation of *Jereslaus' Wife*.
7. ff. 29ʳ–41ʳ *Learn to Die*.
8. f. 41ʳ Prologue to a Lesson on All Saints' Day.
9. ff. 41ʳ–42ʳ A Lesson on All Saints' Day.
10. ff. 42ᵛ–43ᵛ Prologue to *Jonathas*.
11. ff. 43ᵛ–51ᵛ *Jonathas*.
12. ff. 51ᵛ–52ʳ Moralisation of *Jonathas*.
13. ff. 52ᵛ–61ᵛ Lydgate, *Dance Macabre*, Text A.
14. ff. 62ʳ–134ʳ Hoccleve, *Regiment of Princes*.

Paper, with parchment inner and outer bifolia in each quire. ii + 134 + i leaves; 305mm by 220 mm. Collation: I¹⁴ (lacks 2, with loss of *Complaint*

⁹ The scribe evidently followed his exemplar's paging, as a comparison of the paging of his two copies shows. An early discrepancy is due only to the loss of Laud's second leaf, a loss not represented in the current folio numbering.

74–146), II–IX^{14}, X^{16} (lacks 10–16, no loss from *Regiment*). Catchwords; quire and leaf signatures.

Between 5 and 6 stanzas to a page. Each stanza enclosed in a ruled box, with horizontal lines red (as in Yale). Rhymes bracketed in red. Alternating red and blue paraphs mark stanzas. Blue initials, 6– to 2–line, for major text divisions, with red decoration; elaborate 9–line black and red initial at *Complaint* 36. Headings red; marginal glosses red, with blue paraphs.

New Haven, Conn., Yale University, Beinecke Library MS 493.

A copy of the *Series* followed by Lydgate's *Dance Macabre* (*IMEV* 2591) and Hoccleve's *Regiment of Princes*, made in the third quarter of the fifteenth century by the same scribe who copied the Laud MS, in an anglicana script with secretary forms.[10] The two copies were evidently taken from the same exemplar. The same contents, in the same order, are set out in the same way on the page. Their texts are very close; and Yale shares with Laud, as well as the closely related Bodley MS, some Midland and Northern forms derived from or through their common ancestor β.

1. f. 1^{r} Prologue to *Complaint*.
2. ff. 1^{v}–6^{v} *Complaint*.
3. ff. 6^{v}–16^{v} *Dialogue*.
4. ff. 16^{v}–28^{v} *Jereslaus' Wife*.
5. ff. 28^{v}–29^{r} Prologue to Moralisation.
6. ff. 29^{r}–30^{r} Moralisation of *Jereslaus' Wife*.
7. ff. 30^{r}–41^{r} *Learn to Die*.
8. f. 41^{r} Prologue to a Lesson on All Saints' Day.
9. ff. 41^{v}–42^{r} A Lesson on All Saints' Day.
10. ff. 42^{r}–43^{r} Prologue to *Jonathas*.
11. ff. 43^{r}–50^{v} *Jonathas*.
12. f. 51^{r-v} Moralisation of *Jonathas*.
13. ff. 51^{v}–60^{v} Lydgate, *Dance Macabre*, Text A.
14. ff. 61^{r}–133^{v} Hoccleve, *Regiment of Princes* (imperfect).

[10] I have not myself inspected the Yale MS, relying upon photocopies kindly supplied by the Beinecke Library and upon the description of the manuscript in B. A. Shailor, *Catalogue of Medieval and Renaissance Manuscripts in the Beinecke Rare Book and Manuscript Library, Yale University*, 2 vols (Binghamton, NY, 1984–87), II 475–78. Professor T. Lawler very kindly transcribed the glosses for me.

Paper, with parchment inner and outer bifolia in each quire. ii + 134 + i leaves; 288mm by 208mm. Collation: I–IV^{14}, V^{14} (lacks 11, no loss of text), VI–VIII^{14} IX^{14} (lacks 4, with loss of *Regiment* 3976–4049), X^{14} (lacks 12, 14, no loss of text). Catchwords; quire and leaf signatures.

Between 5 and 6 stanzas to a page. Each stanza enclosed in a ruled box, with horizontal lines red (as in Laud). Rhymes bracketed in red. Alternating red and blue paraphs mark stanzas. Blue initials, 6– to 2– line, for major text divisions, with red decoration. Headings red; marginal glosses red, with blue paraphs.

TEXT AND METRE: THE HOLOGRAPH SECTION

Hoccleve's *Complaint* and *Dialogue* present, so far as their text is concerned, a somewhat peculiar challenge. Of their 1239 lines, the last 574 survive in the poet's own fair copy (from *Dialogue* 253 to the end); but that holograph of the *Series*, the Durham manuscript, has lost its first two quires. Hence for the preceding 665 lines (*Complaint* and *Dialogue* 1–252) an editor must depend upon scribal copies. Since editorial treatment of this earlier section of text relies, in a variety of ways, upon evidence provided by the holograph section, it is the latter which must be considered first here.

TEXT

The present edition provides for the first time a full collation of substantive variants in the five scribal copies of the holograph *Dialogue*: the three manuscripts in the Bodleian Library, Bodley, Laud, and Selden, and the manuscripts at Yale and at Coventry.[11] The collation is of some interest in itself, since it offers a rare opportunity to compare scribal copies of a medieval text with one made by the author himself; but there can be no question of these presenting any general challenge to the authority of that holograph. The text of the holograph section must be the holograph text. The only exceptions to this rule occur at ten places where the scribal copies clearly correct a scribal error or omission made by Hoccleve himself in copying out the Durham text: at lines 291, 373, 380, 381, 404, 426, 445, 586, 665, and 667. Authors do naturally

---

[11] Neither Furnivall, Pryor, nor Seymour record variants where the holograph text of the *Dialogue* is available.

make mistakes when transcribing their own works. The two holograph copies of Hoccleve's *Learn to Die*, where they can be compared, show five such miswritings.[12]

The chief purpose of the collation, however, is to establish certain facts about the relationships of the scribal copies to the holograph and to each other, in order to assist in editing that part of the text where holograph evidence is lacking. I have found that the 574 lines of the holograph *Dialogue* are sufficient for the present purpose. Full collation of the whole of the rest of the *Series*, which would provide more evidence, has not been undertaken here.

The Variant Original

One cannot assume that a holograph copy is necessarily the original from which scribal copies descend; and such is indeed demonstrably not the case here.[13] The Durham holograph was a fair copy of the *Series* made, according to its concluding stanza, for presentation to the Countess of Westmorland. The absence of this envoy stanza from all the scribal copies itself suggests that they do not descend from the Durham manuscript—which the Countess may have kept (if she ever received it) shut away in a chest. All the evidence, in fact, points to the descent of these copies from an authorial original other than Durham, what I shall call the Variant Original or VO. This 'Variant Original' may have taken one of two forms: either as the author's working papers showing the text in a different state from the stage represented by the fair copy in Durham, or as another fair copy representing that state.[14] This is an awkward but not a surprising circumstance. It will explain how the scribal copies come to attest the correct reading in the ten lines mentioned above, where Durham has mistakes. It also explains the varying distribution of Latin glosses. The scribal copies have five of the

---

[12] Excursus I here compares the texts in the Durham manuscript and in Huntington HM 744. HM 744 breaks off after line 672. Authorial miswritings in the Capgrave holographs are studied by P. J. Lucas, 'An Author as Copyist of his own Work: John Capgrave OSA (1393–1464)', in *New Science out of Old Books: Studies in Manuscripts and Early Printed Books in Honour of A. I. Doyle*, ed. R. Beadle and A. J. Piper (Aldershot, 1995), pp. 227–48.

[13] One may compare John Capgrave's *Abbreviacion of Cronicles*. Here, according to the editor, the holograph and the scribal copy both descend from a common exemplar, 'presumably an earlier holograph or autograph': John Capgrave, *Abbreuiacion of Cronicles*, ed. P. J. Lucas (EETS, 285, 1983), pp. xl–xlii.

[14] Three authorial fair copies of his poetry survive: the Durham *Series* and Huntington HM 111 and 744. There is also evidence that he made other copies now lost: of the *Regiment of Princes* for John Duke of Bedford, and of 'balades' for Edward Duke of York. See my *Thomas Hoccleve*, p. 23.

six glosses found in the holograph *Dialogue*, but they also share four which are not found there. These presumably were present in the Variant Original.[15] Furthermore, the one Durham gloss lacking in the scribal copies was most probably added in that copy for the particular benefit of the Countess of Westmorland, for it concerns Humphrey Duke of Gloucester, her nephew.

If the scribal copies all descend from a lost Variant Original, not from Durham, it can only be the VO text that we may hope to reconstruct in that earlier part of the *Complaint-Dialogue* where Durham fails.[16] The question then arises: how different were Hoccleve's two texts? The case of a later *Series* item, *Learn to Die*, offers a parallel, for two holographs of this poem have survived. These two copies exhibit some textual variation. In Excursus I here, I identify 69 substantive variants in the 672 lines where the copies can be compared: 15 differences in word-order, 31 substitutions of one word for another, and 23 other variants. Comparison is much more hazardous in the case of the *Complaint-Dialogue*, given the loss of VO; but study of the scribal copies in the holograph section suggests that the relationship between the two authorial texts was not unlike that directly observable in the case of *Learn to Die*.

It cannot be assumed that the scribal copies are witnessing to VO wherever they agree in a reading different from the holograph. I argue below that these manuscripts must all have derived, not from VO itself, but from a scribal copy of that original. This lost copy, the archetype or latest common ancestor of the surviving scribal copies, must be postulated, I believe, in order to account for the many ancestral readings in those manuscripts which cannot, for metrical and other reasons, be attributed to Hoccleve in VO.[17] Leaving these readings aside for the moment, one is left with a set of ancestral readings which at least may be due to Hoccleve himself, since they fail no test of sense or metre. Many of these are slight and trivial, and there is no way of telling for sure which of them are authorial, although the parallel case of *Learn to Die*

---

[15] The six glosses in Durham occur at lines 260, 457, 543, 638, 723, 733. The scribal copies lack Durham's gloss at 543, but have extra glosses at lines 351, 386, 400, and 407. All five have the gloss at 260 in a form different from Durham's. Scribal glosses, since they belong to the Variant Original not to the Durham text, are given here in the notes to those lines. Hoccleve seems to have varied the number and character of his glosses, presumably with some eye on the likely readers of the copy in question. The Durham *Learn to Die* has more than twice as many glosses as the corresponding Huntington lines.

[16] The Stow copy (non-holograph section only) shares the same descent. See below p. xxxvi.

[17] See below, pp. xxvi–xxvii.

suggests that some certainly are. One can be rather more confident only on occasions where the variant is of a sort not normally associated with scribal rewriting or error; but even here, of course, a considerable degree of uncertainty remains.[18]

The following is a complete list of all the archetypal readings in the holograph section, 48 in all, which could possibly represent places where the Variant Original differed from the Durham text. Since I have excluded only those archetypal readings which fail clear tests of sense or metre, the list may well include a significant number of cases where non-authorial readings happen to pass these tests; but the analogy of *Learn to Die*, for what it is worth, suggests that the list may not be grossly overlong. I give the Durham reading first, followed by the possible VO:[19]

272 it is bicomen: þat it bicome is. 329 me hath: hath me. 333 &: or. 350 bond: knotte. 359 And it along for to drawe: And for to drawe it along. 362 Or: And. 364 & dul : ful dul. 399 þat: it. 419 Which thee: And þat. 480 lyth: is. 493 in: by. 502 lightly nat cacche may: nat lightly may cacche. 517 now: thow. 518 þat: the. 522 By: In. 525 now is: is now. 534 is: was. 540 Yee sikir freend: Sikir freend yee. 546 or: and. 549 bownden am I deepe: deepe I bownden am. 550 God: him. 573 Henri: Herry. 584 many a place elles: many anothir place. 595 into: vnto. 659 tyme: whyle. 660 aftir þat (þat *added above line*): aftirward. 660 tolde he: he tolde. 663 man: wight. 670 Which: That. 672 That: Which. 680 Bewar: Be wys. 699 hem haast: haast hem. 706 to: for to. 707 shewen hem: hem shewe. 722 with: thurgh. 727 Now: O. 727 of: on. 731 Thogh: That. 734 Men: Man. 741 haue hokir: hokir haue. 749 Thomas han been: Han been Thomas. 756 swart wrooth: blak wrooth. 760 therof was I: I was therof. 781 neuere it yit I: yit I neuere it. 808 the: his. 824 or: and. 825 shal pourge: my gilt. 826 My gilt: Shal pourge.

Of these, some represent variations in single closed-class, function words: conjunctions (333, 362, 546, 731, 824), prepositions (493, 522, 595, 706, 722, 727), pronouns (399, 670, 672), and a demonstrative

---

[18] On distinguishing between authorial and 'transmissional' variants, see W. W. Greg, *Collected Papers*, ed. J. C. Maxwell (Oxford, 1966), p. 387.

[19] I exclude here places where Hoccleve miswrites, and also VO glosses. In reconstructing archetypal readings here and elsewhere I assume that, where two of the three lines of transmission (S, C, and β) agree in a non-holograph reading against another in the third, they normally represent the archetype. Possible VO readings are given here in the spellings that Hoccleve himself uses elsewhere.

(518). Variations involving other single words occur at 350, 364, 480, 517, 534, 550, 573, 659, 660, 663, 680, 727, 734, 756, and 808. The most striking of these last are: bond: knotte, God: him, man: wight, Now: O, swart: blak. Two minor rewritings occur at 419 and 584. The remaining sixteen items all show variations in word-order: 272, 329, 359, 502, 540, 549, 660, 699, 707, 741, 749, 760, 781, 825, 826. These range from simple two-word reversals (e.g. 329) to more extensive reorderings (e.g. 359). The most drastic occurs in the very last couplet of the *Dialogue*, lines 825–6. Here Durham reads:

> and þat shal pourge, I hope,
> My gilt / as cleene / as keuerchiefs dooth sope.

The alternative represented by the scribal copies has:

> and þat my gilt, I hope,
> Shal pourge as cleene as keuerchiefs dooth sope.

These variations are not unlike, in their general character, those authorial alterations to be observed in the two holographs of *Learn to Die* (Excursus I), though extensive revisions are more common in the latter. On the other hand, comparison with the list (below, pp. xxvi–xxvii) of archetypal readings which cannot be ascribed to Hoccleve will suggest that scribal error has also played a part. Yet even if every one of the variations listed above were, for the purposes of argument, to be credited to Hoccleve himself in VO, the differences between that and the Durham text could still not be regarded as very substantial. The evidence suggests little more than some sporadic tinkering by the author (together with the occasional inadvertent substitution, no doubt) at 48 points in 574 lines of verse.[20] At no point is the sense significantly altered; nor do most of the variants show any distinct superiority in expression. Indeed, the relationship between the two authorial texts can hardly be determined on the evidence provided by the holograph *Dialogue*. Thus, in the closing couplet one might argue that Durham represents a later improvement on VO, since it avoids an awkward placing of the object *gilt* in advance of the verb governing it, *pourge*. Or is it rather that VO improves upon Durham by achieving a more

---

[20] In the 672 lines where the two *Learn to Die* holographs run parallel I find 69 substantive variants. In 938 lines of the complete *Learn to Die*, I find 93 variants which may represent VO as against the Durham holograph. The figures for *Jereslaus* are not dissimilar: 115 possible VO readings in 980 lines. In *Jonathas* there appears to have been more frequent variation: 106 possible cases in 672 lines.

forceful last line? Again, if VO's *knotte* is regarded as a strong revision of Durham's *bond* (350), what is one to make of the place where Durham has *swart* against VO's *blak* (756)?[21]

It might seem important to determine which of the two copies best represents Hoccleve's latest intentions, as a matter of general editorial principle. Yet the present edition—fortunately perhaps—is in no position to make such a choice. There can be no question of replacing Durham with a reconstructed VO text in the holograph section, while in *Complaint* and *Dialogue* 1–252 a reconstructed VO is the only recourse. So the present edition can do no other than offer a text of split authority: a reconstructed Variant Original up to *Dialogue* 252, and a Durham version therafter. Current textual theorists argue forcibly against editions (such as older *King Lear*s) which combine more than one state of a text into a composite version, on the grounds that the resulting composite never existed at any one 'textual moment' in the past.[22] Yet in the peculiar circumstances of the *Complaint-Dialogue* there is no satisfactory alternative. To represent the non-holograph section by an unreconstructed scribal text, as Furnivall does, is to offer the reader much that Hoccleve demonstrably could never have written at any textual moment. Fortunately, the two states of his original do not appear to have differed so much that one should feel any deep concern at joining them together. Modern scholars make much of the instability or 'mouvance' of medieval vernacular texts, often with justice; but in this case the instability was evidently quite slight. It is not, after all, as if one were obliged to transfer in midstream from an A-Text to a B-Text of *Piers Plowman*.

The Scribal Copies

In an edition such as this, which sets out to present as faithfully as possible what Hoccleve wrote—albeit on two separate occasions—reconstruction of the text of the Variant Original section must be a prime task. For this purpose, collation of the scribal copies in the other, holograph, section provides necessary information. Once one has set aside all the 58 variants from Durham which at least might correctly represent

---

[21] Evidence from the rest of the *Series* fails to settle the question of priority between the two versions. For a brief discussion, see Excursus I below. The matter requires further study.

[22] Thus James Thorpe, *Principles of Textual Criticism* (San Marino, Cal., 1972), p. 190: 'It seems to me improper for an editor to try to construct a single "definitive" reading text out of various versions which represent different authorial intentions at different times'. So also Hans Zeller, 'A New Approach to the Critical Constitution of Literary Texts', *Studies in Bibliography*, 28 (1975), 231–64, and many writers since.

VO (including, that is, the ten places where Durham has a miswriting), one is left with variants which may with some confidence be regarded as scribal. From these, certain inferences can be drawn, both about the relations between the scribal copies themselves and also about the text of the scribal archetype from which all five evidently descend.

All five copies are clearly terminal. Each of them, that is, has enough separative or incorrigible errors of its own to exclude the possibility that any of the others might descend from it. There is, on the other hand, very clear evidence of a close relationship between the three mid fifteenth-century manuscripts Bodley, Laud, and Yale (B, L, and Y). In their contents these three books are identical, and unlike either Selden or Coventry. Each begins with the *Series*, following that with Lydgate's *Dance Macabre*, and ending with Hoccleve's *Regiment of Princes*. Each devotes almost the same number of folios to its texts, with between five and six stanzas to a page.[23] Textually, too, they are closely related. B lacks lines 400–551; but its remaining 422 lines show 40 agreements with L and Y.[24] Most of these evidently derive from a common ancestor of B, L, and Y, which may be called β. Some of these β variants belong to common scribal types: changes in word-order (289, 652, 672), addition of *to* before infinitives (359, 392, 745). Others are more singular, for example *depayntest* (670) and the spelling *cretes* for *certes* (328). Furthermore, it can be shown that the three manuscripts relate to β according to the following stemma:[25]

[23] For further details, see above on the manuscripts.

[24] At lines 272, 280, 289, 328, 331 (*truste*), 335, 340, 342 (*So ny*), 347, 349, 350, 356, 359 (*to dilate*), 364, 365, 371 (*not fynde*), 382, 384, 385, 392 . . .557, 570, 580, 583, 593, 595, 611, 619 (*not I not*), 638, 648, 652, 654, 670, 671, 672, 744, 745, 759, 762, 787. BLY are further distinguished by the sidenotes *Amicus* at 369 and also probably *Thomas* at 420 (B defective) and possibly *Amicus* at 449 (not in Y, B defective). In the gloss to 457, L and Y insert *Thomas* (B defective). Elsewhere in the *Series*, BLY share the loss of a stanza, *Learn to Die*, 848–54.

[25] In her stemma of the *Regiment of Princes* manuscripts, M. S. Marzec groups B, L, and Y together, but she relates them differently:

'The Latin Marginalia of the *Regiment of Princes* as an Aid to Stemmatic Analysis', *Text*, 3 (1987), 279. (Also in Greetham, 'Challenges').

B has only three variants in common with L or Y individually, none of them genetically significant (271, 554, 631). On the other hand, L and Y are themselves a closely related pair. They were copied by the same scribe, and quite clearly from the same exemplar, λ. This exemplar was evidently a careful copy of β (better, certainly, than B), but it bequeathed some distinctive variants to the LY scribe: *his* (260), *forward* (386), *ho* (638), and whatever forms lie behind the LY readings at 599, 616, 717, and 756.[26] L and Y also have some individual variants, sufficient to show that neither was copied from the other; but they can safely be regarded as twin witnesses to λ, itself a β witness to be set against the generally less reliable evidence of B.

Where β can be determined with confidence, as is often the case, it takes its place alongside Selden and Coventry as one of three witnesses to the readings of the archetype. S and C are themselves witnesses of unequal, but evidently independent, authority. My critical apparatus to the holograph section shows S varying from presumed VO rather less than once every five lines, whereas C varies at more than twice that frequency, including some variants which must count as quite drastic by the standards set in what is overall a conservative textual tradition (e.g. 301, 382, 620). On this evidence Coventry is, along with Bodley, the least generally trustworthy of the manuscripts, whereas Selden is distinctly the most reliable, as well as the best spelled. Yet C remains an independent witness. It is not descended from the earlier S, which has a number of errors not in C;[27] nor do the two manuscripts show convincing evidence of any other relationship, below the archetype. The readings which they share (excluding those clearly to be regarded as archetypal, where β varies) can all be explained as independent converging errors: 415 (archetypal?), 448, 455 (addition of *to*), 577 (*b/h* confusion), 675 (*b/h* confusion), 740 (addition of *to*), 762 (archetypal?). I therefore treat the C and S texts of the *Complaint-Dialogue* as independent of each other, as the texts of the *Regiment* in the same manuscripts have also been held to be.[28]

Coventry has six minor agreements with β, all of which are readily explained as results of convergent error: 263, 557, 600, 630, 694, 819. C

---

[26] LY variants: 260, 355, 378, 386, 557, 599, 616, 638, 717, 753, 756, 773. LY agreements in the 152 lines missing in B may represent either β or λ, so they cannot be considered here.

[27] C has correct readings where S errs at 300, 330, 331, 392, 415, 549, 559, 631, 686, 746, 770, 791.

[28] Marzec's *Regiment* stemma (n. 25 above) places C far away from S.

also agrees with members of the β group in small variants even more likely to be due to the same cause.[29] I therefore regard Coventry as having no genetic relation, below the archetype, with the BLY group. The evidence leads to the same conclusion in the case of Selden. S has enough errors not found in β to exclude the descent of the latter from it.[30] Some of the variants from Durham that it shares with β or members of the β group prove to represent archetypal readings which have been further varied by C.[31] There remain only two slight agreements: 392 (word-order) and 631. However, Selden's reading at 631 requires further comment. At this point an awkwardness in Hoccleve's syntax serves to explain the addition of *to* after *þat* in both β and S; but in S the addition is made, by the original scribe, as a correction above the line. This could be an independent response by S to the syntactic difficulty; but there are other corrections in S elsewhere which suggest consultation of some copy other than the main exemplar: see below pp. xxxvi–xxxvii.

The Scribal Archetype

S, C, and β, taken together, testify to a large number of readings different from what Hoccleve himself visibly wrote in the Durham holograph *Dialogue*. Of these archetypal readings the 48 listed above (p. xx) can be further assigned, with varying degrees of probability, to the Variant Original; but there remain 73 other common variants which cannot, I believe, go back to VO. The number of these variants, and the character of some of them, excludes the possibility that they may all have arisen through the workings of convergent variation, that is, accidentally. It therefore seems necessary to posit a lost scribal copy of VO from which all five scribal copies descend. The distinction between two types of reading, authorial and scribal, rests in this case very largely upon the analysis of Hoccleve's habitual metrical practice as that is clearly exhibited in his holographs, a matter to be considered in the next part of this Introduction. If that analysis is correct, and if one assumes that his practice in VO matched that consistently observable in Durham and in the two Huntington holographs, then it may safely be taken as a general rule that any line with other than ten syllables (or eleven, with final unstressed syllable) is highly suspect. This metrical

---

[29] With BY at 259; with LY at 569, 654; with B at 273, 681, 727, 798; with L at 526; with Y at 336.

[30] At lines 300, 330, 331, 415, 448, 455, 529, 549, 559, 577, 686, 740, 746, 770, 791. Marzec's *Regiment* stemma is consistent with this conclusion.

[31] At lines 326, 337, 540, 741, 776.

criterion is far more powerful than any other (significant differences of sense are rarely in question); but it can yield only somewhat approximate results. On very rare occasions indeed, the syllable-count does fail in authentic Hoccleve verse, so a very few readings ascribed here to the scribal archetype may just be his. Conversely, and much more significantly, it must be presumed that some among the readings assigned by me to VO are in fact archetypal variants which simply happen not to be unmetrical. Hence I guess that my tally of VO readings is too high, and that of archetypal readings too low; but I can see no sure way of correcting the error.[32]

The following is a complete list of the 73 readings in the holograph section of the *Dialogue* which may be ascribed, subject to the preceding caveats, to the scribal archetype. I give the Durham reading first, followed by the presumed archetypal error:[33]

258 al this: þis. 266 often: ofte. 274 and: and al. 279 knowen: knowen þat. 281 richesse: and ricchesse. 282 lent been: ben lente vs. 284 Paleses: Paleis. 288 syn: siþen. 289 hire haue ofte: here hir haue ofte (?). 314 past: passid. 319 gynneth: bigynneth to. 326 trouble myn: trouble nowe myn. 327 ay: euere. 331 signe: a signe. 331 lyte: a lite. 337 made: haue maad. 358 dwelle: to dwelle. 365 as þat: as. 371 fynde: nowe finde. 372 ay: euere. 382 Syn: Sithen. 396 Syn: Siþen. 399 is: it is. 406 it: *om.* 407 the: but þat the. 408 þat þat: þat. 409 mirour: a mirrour. 415 reewe vpon thee: on þe rewe (?). 419 mochil: moche þe. 432 smal: litile. 443 laboure: to laboure. 466 euene: euere (VO??). 483 Beforn: Bifore. 484 I: þat I. 491 also: as. 492 Syn: Siþen. 495 hem: it. 507 whan þat: whanne. 513 As þat: As. 527 trauaille: to trauaile. 531 it: *om.* 548 with: therwith. 553 it: *om.* 554 lord lige: lege lorde. 561 Vegece: *om?* 568 beforn: bifore. 581 doutelees: and þat is doutelees. 595 worthynesse: prowesse. 643 the deffaute: defaute. 644 tyde: bitiden. 662 Syn: Siþin. 677 syn: sithen. 702 haue in þat: haue þere in (?). 708 syn: siþen. 709 mene: a meene. 710 Putte: Putte it. 721 ay: euere. 727 syn: sithen. 732 haue: to haue. 732 maistrie: þe maistrie.

---

[32] 'The problem of distinguishing between revision, that is, authorial variation, and the scribal variation inevitable in manuscript transmission is probably the most delicate operation in all textual criticism', George Kane, *Chaucer and Langland: Historical and Textual Approaches* (London, 1989), p. 162. A more delicate operation than mine, seeking to distinguish in the case of each individual variant, might be attempted; but the results would here be very uncertain, I believe.

[33] As with VO (n. 19 above), I assume that, where two of the three lines of transmission agree against the third in non-holograph readings, they normally represent the archetype. Archetypal readings are given in Selden's forms, where available.

733 witnesse: witnesse it. 739 twixt: bitwixe (?). 743 thee: þou. 757 ther: *om.* 762 as: and as (?). 763 God woot: God it woote. 776 may: may þei. 778 neuere: not. 779 is: it is. 786 Syn: Siþen. 789 now: and nowe. 800 Stonde: To stonde. 802 do: to do.

This list, subject though it is to caveats, provides definite indications of the kinds of error to be looked for in the archetype, and hence also will offer guidance for conjectural emendations of archetypal readings in the non-holograph section. The only variant which substantially affects meaning occurs at 595, where the archetype showed *promesse* for an original *worthynesse*, probably under the influence of the preceding rhyme-word *promesse*. Otherwise the variants, while disrupting the syllable-count, leave the sense changed little or not at all, very often by adding, dropping, or replacing small words such as conjunctions, prepositions, and articles. The most frequently represented change concerns Hoccleve's word for 'since'. The holographs always (77x) have *syn* or, where two syllables are required, *syn þat;* but the archetype commonly replaces *syn* with *sithen,* a form never found in the holographs. In every case, this substitution produces a line with one syllable too many: 288, 382, 396, 492, 662, 677, 708, 727, and 786. The same unmetrical result follows from the replacement of *ay* by *euere* at 327, 372, and 721. Even such apparently trivial variations as *ofte* for *often* (266) or *bifore* for *beforn* (483, 568) produce the wrong number of syllables.[34] More obvious cases are *bigynneth to* for *gynneth* (319), *bitiden* for *tyde* (644), and *bitwixe* for *twixt* (739).

Omission of small words present in the holograph and presumably also in VO produces other unmetrical lines: *al* (258), *it* (406, 531, 553), *þat* (365, 408, 507, 513), *the* (643), and *ther* (757). The omission of *þat* after conjunctions is notable, since Hoccleve's systematic use or non-use of this optional extra syllable is easily misrepresented by copyists.[35] Archetypal additions of small words occur more commonly than omissions, sometimes where the original appeared elliptical: *a* (331, 331, 409, 709), *al* (274), *and* (281, 762, 789), *haue* (337), *here* (289), *it* (399, 710, 733, 763, 779), *nowe* (326, 371), *þat* (279, 484), *the* (732), *thei* (776), *to* (before infinitives, 319, 358, 443, 527, 732, 800, 802). The addition of *to* before infinitives on seven occasions is notable. Here, as elsewhere, it seems that the scribe who made such additions may have

---

[34] The holograph concordance shows that Hoccleve always writes *often,* not *ofte,* in eliding contexts where two syllables are required, as at 266. Similarly, in non-eliding contexts he always writes *beforn* not *before* where only two syllables are required, as at 483 and 568. [35] See below, p. xxxiii.

been sometimes motivated by a desire to correct the syllable-count, being unaware of the syllabic value of Hoccleve's unstressed *e*. Thus, the original line 'Rial might and eerthely magestee' (274, with trisyllabic *eerthely*) might have seemed to need the added *al*, just as *to* might have appeared to regularise 'If þat me list in this mateere dwelle' (358). So also with, for example, lines 281, 371, and 548. Yet it cannot be said that the archetypal copy of VO, though necessarily even earlier than the early Selden, exhibited much understanding of, or concern for, the metrical rule governing Hoccleve's verse.

It may seem rash to rely so heavily on a metrical rule in distinguishing readings of VO from those of the archetype in the holograph section, and still more rash, perhaps, to use it in reconstructing VO from the archetype in the non-holograph section. However, as has been demonstrated most recently by Judith Jefferson, Hoccleve observed the syllable-count with quite remarkable consistency, not only in Durham but also in the two Huntington holographs, the contents of which, though composed over a period of some twenty years, exhibit no changes in the poet's metrical practice. There is accordingly every reason to believe that VO observed the same rules. It will be necessary to give an account of these before going on to consider the textual problems of the non-holograph section.

METRE

Study of Hoccleve's metre enjoys the very unusual advantage of three holograph manuscripts containing some 7000 lines of verse carefully copied by the poet himself. I leave aside here the question of the rhythmical structure of his verse line. This matter, which awaits further investigation, seems unlikely to have much bearing on decisions about the text. In any case, there can be little doubt that the prime general metrical rule for Hoccleve, as for his French contemporaries, concerned the number of syllables, not the distribution of stresses. It has long been understood that his lines generally conform to a rule of ten syllables, with or without an extra unstressed syllable at the line-end;[36] but two studies in particular

---

[36] Furnivall (*Minor Poems*, xli) observes that 'so long as he can count ten syllables by his fingers, he is content'. Similarly George Saintsbury: 'Occleve did do his best to get ten syllables into each line. His work is almost wholly decasyllabic', *A History of English Prosody*, Vol. I (London, 1906), p. 232. So also Eleanor Hammond: 'Hoccleve manages pentameter badly, and is insensitive to the weave of stressed and unstressed syllables, so long as their number is constant at ten', *English Verse between Chaucer and Surrey* (Durham, NC, 1927), p. 55.

have revealed the extraordinary consistency with which he observes this rule. One is a remarkable but neglected study published as long ago as 1916 by J. H. Kern. Kern had no access to the manuscripts and depended on the EETS texts, unrevised at that time and not trustworthy in every detail; yet he showed a profound understanding of Hoccleve's orthography and metre, even in minutiae.[37] The recent study by Judith Jefferson, drawing on the computer-generated concordance of the whole holograph corpus, fully supports Kern's conclusions and provides further evidence of the poet's meticulous cultivation of the decasyllabic line.[38] My own present analysis, confined to the 574 lines of the holograph *Dialogue*, confirms their results.

It is clear from these lines, as from the more broadly-based studies by Kern and Jefferson, that Hoccleve took pains to ensure that his lines were both constructed and spelled in such a way that their conformity to the syllabic 'rule of ten' would be apparent to readers of suitable competence. In particular, he evidently felt able to assume that such a reader would be familiar with the rules governing unstressed *e* in verse of his kind. There can be no doubt that wherever Hoccleve writes ⟨e⟩ in unstressed position (most often, but not always, final) it is to be pronounced as a syllabic /ə/, subject to certain counter-rules to be specified shortly.[39] By the 1420s, in fact, pronunciation of final /ə/ had already become a thing of the past in general spoken English;[40] but Hoccleve must have had some grounds for confidence that at least those readers acquainted with the practice of French poets and of such English predecessors as Chaucer and Gower would be able to realise his verses appropriately.

The same readers could evidently be relied upon to know that ⟨e⟩ was not always to be sounded. Hoccleve's verse takes for granted certain 'deletion rules', most but not all of which affect final /ə/. These may be stated as follows:

---

[37] 'Zum Texte einiger Dichtungen Thomas Hoccleve's', *Anglia*, 39 (1916), 389–494, supplemented by his note 'Hoccleve's Verszelle', *Anglia*, 40 (1916), 367–9.

[38] 'The Hoccleve Holographs and Hoccleve's Metrical Practice', in *Manuscripts and Texts: Editorial Problems in Later Middle English Literature*, ed. D. Pearsall (Cambridge, 1987), pp. 95–109.

[39] This fundamental fact has been disputed, but ineffectively. A problem arises in cases where strokes added by the author to final consonantal letters may be taken to indicate suspensions of final ⟨e⟩. See further p. li.

[40] 'By the early fifteenth century all final /ə/ have probably dropped', Roger Lass, in *The Cambridge History of the English Language*, Vol. II *1066–1476*, ed. N. Blake (Cambridge, 1992), p. 81.

1. Final unstressed /ə/ is lost by elision when it immediately precedes
a word beginning with a vowel or ⟨h⟩. In Hoccleve's verse, elision occurs
usually before all kinds of word beginning with ⟨h⟩: native lexical words
such as *hoot* (356) and *hond* (713), as well as *he*, *him*, *how* etc. and words
of French origin such as *honurable*. Kern notes elision also before *who*, as
at *Dialogue* 653.[41] A few examples of non-elision before ⟨h⟩ do occur in
the holographs; but the single case in the holograph *Dialogue*, at 805, is
susceptible of explanation: see 1.1 below.

1.1. Rhymes show that elision of final unstressed /ə/ does not occur
across the break at the line-end, that is, before a following line beginning
with vowel or ⟨h⟩; but the mid-line break or caesura, most often marked
by a virgule, does not prevent it. There are, however, three examples of
non-elision in this position in the holograph *Dialogue*: 'The fool thurgh
loue of this lyf present' (260, with a virgule after *love* in Selden, but not
in Durham), 'To muse longe / in an hard mateere' (496), and 'Lo heer
the fourme / how I hem obeye' (805). The same licence at this point in
the line has been observed in Chaucer and in Middle French poets.[42]

1.2. Words ending in consonant + ⟨le⟩, ⟨ne⟩, ⟨re⟩, or ⟨we⟩ commonly
elide. Thus: 'To cronicle his actes / were a good deede' (603), 'Yit
Thomas herkne a word and be souffrable' (369), 'And pardee freend /
þat may nat hyndre a myte' (509), and 'Me for to make / and folwe it
am I prest' (553). There are three exceptions (two of them in mid-line
position): 'Freend / I nat medle of matires grete' (498), 'My lord of
Gloucestre / is it nat so' (534, where *Gloucestre* has three syllables), and
'Passen / as dooth the shadwe of a tree' (276).[43]

1.3. The word-ending ⟨ye⟩ or ⟨ie⟩, when unstressed, counts for only one
syllable, with loss of /ə/, but for two when it carries some degree of
metrical emphasis. Thus, *studie* is disyllabic at lines 379, 398, 422, and 500
(*studies*), but trisyllabic at 659. Similarly, *ladyes* is disyllabic at 806, but
trisyllabic at 706 and 822 (*ladyes*). In the rhymes at 765–8 the syllable-count
requires monosyllabic unstressed endings: *varie* / *contrarie* / *aduersarie*;
but the ending can be, and probably is, disyllabic under secondary stress in
the rhymes at 562–5 (*chiualrie* etc.) and 730–3 (*vilenye* etc.).[44]

[41] 'Zum Texte', p. 413, with other examples, implying initial /h/ in *who* as today.
[42] See Bernhard ten Brink, *The Language and Metre of Chaucer*, 2nd edn revised
F. Kluge, trans. M. Bentinck Smith (London, 1901), pp. 186–7; G. Lote, *Histoire du Vers
Français*, Part I *Le Moyen âge*, 3 vols (Paris, 1949–55), III, 81–2; *The Poetical Works of
Alain Chartier*, ed. J. C. Laidlaw (Cambridge, 1974), p. 55.
[43] Cf. Lote, *op. cit.*, III, 80–2.
[44] It may be noted that, though this ending can lose final /ə/ in rhyme, as at 765–8,

2. Words ending in vocalic ⟨y⟩ may delete that syllable when the sound combines with a following vowel ('synaloepha'). Thus, *many a* commonly counts as two syllables only, at 336, 479, 536, 569, 584, and 649. Similarly *body and* (402) and *bisy ynow* (788). *Studie* (see 1.3 above) is also affected: 'Thy bisy studie aboute swich mateere' (302, also 424, 504). So also *stithie* (440). But this deletion is optional. It does not operate at 441, 551, 557, or 605.[45]

3. Words with two unstressed vowels separated by a liquid or nasal consonant delete one syllable.[46] So *euele* (adverb), *euene, euere, euery*, and *neuere* have two syllables only, reduced to one where the final /ə/ elides. Thus: 'Ones freend / and holde euere therupon' (353, two syllables), 'As euere it was at any tyme or this' (367, one syllable). Similarly, Hoccleve regularly treats the verb *considere* as having three, not four, syllables, as at 760: 'Considereth / therof / was I noon auctour'. The only exception to this rule is *neuere*, disyllabic with elision but no syncope, at 339.

A reader of the Durham holograph *Dialogue* who paid attention to the forms and spellings of words, allowed the seven exceptions noted, and selected the appropriate alternative renderings, would be left with only three lines unaccounted for; and these prove to be among the ten places already noticed where Hoccleve made a slip in copying: lines 373, 380, and 381. In each of these, a reading recoverable from the scribal copies restores the syllable-count (and, in two cases, the sense). To find so few difficulties in strictly applying the 'rule of ten' to these 574 lines may arouse the suspicions of those who question the part played in such demonstrations by hypotheses concerning pronunciation of final ⟨e⟩, 'deletion rules', alternative pronunciations, and the like. These hypotheses, however, play no part in the scanning of some 140 of the 574 lines in question (e.g. 452–5), and every one of these proves to have the requisite number of syllables.

In achieving this striking degree of regularity Hoccleve employs a number of small devices, making 'choices from amongst the options

Hoccleve never rhymes such words with words like *mercy* which have no etymological /ə/ to delete.

[45] Ten Brink noted the same phenomenon ('synklisis') in Chaucer's verse: *op. cit.*, p. 184.

[46] The general principle is stated by Halle and Keyser: 'Two vowels may constitute a single position, provided they adjoin or are separated by a liquid or nasal'. Cited by G. Youmans, 'Reconsidering Chaucer's Prosody', in *English Historical Metrics*, ed. C. B. McCully and J. J. Anderson (Cambridge, 1996), pp. 185–209; p. 185.

available to him in order to maintain his decasyllabic line', as Judith Jefferson has shown.[47] Since reconstruction of the non-holograph text requires some acquaintance with these devices, I give examples here from the holograph *Dialogue*. They fall under three heads: individual word-forms, pleonastic *þat*, and word-order.

Individual Word-Forms

(a) *The*. The vowel of the definite article is subject to no general deletion rule. So on the two occasions where metre requires its deletion, Hoccleve spells to indicate the fact: 'If I lightly / nat cacche may theffect' (502), and 'Yis Thomas yis / in thepistle of Cupyde' (754). Cf. Jefferson, p. 99.

(b) *Ofte / often*. Before a following vowel or ⟨h⟩, *ofte* gives one syllable (289, 668, 684), but *often* secures a second (266).

(c) *Myself / myseluen*. Hoccleve departs from his normal form *myself* (390 etc.) to gain an extra syllable at 337: 'I with myseluen made foreward'.

(d) *Han / haue* (infinitive). Compare 'With ladyes / to haue daliance' (706) with 'Men sholde of hem han dominacioun' (734). Jefferson, p. 104.

(e) *Shul(n) / shole*. Hoccleve's normal present plural form of 'shall' is *shul* or *shuln*, both monosyllabic, but *shole* (283) gives a required extra syllable. Jefferson, p. 104.

(f) *-en / -e* (plural verbs). In eliding contexts, *-en* preserves and *-e* loses a syllable. Compare 'þat they me oghten haue in greet cheertee' (777) with 'Yee knowe it bet than I by many fold' (352).

(g) *-en / -e* (infinitives). Along with (f) and (h), this is the variant most often employed in eliding contexts, e.g. 'Now let vs stynten heere / & make a pause' (434). Compare 287, 288, 294, 303, 315, etc. (with elided *-e*) and 394, 453, 605, 707, etc. (with *-en*). Jefferson, pp. 102–3, also draws attention to variations in infinitive prefixes, *for to / to / zero*. Examples of *for to* are at 359, 570, 606, etc. A striking unprefixed infinitive is at 800 (where scribal copies add an unmetrical *to*).

(h) *-en / -e* (past participles of strong verbs). Compare 'To whom / nature yeuen hath beautee' (269) with 'That they nat foryeue haue / ne foryite' (672). With all past participles weak or strong, as

---

[47] Jefferson, p. 99, followed by discussion and examples on pp. 99–106.

Jefferson observes (pp. 101–2), the *y*- prefix is another syllabic option, employed here at 393, 515, and 726.

Pleonastic 'þat'.

After certain conjunctions and relative pronouns, *þat* may be used to provide an extra syllable (Jefferson, pp. 99–100).

(a) *As / as þat.* Compare *as* at 367, 518, 599, and 623, with *as þat* at 365, 372, 399, 485, 513, 542, 590, and 765.

(b) *If / if þat.* Compare *if* at 684 with *if þat* at 458, 686, and 787.

(c) *Til / til þat.* Compare *til* at 572 with *til þat* at 307, 402, and 406.

(d) *Syn / syn þat.* Compare *syn* at 382, 662, 677, and 786, with *syn þat* at 288, 396, and 492.

(e) *Whan / whan þat.* Compare *whan* at 610 with *whan þat* at 507.

(f) *Which / which þat.* Compare *which* at 419 with *which þat* at 464.

(g) *Whoso / whoso þat.* Compare *whoso* at 600 with *whoso þat* at 764.

Word-Order.

Cases where Hoccleve's choices in the order of words are dictated by the syllable-count cannot in their nature be entirely clear-cut. At 554, however, the unusual word-order *lord lige*, 'corrected' in all scribal copies to the customary *lige lord* (cf. *Dialogue* 180), must have been prompted by the need to lose the second syllable of *lige*: 'Next our lord lige / our kyng victorious'. Less clear examples may be seen at 269 ('yeuen hath'), 297 ('nat wole'), 334 ('nat worth were'), 357 ('were it'), 420 ('answere I shal*'*), 672 ('nat foryeue haue'), and 819 ('me putte').

It will be evident from the foregoing analysis of the holograph *Dialogue* that Hoccleve's decasyllabic verse was a delicate creation, extremely vulnerable to even the slightest of scribal variations. The evidence of scribal copies in this section fully bears this out. The Selden manuscript is a well-spelled and relatively error-free copy; but even Selden can by no means be trusted in those small matters upon which the syllable-count so often depends. Comparison with the holograph shows that Selden (and *a fortiori* the other copies) frequently fails to represent a medial or final syllabic /ə/, writes ⟨e⟩ where no /ə/ is in question, and selects a wrong alternative form. The following examples may stand for many:

> Thyng þat or this me thoghte game & play (D 255)
> Thing þat or þis / me þouȝt game & play (Selden)

Thoghte as a past tense form is always so spelled in the holographs, distinct from the past participle *thoght*. Selden reduces the line to nine syllables. Similarly:

> With soote smellynge also and odour (D 271)
> With swoot smellyng / also and odour (Selden)

Hoccleve himself varies between *-yng* and *-ynge* in gerunds (Jefferson, p, 104), and Selden's *smellyng* may correctly represent VO; but *swoot* for *soote* reduces the line to nine syllables. More commonly, however, Selden will write ⟨e⟩ where no /ə/ is in question and so produces a line which, read according to Hoccleve's practice, has too many syllables:

> Shul vs bireft be / by deeth þat ful sour is (D 285)
> Shul vs birefte be / by deeþ þat ful sour is (Selden)

Unlike strong past participles, such weak ones do not have an unstressed syllabic ending: Selden's *birefte* is both unhistorical and unmetrical. Selden also selects wrong alternative forms. Thus, in the first five types of variation in individual words given above (p. xxxii), Selden fails to represent elision of *the* (502, 754), and writes *ofte* for *often* (266), *mysilfe* for *myseluen* (337), *haue* for *han* (734), and *shal* for *shole* (283). Alternative verb forms in *-e* or *-en* can also very easily go wrong, as in:

> But he wel rule him / may in slippen eft (D 394)
> But he wel rule him / may in slippe efte (Selden)

Or again:

> þat they me oghten haue in greet cheertee (D 777)
> That they me ouȝte haue / in greet chirtee (Selden)

Such comparisons have an obvious bearing on the reconstruction of the Variant Original in the non-holograph section, a matter to which I now turn; but one incidental observation may be made here. To see how easily Hoccleve's careful syllabic practice may be misrepresented in even such a good copy as Selden can hardly fail to suggests thoughts about his master Chaucer, whose verse survives only in scribal copies. How like Hoccleve's metrical usage would Chaucer's prove to be if we had Chaucer holographs? Chaucer may well have been less fussy about details than his somewhat obsessive disciple; and in the *House of Fame* he prays to Apollo that his rhyme prove 'sumwhat agreable' even though 'som vers faile in a sillable' (1097–8). Yet that concession itself shows attention—perhaps a primary attention—to the counting of syllables; and there is every likelihood that his usage in this matter will have been much misrepresented by the scribes, as Hoccleve's was.[48]

TEXT AND METRE:
THE NON-HOLOGRAPH SECTION

The foregoing study of the holograph section of the *Dialogue* has provided two kinds of information useful for the establishment of the text in *Complaint* and *Dialogue* 1–252. Comparison with the holograph text there established some facts about the character and relationships of the scribal copies, notably the close affinity between B, L, and Y, and also about the character of the scribal copy of the Variant Original from which all five evidently descend. Since the non-holograph section is simply an adjacent part of the same text, distinguished only by the fact that the Durham MS happens to have lost the original leaves containing it, one may expect to find the same situation there, and to employ knowledge of it in determining the readings of the archetype. Furthermore, since archetypal readings most often represent those of VO itself, choices between variants in the surviving copies can draw upon knowledge of Hoccleve's metrical practice, as that is clearly displayed in the holographs: his decasyllabic line with its occasional licences, and the devices by which he achieves it. This same metrical information also plays a more essential part, once the archetypal text has been determined, in identifying unoriginalities there (what Maas calls *examinatio*) and restoring the VO which lies behind it (*divinatio*).[49] At that last stage, however, it will be necessary to draw on another kind of information, that concerning the poet's linguistic practice; for the metrical structure of his lines commonly depends for its realisation upon his customary words and word-forms.

TEXT

The Scribal Archetype

The first stage of this operation, determining the readings of the archetype, involves six copies, not five as in the holograph section.

[48] George Kane observes: 'the fact of the matter is that the manuscripts of Chaucer's poetry abound in minor variation which either certainly or possibly affects the syllabic value of the line', *Chaucer and Langland*, p. 231

[49] Paul Maas, *Textual Criticism*, trans. Barbara Flower (Oxford, 1958), p. 1.

This is because the holograph leaves missing from the Durham MS were replaced by the Tudor antiquary John Stow (1525?-1605), copying from some other source onto ten paper leaves. The relationship of his text, St, to that of the other scribal copies will be considered later; for the moment it is enough to notice the clear evidence linking St back to the same common archetype. It shares with the other copies, in fact, the majority of the 47 readings which I list below as unoriginal in that archetype (p. xlvi).

Recovering the archetypal text is not as difficult here as in many manuscript traditions of medieval writings. For one thing, some 260 of the 665 lines in question display what can only be their archetypal form, without substantive variation in any of the copies.[50] There are also many lines whose archetypal form can be determined with almost equal ease, where a variant, often in only one manuscript, shows an obvious sub-archetypal departure from the text found in the other copies (e.g. *Complaint* 3, where Laud has *rubbe* for *robbe*). In less obvious cases, consideration of the manuscript evidence is simplified by the fact that here, as in the holograph section, the three manuscripts B, L, and Y demonstrably represent an exclusive common ancestor, β. These three agree in significant sub-archetypal readings peculiar to themselves on 66 occasions—much the largest total of such agreements in any group or pair of copies—and some of their readings are very distinctive: *Complaint* 28, 148, 217, 224, 326 (a line omitted); *Dialogue* 81, 102, 118. B and Y also agree on seven occasions where L has lost a leaf, most probably representing β there too. L and Y, as previously noted, were copied by the same scribe and form a pair within the β group: [B(LY)]. Their common source, λ, is represented by eight variants only. It was evidently a more careful copy than B (or B's exemplar), which has a much larger number of variants peculiar to itself.[51]

There remain the three copies Selden, Coventry, and Stow. Selden, the earliest of the manuscripts, has only a handful of agreements with C or St, all of them easily understood as independent converging errors.[52] S is also independent of β; but, in addition to four trifling agreements, it has three other readings, introduced as 'corrections' by the original scribe, which suggest that he was there consulting a second copy

---

[50] This total includes 28 lines where manuscripts show marginal or interlinear insertions, erasures, or wrong ordering of lines, but agree otherwise in their readings.

[51] The eight LY variants are at C13, 177, 314, 316, 319, 342; D37, 160. B, by contrast, has more than 80 variants of its own.

[52] With Coventry: C136, 316, 342; D109. With Stow: C119, 157, 278; D15.

somehow related to β, in addition to his regular exemplar. At *Complaint* 126, S introduces *he* interlineally before *yeue*, thus joining BY (L is defective) in what is most probably a sub-archetypal variant. At *Complaint* 148, S writes *euere ful bisily* over an erasure whose length suggests an earlier *bisily*, the archetypal (and VO) reading preserved in C and St. The line in its original form evidently seemed too short to Selden, as it did to β, whose expansion is similar: *þen full besely* (B). At *Complaint* 238, S shares another unmetrical expansion with β, this time in identical form. The scribe writes *greuous pine* over an erasure whose length suggests that he originally copied just *pine*, the archetypal and VO reading correctly preserved, again, in C and St.[53] A similar 'correction' by S to a β reading was noted in the holograph section, at *Dialogue* 631 (p. xxv above). None of the Selden scribe's other alterations, rather frequent in the *Complaint* and *Dialogue*, point towards β, or indeed to C or St; but those just noticed, few as they are, provide visible evidence that lateral transmission, as well as accidental convergence, is to be reckoned with in analysing the distribution of variants. However, it cannot be said that S is a seriously contaminated manuscript; and it must in general be treated as an independent witness to the readings of the archetype, which it preserves with considerable fidelity. Selden was accordingly adopted as the basis for collation in reconstructing those readings.

The Coventry MS has very much more variation in its text than Selden, here as in the holograph section, and it agrees with S only in four unremarkable variants (n. 52 above). There are thirteen agreements between C and β: *Complaint* 99, 150, 289, 291, 293, 350, 412; *Dialogue* 16, 25, 78, 110, 127, 204.[54] It is not surprising that C should agree in variants more often with β than with S, given the low level of variation in the latter; and most of the Cβ variants are easily explained as the results of accidental convergence, in small changes of word-order and the like. Most challenging are the omission of *waar* at *Dialogue* 25 and the substitution of unmetrical *truly* (trisyllabic in Hoccleve) for *soothly* at *Dialogue* 78. Yet on this evidence C can hardly be regarded as other than independent of β, as it is of S.

John Stow's copy remains to be considered. It is clear that Stow

---

[53] Ultra-violet light did not enable me to see the erased readings in either 148 or 238. In the former Selden also added the *-en* to *labouriden* as part of the 'correction', just as BLY add a reflexive *hem* also to lengthen the line.

[54] Coventry also has four agreements with B alone, one with L alone, and three with BL; but all these are obviously accidental.

cannot have taken his text from any of the other surviving manuscripts. Both C and the β copies have a large number of separative errors not followed in St; and even Selden, the most likely candidate, varies from what I take to be original readings in more than forty places where St does not follow.[55] Since in his treatment of other texts Stow has been shown to have consulted more than one copy, conflation must be reckoned with again here;[56] but St shares few variants with any one of the other copies: four with S, five with β, and six with C.[57] Of these, the only ones that may suggest some relationship are the agreements with C at *Complaint* 2 (the curious reading *brome*) and 294 (*thay* for *ay*), and especially at *Dialogue* 179, where St and C have *entendement* against the likely archetypal reading in S and β of *enditement*. But there is some complication here: B gives the line in the margin, Y shows signs of hesitation, and S evidently wrote *entendement* before erasing it and substituting *enditement*.[58] Such evidence is hardly enough to challenge the conclusion that St must in practice be treated as a fourth independent witness, alongside S, C, and β.

In reconstructing the archetype, accordingly, we can treat the six manuscripts as representing four generally independent lines of descent: S, C, β, and St. In very many places, as has already been observed, their unanimous or nearly unanimous evidence presents no problem; but in other cases decisions have to be made.[59] Some such decisions have already been implied in the preceding discussion, which assumed that certain readings shared by two of the four witnesses represented departures from the archetypal text. Where only two rival readings are concerned, each supported by two witnesses, balance of manuscript support provides no evidence. Among the thirty-seven variations of this kind, five suggest no clear arguments in favour of either reading: *Complaint* 233, 350; *Dialogue* 16, 204, 222. Here I have followed Selden. At *Complaint* 99 and 294, the more difficult variant has been preferred. In nine other cases superiority of sense has been the criterion: *Complaint* 74, 119, 126, 150, 268, 289; *Dialogue* 133, 179, 249. Other choices are made wholly or partly on the evidence of Hoccleve's known

[55] The most significant are: C28, 29, 53, 55, 62, 71, 126, 136, 148, 153, 160, 167, 234, 238, 248, 266, 279, 308, 326, 327, 342, 352, 378, 412; D109, 136, 151, 204, 210, 234, 247.

[56] See below, p. xxxix.

[57] With Selden: C119, 157, 278; D15. With β: C74, 233, 268; D157, 249. With Coventry: C2, 247, 294; D133, 179, 222.

[58] The third letter of Selden's *enditement* is altered from a *t*, and the rest of the word is written over an erasure long enough to have dealt with the extra letter of *entendement*.

[59] Comments on the more difficult cases will be found in notes on the lines in question.

linguistic usage, such as his consistent use in the holographs of *betwixt*, not *bitwixe*: *Complaint* 20, 249; *Dialogue* 157. Again, knowledge of the poet's metrical usage determines, or enters into, decisions at fifteen points: *Complaint* 126, 136, 148, 238, 248, 249, 293, 412; *Dialogue* 15, 25, 78, 109, 110, 117, 127. The use of such criteria assumes that at these points the archetype did not itself vary from what Hoccleve wrote in VO. The assumption may be questioned, but there is no practical alternative to it.

Where three lines of transmission agree against one, the presumption lies with them; and in many cases the minority reading can easily be rejected, on a variety of grounds. However, there are thirteen such places where a single witness may be judged to carry the VO reading, either by transmission from the archetype (in which case the agreement of the other three requires explanation) or by correction of some kind.[60] These are considered individually in notes to the lines in question. By far the most striking are the seven lines where Stow alone has what I regard as original readings: *Complaint* 28, 71, 266, 308, 342, 352; *Dialogue* 234. In one or two of these (notably *Complaint* 308) originality may be doubted; and in others (e.g. *Complaint* 266) a difficult reading in the archetype may be supposed to have given rise to the same easier reading independently in S, C, and β. But when all seven are considered together, it seems hard to avoid the conclusion that John Stow (if he was not a master of conjectural emendation) had access to a second copy of the *Series* which was, unlike his main exemplar, independent of the scribal archetype, and that he introduced some readings from it. His version of *Complaint* 352, where Hoccleve's Latin source supports him, could be an intelligent emendation; but his *Whiche that* at *Complaint* 71 looks very much like a reading taken from outside the archetypal tradition. If this were so, it would not be surprising; for Stow has been shown to have used more than one manuscript in copying other texts.[61]

---

[60] Kane and Donaldson comment on cases where 'an original reading may be present in a single manuscript': 'It can have been restored by genuine correction; or fortuitously restored by felicitous scribal variation, in particular by skilful sophistication; or it can have been preserved by faithful vertical transmission and isolated by coincident substitution in the other manuscripts' (*Piers Plowman: The B Version*, p. 165).

[61] See A. S. G. Edwards and J. Hedley, 'John Stow, *The Craft of Lovers* and T. C. C. R. 13. 19', *Studies in Bibliography*, 28 (1975), 265–8; and A. S. G. Edwards and J. I. Miller, 'Stow and Lydgate's "St. Edmund"', *Notes and Queries*, 218 (1973), 365–9. Stow collated two exemplars for his text of Lydgate's *Balade of Good Counsel* in his 1561 edition of Chaucer: see Anne Hudson, 'John Stow (1525?–1605)', in *Editing Chaucer: The Great Tradition*, ed. Paul G Ruggiers (Norman, OK, 1984), p. 61.

From Archetype to Variant Original

If we had only scribal copies of the *Complaint-Dialogue* and knew of no
other verse by the same writer—as is most often the case with Middle
English poems—it would be hard to do more than collate the other
copies against a base text, and adopt into that text, which could only be
Selden's, such other readings as seemed preferable to its own. Nor, in
those circumstances, would the need for any further improvement by
conjecture appear very pressing: Michael Seymour, after all, was able to
derive a presentable text of the *Complaint* direct from Selden, with only
half a dozen readings adopted from other manuscripts.[62] In reality,
however, we are in the highly unusual position of being able to draw
upon the evidence of more than 7000 lines composed by the same poet
and copied by him into the Durham and Huntington MSS. This
holograph material displays a high degree of consistency, especially in
the poet's cultivation of the decasyllabic line, and also in his linguistic
usage (lexical, morphological, and orthographic). Comparison with those
holographs makes it clear, in fact, that any archetypal text based on
Selden—even one which takes account, as I did in the last section, of
holograph evidence in the assessment of manuscript variants—will
seriously misrepresent what Hoccleve must have written, and especially
the delicate texture of his syllabic verse.

In what follows, accordingly, I set out to reconstruct the Variant
Original, starting from the archetypal text represented by Selden as
corrected from the other scribal copies. I distinguish three phases in the
reconstruction. In the first, the archetypal text is altered to bring it into
conformity with Hoccleve's practice in spelling and inflecting words, so
far as that can be determined from the holographs. In effect, this means
taking the holograph corpus as copy text, in Greg's sense.[63] The
resulting 'normalised' archetype, as it might be called, must then be
reviewed in order to identify those places where it fails in sense, or
where it still, even after normalisation, fails in metre. Where possible,
finally, these places are repaired by conjecture, a process guided by
knowledge of the failings of the archetype in the holograph *Dialogue*.

The first stage of this operation corresponds to that 'normalisation of
accidentals' proposed by D. C. Greetham for a new edition of
Hoccleve's *Regiment of Princes*. The *Regiment*, by far the most widely

[62] *Selections from Hoccleve*, pp. 75–87. His text is the best at present available,
representing a marked improvement on that given by Furnivall and Pryor from Stow.
[63] W. W. Greg, 'The Rationale of Copy-Text', *Studies in Bibliography*, 3 (1950–1), 19–
36, reprinted in Greg, *Collected Papers*, ed. J. C. Maxwell (Oxford, 1966), pp. 374–91.

read of the poet's works, survives in no less than forty-three scribal copies, but not in any made by Hoccleve himself. Greetham argues convincingly that the accidentals of the edited text should be 'normalised' in accordance with the poet's consistent usages, to be discovered from a concordance of his holograph forms.[64] As he observes, 'there is in the Hoccleve holographs a quite remarkable degree of consistency in accidentals, much more than in Fisher's Chancery English . . . and perhaps more than in any other English author before the eighteenth century'.[65] He states his main conclusion as follows: 'the Hoccleve holographs may not be denied their status as valuable evidence for the editorial process: to do so would be to accept an acknowledged non-auctorial condition of the text in favour of one which can, with careful scholarship, be shown to rely upon the demonstrable preferences of an author who clearly cared very much about the exact form of his language'.[66]

Comparison of the scribal copies with the holograph material makes it clear that Selden is much the closest to the spellings and inflexional forms used by Hoccleve himself. However, S does itself frequently depart from that usage, often to the detriment of the syllable-count; and I have aimed to correct it wherever possible. The various grounds for such correction must be set out here.

(1) Very often, among the more than 6000 lexical items in the holograph concordance, a word will be found recorded in an absolutely invariable form different from that given by Selden. This is the simplest kind of case. A cluster of examples may be found in *Complaint* 141–3, where S has:

> And this I demed wel / and knewe wel eke
> What so þat euere / I shulde answere or seie
> They wolden not / han holde it worth a leke

---

[64] D. C. Greetham, 'Normalisation of Accidentals in Middle English Texts: the Paradox of Thomas Hoccleve', *Studies in Bibliography*, 38 (1985), 121–50. See also Greetham, 'Challenges of Theory and Practice in the Editing of Hoccleve's *Regement of Princes*', in *Manuscripts and Texts*, ed. D. Pearsall (Cambridge, 1987), pp. 60–86. The edition of the *Regiment*, now in the hands of Charles Blyth, will adopt Greetham's principles: see Charles Blyth, 'Editing *The Regiment of Princes*', in *Essays on Thomas Hoccleve*, ed. C. Batt (London, 1996), pp. 11–28.

[65] 'Normalisation', pp. 136–7, referring to John Fisher's computer-generated analysis of English in Chancery documents.

[66] 'Normalisation', p. 150. On 'remarkable consistency' in the orthography of another Middle English holograph, see P. J. Lucas, 'Consistency and Correctness in the Orthographic Usage of John Capgrave's *Chronicle*', *Studia Neophilologica*, 45 (1973), 323–55.

Here, as it happens, the only changes required all involve invariable Hocclevian forms: *deemed* for *demed*, *kneew* for *knewe*, *eek* for *eke*, *sholde* for *shulde*, *seye* for *seie*, *nat* for *not*, and *leek* for *leke*. It is a measure of the consistency commonly achieved in the holographs that the negative adverb is always spelled *nat* (491x), the form *not* being strictly reserved for contracted *ne wot* (3x). These slight changes may appear no more than cosmetic; but it should be noted that the final ⟨e⟩ in *knewe*, *eke*, and *leke* would all, if read according to the strict Hocclevian rules, add an extra syllable (unmetrical in one case) to the lines in which they occur. Since S conforms more closely than any of the other copies to the poet's customary usage, reference to the holograph concordance will quite often serve only to confirm the Selden form; but where this is not the case, the simple act of substituting the invariable form very commonly restores or helps to restore the syllable-count at a stroke. Since this is an important consequence of the 'normalisation of accidentals', I give some further examples here: *hoom* for Selden's *home* (*Complaint* 155, 278), *suspect* for *suspecte* (*Complaint* 165), *his* for *hise* (*Complaint* 202, 213), *lewde* for *lewide* (*Complaint* 219, *Dialogue* 36), *hoomly* for *homely* (*Complaint* 221), *likne* for *licken* (*Complaint* 242), *betwixt* for *bitwixe* (*Complaint* 249), *encombrous* for *encomborus* (*Complaint* 318), *thurgh* for *thoruʒ* (*Complaint* 393), *narw* for *narowe* (*Dialogue* 123), *shuln* for *shullen* (*Dialogue* 188, 233), *rekne* for *recken* (*Dialogue* 221). In only one place, significantly, does such a substitution create rather than resolve a metrical anomaly (*blisse* for *blis* at *Complaint* 357).

(2) Things are less simple in cases where the concordance offers more than one form of a word. Here one must first take care to distinguish between motivated and free or unmotivated variation. Given the general consistency of Hoccleve's writing practice, one should consider all possible motives for a variation (grammar, metre, rhyme) before concluding that it has none. Thus, Greetham refers to holograph variation between *maad* and *made* as comparable with unmotivated *whilom/whylom*; but all thirty occurrences of *maad* there are past participles, and all thirty-eight occurrences of *made* are past tenses— as indeed the morphology of weak verbs would lead one to expect.[67] Yet Hoccleve does on occasion vary forms for no perceptible reason. Examples involving words occurring in the non-holograph section are: *i/y* variation: *riche/ryche* (*Complaint* 16), *maist/mayst* (*Complaint* 370);

---

[67] 'Normalisation', p. 137. On forms of weak verbs in Hoccleve, see p. liii below.

an/on variation: *stande/stonde* (*Complaint* 172, 189, etc.); *a/aa* variation: *hast/haast* (*Dialogue* 23); *an/aun* variation: *chaunge/change* (*Complaint* 7, 10, etc.), *straunge/strange* (*Complaint* 70).[68] *Mateere* varies with *matire*, *honour* with *honur*, *resoun* with *reson*. Since there is, in the nature of these cases, no way of telling which alternative Hoccleve might have used, I have allowed Selden to stand where its form is among those found in the holographs. Where it is not, I have adopted whichever form appears most frequently in the concordance.[69] Three difficult cases should be mentioned here. Like the holographs, Selden exhibits variant forms of the present plural and past participle of the verb 'to be': *been* and *be*. Since I can find no consistent motivation for these variants, I have allowed Selden's forms to stand. The word 'that' presents a different problem. Unlike S, Hoccleve uses runic thorn only when writing this word in its abbreviated form *þ^t*.[70] This abbreviated form is very much more common than the full form *that* in the Durham holograph (699x as against 48x), and I have therefore adopted it throughout, having failed to discover any consistent motivation for the writing of *that*. Neither grammatical function nor line-length seem to be involved; and, although most of the occurrences of *that* are at the beginnings of verse lines (43x out of 48), it is outnumbered even there by *þ^t* (115x).[71] The personal pronoun 'I' presents another problem. In Excursus I, it is suggested that Hoccleve can be seen shifting towards a preference for *y* rather than *I* in mid-line position in the course of copying Durham; but the *I* form still prevails in the holograph *Dialogue* (*I* 123x, *y* 4x). There seem no grounds, therefore, for replacing Selden's regular *I* with *y* at any point.

(3.1) One motive for small spelling variations in the holographs is to distinguish confusible words. Thus Selden's form *feer* at *Complaint* 151 is to be corrected, in part because Hoccleve consistently distinguishes

---

[68] Similar cases of unmotivated variation in accidentals may be observed in the two holograph copies of *Learn to Die*: see Excursus I here.

[69] A more sophisticated statistical method is presented by Greetham, 'Normalisation', pp. 132–3.

[70] Thorns elsewhere in Selden are replaced by *th* in accordance with the poet's practice. Selden's yogh, a letter not used by Hoccleve, is replaced by *y* or *gh* as appropriate, e.g. *yelownesse* (C5), *wightes* (C14).

[71] M. L. Samuels discusses variation between *þ^t* and *that* in his essay 'The Scribe of the Hengwrt and Ellesmere Manuscripts of *The Canterbury Tales*', reprinted in *The English of Chaucer and his Contemporaries*, ed. J. J. Smith (Aberdeen, 1988), pp. 38–50; see pp. 44–6. Hoccleve's use of 'obsolescent' thorn is distinctly more conservative than that of the Hengwrt-Ellesmere scribe; nor do the grammatical considerations adduced by Samuels (p. 45) apply to him.

fere 'fear' from *feere* 'company'. Similarly, Selden's *ʒe* cannot stand as *ye* for the personal pronoun at *Dialogue* 39 and 148, since the poet always spells that pronoun *yee*, reserving the form *ye* for 'eye'. Again, with only one exception Hoccleve distinguishes *mene*, 'moderate, intermediary', from *meene*, 'intend', so I have altered the first *mene* in Selden's *Complaint* 218, but not the second. More significant, however, are motivated variants in the form of the same word. A rare example where sense enters into such variation appears in *ther/there*. All 36 examples of *there* in the holographs mean 'in that place' (as at *Dialogue* 77), whereas anticipatory or 'existential' uses of the word are always represented by *ther* (as at *Complaint* 9 but not 10).[72] Selden generally preserves this distinction; but at *Complaint* 128 the syllable-count requires *ther* for 'in that place', a departure from his usual practice which Hoccleve occasionally allows himself elsewhere *metri causa*.

(3.2) Much the most frequent motives for variation are metrical: to facilitate syllable-count and rhyme. Hoccleve is generally careful to match his rhyme-forms. Thus, of his two forms of 'well', *wel* and *weel*, he would certainly have used the latter at *Complaint* 298, where the word rhymes with *seel* and *euerydeel*. Some forms are used only in rhyming position, for example trisyllabic *aweye* (*Complaint* 80) as against regular *away* (*Complaint* 79). S here has *a wey*, which reflects the original *ey* form but rhymes imperfectly with *seye* (compare *aweye/seye*, *Jereslaus* 732–3). Another form used only in rhyme is *spiryt*, as against regular *spirit* (compare *Jonathas* 121). Selden's *spirite* must be changed to *spiryt* at *Complaint* 27 (rhyming with *delyt*) and at *Complaint* 282 (rhyming with *qwyt* and *plyt*). Hoccleve regularly writes *y* to represent /i:/ before a single final consonant, and here it presumably marks a lengthening associated with stress on the second syllable of the word. A similar case is *maneere*, rhyming with *appeere* and *cheere* (both regular forms) at *Complaint* 163. This form, along with its variant *manere*, is used in contrast with *maner*, to mark the trisyllabic form with stress on the second syllable. However, it is syllable-count rather than stress position that Hoccleve's variants most commonly and consistently indicate.[73] The most frequent variation of this kind is that between *-e* and *-en* in verb endings (infinitives, present and past plurals, and strong past participles). In eliding contexts this allows a syllable to be secured

[72] Mustanoja, p. 337.

[73] One might expect that the variants *honur/honour* or *reson/resoun* would consistently indicate stress on, respectively, the first or second syllable; but the holographs have many counter-examples. I have therefore included them as unmotivated variants above.

or lost, as the metre requires. Scribes often write the wrong form, as one might expect; and I have corrected S accordingly at, for example, *Complaint* 120, 131, 200, 203, 255. Similarly, in non-eliding contexts *seyn* and *han* are used where only one syllable is required, as against disyllabic *seye* and *haue*. This has prompted alterations of Selden at *Complaint* 171, 264, *Dialogue* 89, 188. Other common morphological variants are *-yng/-ynge* for present participle and verbal noun (e.g. *Complaint* 179) and *had/hadde* for the past tense of 'had' (e.g. *Complaint* 28).[74] A similar purpose is served by lexical variants such as *than/thanne* (e.g. *Complaint* 337), *whan/whanne* (e.g. *Complaint* 104–5), and *lewdnesse/lewdenesse* (*Complaint* 101). A recurrent small example is the word for 'her' or 'their', *hir/hire*. *Hir* represents these pronouns as monosyllables in non-eliding contexts, where *hire* would give two syllables. In eliding contexts, Hoccleve favours the latter form. Thus *Male Regle* 232: 'No more / than hir wit were in hire heele'.[75]

(4) Where a word does not occur at all, varied or unvaried, in the holograph corpus, one may have recourse to general rules of authorial spelling or morphology, where those apply without exceptions. Thus, Selden's uses of yogh and thorn must be replaced (except in *þat*). Again, Selden's *sanke* (*Complaint* 7) cannot stand, because the past tense singular of strong verbs never has *-e* in the holographs. An *-e* is added to Selden's *affriȝt* (*Complaint* 46), because past tense singular forms of such contracted weak verbs always have *-e*; but *-e* is struck off Selden's *spilte* (*Complaint* 368), because weak past participles never have it. Both these last changes are supported by rhymes. A rather more complex case is the alteration of Selden's *knockede* to *knokkid* (past tense singular, *Dialogue* 11), supported by holograph *knokkith*. Weak verbs with syllabic *-ed* in the past tense do not add *-e*; but Hoccleve also varies between *-ed* and *-id*, as well as *-est/-ist*, and *-eth/-ith*. Since all three endings show *i* rather than *e* forms after stems ending in *-k*, *i* has been adopted here.[76] Other occasions for correction arise where an unrecorded word can safely be analysed into parts which are themselves recorded. Thus Selden's *brainseke* (*Complaint* 129) is corrected to

[74] These and other morphological variants in service of the syllable-count are studied by Jefferson, *art. cit.*, pp. 101–4.
[75] Only eight of the 230 instances of *hir* in the concordance precede words beginning with a vowel or ⟨h⟩.
[76] I have made such changes only where Hoccleve's usage is consistent, as after stems ending in *k*. Thus, he always writes *-est*, *-eth*, or *-ed* after stems ending in *m*. In inconsistent cases (e.g. after stems ending in *r*) I have let Selden stand. It may be that factors other than the final stem consonant are involved.

braynseek on the strength of invariable holograph *brayn* and *seek*, *myschese* (*Dialogue* 75) is altered to *mischeese* (always *mis-* and *cheese*), and *biþou3te* (*Complaint* 274) becomes *bethoghte* (*be-* usually, *thoghte* always).

Such 'normalisation of accidentals' serves to bring the archetypal text, as that is represented in the emended S readings, closer at many points to what Hoccleve must have written in the Variant Original. It also has the effect of excluding from further consideration any places where an unmetrical reading may have arisen, not by substantive variation, but merely by scribal substitution of a non-authorial form. Once this process of normalisation is completed, therefore, the text stands ready for conjectural emendation at those points where substantive variation appears to have given rise to readings which fail tests of either metre or—less often—sense. I find 47 such places in the 665 non-holograph lines, a figure which may be compared with the 73 archetypal errors listed above (pp. xxvi–xxvii) in the 574 holograph lines. For purposes of comparison with that list, I give the 47 readings in the same form here, but in this case it is my conjectural reading which is followed by the presumed archetypal error:[77]

C19 thoght: þou3tis. C22 syn: sithin. C45 euery: euery mannes. C57 syn: sithin. C58 good: good and gracious. C71 Which: With. C71 gan: gan to. C87 past: passed. C96 syn: sithen. C124 Seide: And seide. C176 Syn: Sithen. C189 Syn: Sithen. C221 nathelees: neuerethelees. C228 can: ne can. C231 were: were it. C236 souerain: moost souerain. C246 algate: algatis. C247 twixt: betwixt. C260 Syn: Sithen. C264 but: but if. C265 Syn: Sithen. C266 sepulture: sepulcre. C269 Syn: Sithen. C278 Syn: Sithen. C308 dreeme: deeme. C342 heuynesses: heuynesse. C350 aylastynge: euere lastynge. C352 Commune: Comen. C352 men: me. C357 go: to go. C371 repente: me repente. D5 Syn: Sithen. D33 speke: to speke. D41 Syn: Sithen. D55 thynke: to þinke. D58 Syn þat: Sithen. D73 syn: siþen. D80 syn: sithen. D90 Ihesu: curteis Ihesu. D93 Syn: Sithen. D115 Take: Take it. D132 Syn: Sithen. D137 syn: sithen. D140 Syn: Sithen. D213 Syn: Siþen. D228 gynne: bigynne to. D234 monicioun: mocioun.

[77] As before, archetypal readings are given in Selden forms, where available. The list includes the seven places where Stow may be supposed to have gathered an original reading from outside the archetypal tradition (C28, 71, 266, 308, 342, 352; D234): see above, p. xxxix.

Since individual cases are discussed in notes on the lines in question, I confine myself here to general observations. It may be noted that 29 of these 47 emendations suppose scribal errors exactly like those observed in the scribal archetype in the holograph *Dialogue*. The most numerous cases are: archetypal *sithen* for authorial *syn* (18x here, 9x in holograph *Dialogue*); archetypal addition of *to* before infinitives (5x here, 7x in holograph *Dialogue*); and archetypal addition of *it* where a verb might seem to need expression of a subject or object (2x here, 5x in holograph *Dialogue*).[78]

Emendations have been prompted by the following types of consideration:

(a) *Syllable-Count*: *Complaint* 19, 45, 58, 71, 228, 231, 236, 246, 247, 264, 266, 350, 357, 371; *Dialogue* 33, 55, 90, 115, 228, 234. These corrections depend upon belief in the poet's consistent counting of syllables.[79] Of the twenty, nine gain support from occurrence of the same errors in scribal copies of the holograph section. In three other cases (*Complaint* 58, 236; *Dialogue* 90), unmetrical additions seem to be prompted by pious zeal. Most doubtful is the emendation at *Complaint* 45.

(b) *Syllable-Count and Linguistic Usage*: *Complaint* 22, 57, 87, 96, 176, 189, 221, 260, 265, 269, 278; *Dialogue* 5, 41, 73, 80, 93, 132, 137, 140, 213. In these twenty places correction to Hoccleve's lexical usage also restores the syllable-count: *syn* for *sithen* (18x), *past* for *passed* (*Complaint* 87), and *nathelees* for *neuerethelees* (*Complaint* 221).

(c) *Linguistic Usage*: *Dialogue* 58. See note *ad loc.*

(d) *Sense*: *Complaint* 71, 124, 308, 352, 352. These are the only substantive emendations of the archetype that do not depend upon knowledge of the poet's language and metre. In four of the five places (*Complaint* 71, 308, 352, 352), Stow has what I take to be the original reading derived from outside the archetypal tradition.

METRE

Since the scribal copies present in their substantive variants rather few problems, the most conspicuous differences between the Selden and Variant Original texts as printed here concern not sense but metre. 'Normalisation of accidentals' itself has the immediate effect of restoring

---

[78] Other examples are the variants at C19, 87, 124, and 350.

[79] One other emendation serves to correct a rhyme: C342.

the syllable-count in many lines; and the counting of syllables has played a major part in my discriminations between scribal readings, and also in the determining of conjectures. A relevant test of the resulting VO, therefore, is to compare its syllabic regularity with that of the holograph *Dialogue*, a text of not dissimilar length (574 lines as against 665 non-holograph lines). The method must be to apply the same 'deletion rules' that were earlier applied to the holograph section (pp. xxix–xxxi), noting and allowing the same specific kinds of exception or licence as were allowed there.[80] The results are as follows:

Rule 1 (general elision of final unstressed /ə/ before words beginning with a vowel or ⟨h⟩). No exceptions in the holograph *Dialogue*;[81] four exceptions here: 'Syn God hath maad / myn helthe hoom repeire' (C278), 'To the man / as aboue haue I said' (C377), 'If thow be wys / of þat mateere ho' (D26), 'Am I nat holden it oute / O yis' (D81). In the two *Dialogue* lines, an exceptional syntactic break before the following word may explain non-elision. The hiatus at D81 could be avoided by adding -*n* to the infinitive ending of the verb *oute*; but I have preferred to avoid the jingle with *holden*.

Rule 1.1 (elision of final unstressed /ə/ across the mid-line break). Three exceptional examples of non-elision there in the holograph *Dialogue*; five exceptions here: 'Whan I hem mette / as they nat me sy' (C77), 'I soghte reste / and I nat it fonde' (C195), 'By communynge / is the beste assay' (C217), 'Thank of myn elde / and of my seeknesse' (C410), 'Swich multitude / of þat false secte' (D191).[82]

Rule 1.2 (elision in words ending in consonant + ⟨le⟩, ⟨ne⟩, ⟨re⟩, or ⟨we⟩). Three examples of non-elision in the holograph *Dialogue*, one here: 'For ofte whan I / to Westmynstre halle' (C72).

Rule 1.3 (word-ending ⟨ye⟩ or ⟨ie⟩ monosyllabic or disyllabic according to stress position). Regular in all cases here, as in holograph *Dialogue*. Compare, for example, C50 and 52 (monosyllabic after stress) with C93, 95 and 96 (disyllabic with stress). The same principle applies to the

---

[80] For purposes of this comparison, it does not matter whether these exceptions are regarded as allowable licences or as simply unmetrical.

[81] In the rest of the Durham *Series* I find three examples of elision failing outside the mid-line position: *Jereslaus* 758 (*face*), *Learn to Die* 384 (*mighte*), and *Jonathas* 529 (*helthe*, much like C278).

[82] The rest of the Durham *Series* provides clear evidence that Hoccleve did allow occasional non-elision at the mid-line break (marked by a virgule in D or, failing there, in S): *Jereslaus* 144, 393, 711, 761, 763, 881, 900; *Learn to Die* 2, 44, 64, 100, 150, 545, 563, 696, 734; *Jonathas* 25, 165, 183, 212, 240, 358, 420, 653.

word-ending in the verb *continue*, which has three syllables, or two with elision (C216, 226; D164).

Rule 2 (synaloepha in words ending in vocalic ⟨y⟩). Variation as in holograph *Dialogue*. Compare, for example, disyllabic *many a* (C19, 41, etc.) with trisyllabic *many a* (C201, D103).

Rule 3 (syncope in words such as *euene, considere*). One exception in the holograph *Dialogue*, none here. See for example C14 (*euery*), C96 (*someres*), C176 (*recouered*), D227 (*considere*).[83]

By this point in the analysis, every one of the 574 holograph lines was accounted for; but of the 665 non-holograph lines, nine remain to be considered here. Five of these, read according to the rules so far noticed, will have one syllable too many in the reconstructed VO text. Four of the five can be saved by invoking the rule accepted by students of Chaucer's metre: that two successive unstressed or weakly stressed monosyllabic words may count as a single syllable for metrical purposes.[84] Thus: *at the* in C113, 'He suffrith longe / but at the laste he smit'; *be a* in C336, 'No force how soone / I stynte to be a man'; *it a* in D140. 'Syn þat the parlement / hath maad it a lawe'; and *of the* in D173, 'The vois of the peple / vengeance on yow gredith'. Alternatively, C113 and D173 can be read as having a supernumerary unstressed syllable at the mid-line break. The remaining line, D137, must be read so: 'But syn gold to weye / charged now been we'.[85] All but one of these lines is open to emendation: see notes *ad loc.*

The four remaining lines have fewer than the required number of syllables. The first is C185, 'Thus thoghte I / A greet fool I am'. Even if one assumes non-elision of *-e* in *thoghte*, the line still lacks a syllable. Kern suggests adding *thanne*; but the exceptionally heavy mid-line break, marking the introduction of reported speech, can surely here be accepted as taking the place of the missing syllables.[86] D118, 'It seemeth but smal / other is ther', is defective in both metre and sense. I have let the line stand, in the absence of a convincing emendation,

[83] See p. xxxi, n. 46 above.
[84] See discussion by Gilbert Youmans, 'Reconsidering Chaucer's Prosody', in *English Historical Metrics*, ed. C. B. McCully and J. J. Anderson (Cambridge, 1996), pp. 185–7.
[85] Chaucer scholars disagree about whether he allowed a 'redundant syllable at the caesura': see ten Brink, *Language and Metre*, pp. 216–8; Janet Cowen and George Kane (eds), *Geoffrey Chaucer: The Legend of Good Women* (East Lansing, Mich., 1995), pp. 121–2. Possible examples elsewhere in the Durham *Series* are *Learn to Die* 270 and 872.
[86] Kern, 'Zum Texte', p. 422. With non-elision at the mid-line break, *thanne* would supply the necessary syllables. The manuscript variants give no help.

marking it as suspect with a dagger. There remain D169, 'By commune harm / is nat smal to sette', and D247, 'Ripnesse of deeth / faste vpon me haastith', both as they stand instances of a metrical type not found anywhere in the holograph *Series*, the 'broken-backed' or 'Lydgate' line.[87] D169 could be saved by reading *it is* with the Coventry MS, and D247 by reading *now* before *haastith* with Selden; but see the notes to these lines.

LANGUAGE: ORTHOGRAPHY, MORPHOLOGY, PUNCTUATION

Hoccleve's English has been assigned by M. L. Samuels to the third of the four types of London English which he distinguishes. Samuels lists the three Hoccleve holograph manuscripts as representatives of 'early fifteenth-century Type III', along with the Hengwrt and Ellesmere copies of Chaucer's *Canterbury Tales*, the Corpus Christi Cambridge *Troilus*, and the Trinity Cambridge *Piers Plowman*.[88] A full study of Hoccleve's usage based on the holographs has yet to be produced, despite the fact that, as Norman Davis observed, 'Hoccleve is especially important for historical study because a number of his surviving works are written in his own hand, so that the language is free from the scribal interference that often disguises an author's usage.'[89] At present the most substantial study remains that by Erich Vollmer, published as long ago as 1899. Vollmer treats phonology and, more briefly, accidence.[90] The following notes refer only to the holograph *Dialogue* (ll. 253–826), from which all illustrations are taken.

ORTHOGRAPHY

1. Where /a:/ precedes a single final consonant, it is regularly written ⟨aa⟩: *baar, maad, waar*. Before consonant clusters also, ⟨aa⟩ is sometimes written for the long vowel: *taastid, haast* (D518, but *hast* D295).

---

[87] See E. P. Hammond, 'The Nine-Syllabled Pentameter Line in some Post-Chaucerian Manuscripts', *Modern Philology*, 23 (1925), 129–52.

[88] M. L. Samuels, 'Chaucer's Spelling', in *The English of Chaucer and his Contemporaries* (Aberdeen, 1988), ed. J. J. Smith, pp. 23–37; p. 24.

[89] Norman Davis, 'Notes on Grammar and Spelling in the Fifteenth Century', in *The Oxford Book of Late Medieval Verse and Prose*, ed. D. Gray (Oxford, 1985), pp. 493–508; p. 493.

[90] E. Vollmer, 'Sprache und Reime des Londoners Hoccleve', *Anglia*, 21 (1899), 201–21. There are also valuable observations in Kern, 'Zum Texte', *passim*.

2. Although Hoccleve's rhymes generally respect the distinction between /e:/ and /ɛ:/ (Vollmer, 'Sprache und Reime', pp. 201–2), his spellings do not consistently mark it. When preceding single final consonants, both sounds are represented by ⟨ee⟩: *been*, *deeth*. In other positions, Hoccleve commonly prefers ⟨e⟩ for /ɛ:/, as in *rede*, and ⟨ee⟩ for /e:/, as in *weene*.

3. Unstressed /ə/ is written ⟨e⟩. In final positions it is represented by a suspension only after ⟨r⟩ (with a flourish) and ⟨ll⟩ (crossed with a bar).[91] These suspensions are expanded as italic -*e* in the present holograph text.

4. Short /i/ is represented by ⟨i⟩, except before ⟨m⟩ and ⟨n⟩, where ⟨y⟩ is commonly preferred.

5. Where /i:/ precedes a single final consonant, it is regularly written ⟨y⟩: *fyr*, *lyf*, *plyt*. In the majority of other words with /i:/, Hoccleve commonly prefers ⟨y⟩ also. Thus, the holographs consistently distinguish the infinitive *wryte*, with its long vowel (e.g. D508), from the past participle *write*, which has a short vowel (e.g. D671). On his writing of the first person singular pronoun *I*, see p. 116.

6. Although Hoccleve's rhymes generally respect the distinction between /o:/ and /ɔ:/ (Vollmer, 'Sprache und Reime', pp. 201–2), his spellings do not consistently mark it. When preceding single final consonants, both sounds are represented by ⟨oo⟩: *anoon*, *book*. In other positions, Hoccleve commonly prefers ⟨o⟩ for /ɔ:/, as in *lore*, and ⟨oo⟩ for /o:/, as in *soone*.

7. Spellings of /u:/ vary between ⟨ou⟩ and ⟨ow⟩. The latter, less common, type occurs mainly before ⟨n⟩ and in final position: *sowneth*, *thow*.

8. Hoccleve employs the consonantal symbol thorn, ⟨þ⟩, only when abbreviating the word *that* as *þᵗ* (see p. xliii). Unlike the Selden scribe, he does not use yogh, ⟨ȝ⟩.

---

[91] By contrast, strokes added to other final letters (⟨d⟩, ⟨f⟩, ⟨g⟩, ⟨gh⟩, ⟨ght⟩, ⟨k⟩, ⟨ssh⟩, and ⟨t⟩) are not to be expanded. This conclusion was reached independently by Kern, 'Zum Texte', pp. 390–95, and Jefferson, p. 96 n. 8. When writing Latin, Hoccleve also uses suspensions for ⟨e⟩ after final ⟨ll⟩ and ⟨r⟩: thus, 'fundare' in his gloss to D638–9, and 'mille' in the gloss to D456–8. The EETS editions cannot be relied upon in this matter, which has considerable metrical significance.

9. The following consonantal writings are common or regular: ⟨cc⟩ in words such as *affeccioun*; ⟨cch⟩ in words such as *cacche*; ⟨gg⟩ in words such as *allegge*, *logged*; ⟨k⟩ initially before back vowels as in *kaght*, and finally as in *blak*; ⟨kk⟩ in medial position, as in *rekke*; ⟨l⟩ in final position, as in *al*, *ful*; ⟨qw⟩ in words such as *qwyt*, *acqweynte*; ⟨ssh⟩ in words such as *fressh*, *finisshid*.

MORPHOLOGY

1. Adverbs are formed by adding *-e* (*sore, hye, longe, neede*), *-es* (*needes, needis* in rhyme D822), *-ly* (*treewely*), and in one case *-liche* (*largeliche* D755). Comparative forms of adverbs take either *-er* (*sonner*) or *-ere* (*heuyere, lightlyere*) as metre or rhyme require. Compare *lenger* D441 with *lengere* D508.

2. Monosyllabic adjectives ending in consonants commonly (almost always in the holograph *Dialogue*) add *-e* when qualifying plural nouns: 'longe & faire dayes' (D275), 'matires grete' (D498), 'wommen been felle and wyse' (D681), 'my ladyes alle' (D806); but 'they been swart wrooth' (D756). The holograph *Dialogue* also has a few examples of the weak singular inflection with *-e* in monosyllabic adjectives: 'this wyde world' (D555), 'þat selue same' (D731); but endingless forms are here more frequent: 'the wys man' (D261), 'þat hy bond' (D340), 'the good plyt' (D487). Apart from regular comparative forms in *-er*, note 'the lattere errour' (D407), a form which supports the *grettere* required by rhyme at C345. See Kern, 'Zum Texte', pp. 417–19.

3. In the personal pronoun, third person plural forms are *they, hir(e), hem*. *Hir(e)* is also the form for the oblique cases of *shee*.

4. In nouns, the plural ending, normally *-(e)s*, appears as *-is* twice in rhyming position: *touris* D284, *deedis* D820. 'On hoonde' D520, also in rhyme, preserves the old dative singular ending *-e*.

5. In verbs, the forms of the second and third persons singular present indicative show variation between *-est*, *-eth* and *-ist*, *-ith*. The distribution of these types bears some relation to the final consonant of the verb stem. Thus, stems ending in *-m* always, in the holographs generally, take *-est*, *-eth*, whereas those ending in *-s* always take *-ist*, *-ith*; yet those ending in *-r* show both types. In the present plural of verbs, *-en* varies freely with *-e* in non-eliding contexts. In eliding contexts, a syllable is secured by the *-en* form. The infinitive ending *-e(n)* varies in the same way.

6. The present participle and gerund ending varies between *-ynge* and *-yng*: see Kern, 'Zum Texte', pp. 435–9. The former is disyllabic in non-eliding contexts (rhyming with imperative *mynge* at D431, 432).

7. Imperative inflections are *-e* in the singular, and in the plural *-eth* or *-ith* (varying as in 5 above). On their distribution, see D617n.

8. In the past tense of strong verbs, first and third person singular forms are identical and endingless: *cam, knew, spak, wroot*. Strong past plurals (not represented in the holograph *Dialogue*) take *-e* or *-en*, as do strong past participles: *holden, slayn* (with contraction), *write, writen*. The participial prefix *y-* appears in *yfalle* D393.

9. In the past tense of weak verbs, singular forms are: first person *-e*, second person *-est* or *-ist*, third person *-e*: *redde, seidist, made*. Weak past plurals (not represented in the holograph *Dialogue*) take *-e* or *-en*. However, singular *-e* and plural *-e(n)* are lost after syllabic *-ed* or *-id*: 'he logged him' (D615). Weak past participles vary between *-ed* and *-id* (as in 5 above): *causid, lerned, thankid*. Short past participle forms include *maad, swept, taght, told*.

10. Present plural forms of the verb 'to be' are *be* or *been* (though *arn* occurs elsewhere in the holographs, and at C352 here). The past participle is also *be* or *been*. Plural forms of 'shall' vary between *shuln* and *shul*; but D283 has disyllabic *shole*.

PUNCTUATION

The edited texts in this edition represent Hoccleve's own orthography and morphology, directly in the holograph *Dialogue* and by editorial intervention elsewhere; but this is not the case with his punctuating practice. That can here be seen only in the holograph *Dialogue*; and even there only the poet's paraphs and virgules are represented in the present text, which is otherwise supplied with modern punctuation in accordance with EETS practice.[92]

1. *Paraphs*. The holograph *Dialogue* has paraph signs (¶) in either blue or gold, generally in alternation. The main function of the sign here is to mark the beginnings of speeches. Every change of speaker is so indicated

---

[92] Punctuation in the Durham MS is discussed in Pryor's thesis, Introduction, pp. 135–44. Pryor attempts to reproduce all Hoccleve's marks in her text. On punctuation in the non-holograph section here, see below, p. lxiv. See generally M. B. Parkes, *Pause and Effect: An Introduction to the History of Punctuation in the West* (Aldershot, 1992).

(e.g. D620–28). On three occasions, paraphs mark a return to direct address towards the end of a longer speech: D291, 617, 739. They also signal the beginnings of the only two passages of authorial narration in this part of the *Series*: D659, 799. Six other paraphs draw attention to *notabilia*: D344 (citation of Cicero), 400 (simile), 575 (reference to Cherburgh), 715 (advice about women), 722 (example of Adam), 806 (balade to women).

2. *Virgules.* The oblique stroke or *virgula suspensiva* is found in 353 of the 574 lines in the present edition of the holograph *Dialogue*. (For comparable statistics in the Selden text of the non-holograph lines, see below p. lxiv). As the following figures show, lines with a single virgule have it most often towards the middle, especially after the fourth syllable: 4 virgules after the first syllable, 22 after the second, 33 after the third, 139 after the fourth, 73 after the fifth, 45 after the sixth, 12 after the seventh, 3 after the eighth, and none after the ninth. There are also 21 lines with two virgules, and one (D281) with four. The placement is commonly determined by considerations of syntax and rhetoric. Virgules approaching either end of a line are drawn there only by unusually strong syntactic or rhetorical features, as at D322, 401, 410, 488, 757, 763. Yet Hoccleve's metrical system cannot strictly be said to employ a 'caesura'—a regular mid-line break, that is, such as that after the fourth syllable in much medieval French verse.[93]

3. *Other marks of punctuation.* Such marks are not reproduced in the present edition of the holograph *Dialogue*, being replaced there by the appropriate modern punctuation, either comma or question mark. Hoccleve employs the *punctus elevatus* in two forms: an S-shaped stroke sloping to the right, with or without a dot or *punctus* at its base.[94] Both types vary considerably in size and form. The function of the modern question mark is performed on seven occasions by the dotted version (D294, 322, 455, 472, 739, 780, 782) and on three by the version without the *punctus* (D382, 613, 626). Many questions, however, are left unmarked. The more common functions of the undotted *punctus*

---

[93] See the discussions by G. G. Killough, 'Middle English Verse Punctuation: A Sample Survey', *Text*, 4 (1988), 163–88; and 'Punctuation and Caesura in Chaucer', *Studies in the Age of Chaucer*, 4 (1982), 85–107.

[94] Parkes discusses variants of the *punctus elevatus* on pp. 42–3 of *Pause and Effect*. His distinction between that and the *punctus interrogativus*, used for questions, does not seem applicable to Hoccleve, where no distinct shape for the latter (Parkes, p. 306) is perceptible.

elevatus resemble those of the modern comma. It marks the end of sentence-initial subordinate clauses, as at the ends of D314, 403, 664, 679, as well as other places where the structure of a sentence may seem to require that the reader be prompted to an upward intonation in expectation of more to come (e.g. after a long subject-clause, at the end of D601). The same ancient association of the *punctus elevatus* with rising pitch, it may be noted, seems relevant also to Hoccleve's use of the mark for questions. All but one of the ten such uses listed above mark yes/no questions—a type commonly ending in a rising tone. By contrast, questions of the open or WH- type, whose intonation normally falls at the end, are left unmarked, except in the single case of D739.[95]

4. It would be wrong to leave the impression that Hoccleve's virgules and *punctus elevati* are consistent in their shapes or always clearly distinguishable. Some are very faint; and variations in size and shape are dictated by line-position and also, sometimes, by need to emphasise a particular mark: thus, the *punctus elevatus* after *report* D770 is exceptionally large, indicating that the sentence remains to be completed in the next stanza. Especially troublesome are the occasional very small marks, in a variety of shapes resembling acute accents, circumflexes, and commas. Some of these I have treated as vestigial virgules, and some might be seen as fragmentary writings of the *punctus elevatus*; but their interpretation is quite uncertain. They seem too various to form a category of their own; but some of them can be assigned to existing categories only by allowing a great deal for the fluidity of handwritten punctuation marks.

THE MAKING OF THE 'SERIES'

HUMPHREY DUKE OF GLOUCESTER

In the *Dialogue*, lines 526–41, Hoccleve represents his present book as fulfilment of a promise made 'many a day ago' to write something for Humphrey Duke of Gloucester. If it is the case that the poet began work on 'this book' shortly after the Duke's return from his absence

---

[95] On the distinction in intonation between questions of the yes/no or 'polar' type and open or WH- questions in Modern English, see, for instance, P. Hawkins, *Introducing Phonology* (London, 1984), pp. 207–9. D739 may be regarded as one of those minority cases where an open question may nevertheless 'be spoken with one of the rising tones, which would add a connotation of "politeness" or "tentativeness"'—or in this case, perhaps, archness (Hawkins, p. 207).

campaigning in Normandy from July 1417 until late in 1419 (see below), this promise may date from 1417 or even earlier. This would explain why Hoccleve felt called upon to apologise for the delay: 'seeknesse and vnlust / and othir mo | Han be the causes of impediment' (D537–8). Elsewhere the poet speaks of Humphrey as his 'good lord', who has been gracious to him for many years (D554–60, 708), and there is no reason to doubt that they were acquainted. Humphrey, the youngest brother of Henry V (b. 1390), was a member of the king's council by April 1415; and that body met in the Star Chamber, next door to the offices of the Privy Seal in the Palace of Westminster.[96] So a senior Privy Seal clerk such as Hoccleve would have had many opportunities, both official and informal, to encounter members of the council.[97]

Humphrey was to acquire a great reputation as a patron of letters, and even as an early 'humanist'; but surviving evidence for his active literary interests dates from later in his life.[98] As early as 1422, John Lydgate did describe the Duke as 'expert in poetrye', but his eulogy places its main emphasis upon Humphrey's prowess as a knight: he is 'Martys sone'.[99] This agrees with the account given by Hoccleve some two years earlier, in *Dialogue* 563–616. That passage is devoted entirely to proving the Duke's surpassing *knyghthode*, by descriptions of his martial feats in the Normandy campaign, at Cherbourg, the Cotentin, and Rouen. Elsewhere Hoccleve discusses with the Friend what kind of book the Duke might like to receive; but their discussion reveals no distinct impression of his literary tastes. Indeed, the Friend suggests that any subject will do, 'so þat it be mateere of honestee' (D627). When he then advises Hoccleve to offer something in praise of women, as a penance for his previous offence again them, the poet expresses doubts. But the Friend

[96] The standard life is still that by K. H. Vickers, *Humphrey, Duke of Gloucester: A Biography* (London, 1907). 'In April [1415] he appears as a member of the King's Privy Council for the first time' (Vickers, p. 14). On the Palace of Westminster, see note to *Complaint* 72.

[97] The Privy Seal acted, among other things, as secretariat to the council: see T. F. Tout, *Chapters in the Administrative History of Mediaeval England*, Vol. V (Manchester, 1930), pp. 59–61, and J. F. Baldwin, *The King's Council in England During the Middle Ages* (Oxford, 1913), pp. 255–61. As a member of the council, 'H. Gloucestre' was among those granting Hoccleve's petition for a corrody in 1424: see my *Thomas Hoccleve*, p. 48 (document no. 63).

[98] See L. C. Y. Everest-Phillips, 'The Patronage of Humphrey, Duke of Gloucester: A Re-Evaluation', Ph. D. Thesis (York, 1983), p. 309: 'It is clear from a chronological analysis of Duke Humphrey's patronage that his interest in being a patron was largely confined to the years 1430–1441 and more particularly to the second half of this period.'

[99] *Epithalamium for Gloucester*, lines 141–47, 155, ed. E. P. Hammond, *English Verse between Chaucer and Surrey* (Durham, NC, 1927), pp. 142–48.

reassures him: Humphrey, he says, enjoys *daliance* with ladies and may do Hoccleve's reputation with them some good by drawing their attention to the book (D701–10). This little vignette imagines the Duke as something other than a solitary or scholarly reader.

There is no evidence that Humphrey himself requested or commissioned the *Series*; yet Hoccleve no doubt hoped that the book would strengthen his relationship with his 'good lord'. Later evidence suggests that Humphrey might have found much to admire in Hoccleve's verse.[100] Although none of the surviving copies of the *Series* can be associated with the Duke, it is hard to believe that the poet failed to present him with one.

DATING THE 'SERIES'

According to Hoccleve himself, he started work on the *Series*— presumably on the *Complaint*—immediately upon hearing of Humphrey's return from France: 'As blyue as þat I herde of his comynge | Fro France, I penne and ynke gan to take' (D542–3). In the Durham copy, made by the poet himself, these lines are accompanied with a gloss: 'Scilicet de secundo reditu suo de Francia' ('Concerning, that is, his second return from France'). As this gloss is found in none of the other surviving copies, it may be supposed to have been added for the benefit of the lady for whom Hoccleve made the Durham copy, Joan Neville, Countess of Westmorland. Since the Countess was Humphrey's aunt, she might take a particular interest in the matter; and she would have known that her nephew returned first from France in 1415, after the Agincourt campaign, and that his 'second return' occurred late in 1419, after campaigning in Normandy. This journey was followed by the period of Humphrey's regency to which Hoccleve refers at D533. The purpose of the gloss may therefore have been to distinguish this occasion from a later, third, return from France, in March or April 1422, for that was also followed by a period when Humphrey acted as regent (up to September 1422).[101] If the Durham copy was made later than that, as seems likely, Hoccleve may have anticipated misunderstanding on the part of its recipient.

[100] The author of *Palladius on Husbandry*, writing in 1440 for his patron Humphrey, says of him that 'he taught me metur make', and that he marked faults in the text with a plummet, evidently in part to correct metre: ed. Hammond, *English Verse*, Prohemium, line 109 (p. 205), and the final stanza of Book II (p. 206). In the Fitzwilliam MS, the *Palladius* observes the count of syllables almost as strictly as do the Hoccleve holographs.

[101] I derive my dates from the biography by Vickers, here as in my earlier discussion: 'Thomas Hoccleve: Some Redatings', *Review of English Studies*, NS 46 (1995), 366–72.

The poet's gloss, therefore, gives reason to believe that he began work on the *Series* shortly after Humphrey's return to England in late November or very early December 1419, and that the reference to the Duke as regent was made during the first of his two period of regency in the absence of Henry V, that is, between 30 December 1419 and 2 February 1421. A little later in the *Dialogue*, at l. 662, the Friend remarks that it is now the holy season of Lent. Since the conversation is represented in the poem as taking place on the day immediately following the poet's troubled night at the end of November (*Complaint* 17), the reference to Lent introduces a chronological inconsistency, and so may be taken as indicating the actual time of writing, in Lent 1420 (21 February to 7 April). This speculation gains some support from the fact that the reference in the *Complaint* to the end of November agrees with the actual time of year at which Hoccleve evidently began work on that piece.[102] Yet both datings serve internal poetic purposes—late November as appropriate for gloomy thoughts, and Lent for penance (*Dialogue* 661 ff.)—and the inconsistent reference to Lent may have no other explanation.

There remains, however, one other piece of evidence in the *Dialogue* which appears to point to a somewhat later date. This is the stanza, D134–40, which refers to a parliamentary statute requiring that gold coins should be weighed by their users. Furnivall was certainly right in identifying this as a statute made by the parliament of 2 May 1421: see the discussion in Excursus III here, where the text of the statute is given. Furnivall's identification has led almost all scholars to suppose that the *Dialogue* was composed after May 1421, and so during Humphrey's second period of regency, in 1422, since the first such period had ended three months before the May parliament.[103] This supposition requires them also to suppose that, when Hoccleve referred

---

[102] The Norman Rolls record a licence to James Celestre to impress forty sailors for the voyage of Humphrey back to England, an entry dated November 21? 1419 in *Calendar of Norman Rolls, Reports of the Deputy Keeper of Public Record*, no. 42 (London, 1881), Appendix, p. 331. 'It is probable that he crossed the Channel within a few days of this provision' (Vickers, p. 80).

[103] So J. H. Kern, 'Die Datierung von Hoccleve's Dialog', *Anglia*, 40 (1916), 370–73; Pryor, p. 12; Seymour, pp. xiv, 135, 136. Furnivall mistakenly supposed that Humphrey's second regency began in June 1421 and therefore dated the *Dialogue* 1421–22 (*Minor Poems*, pp. viii, xxii). The earlier dating proposed here was first suggested by A. I. Doyle and M. B. Parkes, 'The Production of Copies of the *Canterbury Tales* and the *Confessio Amantis* in the Early Fifteenth Century', in *Medieval Scribes, Manuscripts and Libraries: Essays Presented to N. R. Ker*, ed. M. B. Parkes and A. G. Watson (London, 1978), p. 182, n. 39.

to the Duke's second return, he meant in fact the third, in March or
April 1422. But it seems unlikely that he would make such a mistake, for
such a reader. And why, if he was writing in 1422, did he speak only of
Humphrey's martial feats in the 1417–19 Normandy campaign, with no
reference to the Duke's more recent successes in the French campaigns
of 1421–2?[104]

The solution to this problem lies in the text of the stanza itself; for
this clearly declares itself as a postscript, not having formed part of the
Dialogue in its original form. The immediately preceding stanzas
(D103–33) had complained that people would not accept gold coins
without weighing them; but now, since the recent statute has required
just that, the situation is changed. Weighing of such coins, previously
unauthorised, is now not only authorised but actually required by law.
The contrast between an earlier time when the surrounding stanzas were
written and present time, 'now', is emphatic:

> '*Whan I this wroot* / many men dide amis,
> They weyed gold / vnhad auctoritee;
> No statut maad was *thanne* / as *now* is.
> But syn gold to weye / charged *now* been we
> Resoun axith / þat it obeied be;
> *Now* tyme it is / vnto weightes vs drawe
> Syn þat the parlement / hath maad it a lawe.'

So understood, the stanza requires no 1422 dating for the *Dialogue*; on
the contrary, it proves that Hoccleve had already produced a draft of it
before May 1421—the version to which he later felt bound to add,
somewhat awkwardly, his postscript.

The evidence suggests, then, that Hoccleve began the *Complaint* in
the winter of 1419/20, and that the greater part of his work on it and the
Dialogue had been completed by early 1421. These two poems together
provide an introduction and setting for the texts which follow in the
Series: the story of Jereslaus' wife from *Gesta Romanorum*, *Learn to Die*,
and another story from the *Gesta*, that of Jonathas. Monologue and
dialogue here give place to writings produced for third parties: *Jereslaus*
for Humphrey, *Learn to Die* for the devout man who requested it
(D232–8), and *Jonathas* for the Friend's wild fifteen-year-old son. The
resulting structure resembles that of the *dits* of Middle French poets
such as Machaut or Froissart (though with very different content). Like

---

[104] Thus Vickers, pp. 98–9, stresses the prominent part played by Humphrey in the
siege of Dreux, July and August 1421.

them, the English poet represents himself, in the foreground, as the author of those various texts which the work incorporates. The technique is described as 'montage' by one writer on the French *dit*, Jacqueline Cerquiglini: 'le montage . . .consiste précisément a faire tenir ensemble, selon une technique de l'étagement, des choses qui existent ou qui peuvent exister par ailleurs, antérieurement.'[105] Since such embedded texts may have origins independent of the *dit* itself, conclusions about the date of the *Complaint* and *Dialogue* do not necessarily apply to the *Gesta* stories or *Learn to Die*. One or more of these may have been composed as free-standing items before Hoccleve conceived the *Series*. However, there is no positive evidence to suggest this. The *Gesta* stories are closely integrated into the argument of the *Series*, and one may suppose that they had no existence anterior to 1420–1. *Learn to Die* presents a slightly more doubtful case. It is said to have been separately requested by the 'devout man'; and it follows *Jereslaus* with no textual link save a heading ('Explicit moralizatio et incipit ars vtillissima sciendi mori'). The existence of another holograph copy of this poem as a separate item in MS HM 744 may also arouse suspicion. However, the Huntington manuscript itself dates, in all probability, from after 1422; and textual analysis of its copy suggests that it was taken from Hoccleve's working draft or master copy of the *Series* itself.[106]

HOCCLEVE'S 'WYLDE INFIRMITEE'

The *Complaint* and *Dialogue* both look back to a period of illness when, Hoccleve says, 'the substance / of my memorie | Wente to pleye / as for a certein space' (C50–1). This episode is said to have ended when God restored the poet's mind to health, an event which is then dated very precisely to five years ago at the last All Saints' Day (1 November). If the present dating of the *Complaint* to the winter of 1419–20 is correct, the latest All Saints' Day was that of 1419; so the recovery may be assigned to 1 November 1414. Hoccleve stresses the completeness of

---

[105] J. Cerquiglini, 'Le Clerc et l'écriture: le *Voir Dit* de Guillaume de Machaut et la définition du dit', in *Literatur in der Gesellschaft des Spätmittelalters*, ed. H. U. Gumbrecht (Heidelberg, 1980), pp. 151–68; p. 159. See further J. A. Burrow, 'Hoccleve and the Middle French Poets', in *The Long Fifteenth Century: Essays for Douglas Gray*, ed. H. Cooper and S. Mapstone (Oxford, 1997), pp. 35–49.

[106] On the Huntington *Learn to Die*, see Excursus I here. Recent criticism has stressed the thematic unity of the *Series*. Thus, Christina von Nolcken sees *Learn to Die* as central to the whole work, which she describes as a 'text about death': '"O why ne had y lerned for to die?": *Lerne for to Dye* and the Author's Death in Thomas Hoccleve's *Series*', in *Essays in Medieval Studies*, ed. A. J. Frantzen, 10 (1993), 27–51.

his recovery and the precise length of time that has elapsed since, evidently because his chief concern is with the failure of his acquaintances and even, to begin with, of the Friend to acknowledge his restored mental health—a fact which the whole *Series* itself serves to demonstrate by virtue of its very existence.[107]

There is no reason to doubt that Hoccleve did in reality suffer some kind of mental breakdown, probably in 1414.[108] Its exact nature, however, can hardly be determined, since the poet is concerned to vindicate his present sanity, not to describe its past loss. The prognostic speculations of his acquaintances point to conflicting diagnoses (C85–98, and see notes to C88, 92–3, 120, 127–33); and Hoccleve rejects the Friend's suggestion that his trouble was caused by excessive study (D302–4, 379–82, 398–9, and see note to D302–4). He himself speaks of a period of 'wylde infirmitee' (C40, compare *wyldenesse* C107 and *wyldhede* D52), when his *wit* and memory 'wente fer from hoom' (C233, compare C50–1, 64, 248–9). The illness, he says (C42), threw him 'out of himself'—something more than a mere metaphor at the time. He repeatedly ascribes both the illness and his recovery to the visitations of God (e.g. C36–9, 382, D96), and in one place speaks of God as punishing him justly for his 'synful gouernance' (C393–406).[109] Yet in his final statement before the matter is dropped, he singles out an immediate physical cause: 'it was causid of my long seeknesse' (D426). A clue to his conception of the aetiology may be found in his reference in the *Complaint* to 'the greuous venym | þat had infectid / and wyldid my brayn' (C234–5). Medical authorities at the time ascribed some types of mental derangement to noxious 'fumes' ascending to the brain from

---

[107] J. A. Burrow, 'Hoccleve's *Series*: Experience and Books', in *Fifteenth-Century Studies: Recent Essays*, ed. R. F. Yeager (Hamden, Conn., 1984), pp. 259–73.

[108] It may be relevant that the Issue Rolls of Michaelmas 1414 record no payment of Hoccleve's annuity: *Thomas Hoccleve*, p. 22, n. 89. Doubts are expressed by P. B. R. Doob in her influential discussion: *Nebuchadnezzar's Children: Conventions of Madness in Middle English Literature* (New Haven, Conn., 1974), pp. 210–30, especially pp. 226–9. S. Medcalf cites a modern medical diagnosis of Hoccleve as having suffered from 'a bi-polar manic-depressive illness . . .terminating in an attack of mania or hypomania', *The Later Middle Ages*, ed. S. Medcalf (London, 1981), pp. 129–30. G. MacLennan discusses Hoccleve together with Tasso as a case of 'melancholic madness': *Lucid Interval: Subjective Writing and Madness in History* (Leicester, 1992), pp. 18–23. The most elaborate attempt at a modern diagnosis concludes that the poet's psychosis was primarily of a depressive character, many of its symptoms 'meeting the modern criteria for severe depression': G. Claridge, M. R. Pryor, G. Watkins, *Sounds from the Bell Jar: Ten Psychotic Authors* (London, 1990), pp. 62–7, 69–70.

[109] Doob, pp. 220–25, stresses 'Hoccleve's concern with physical and mental disease as the consequence of moral failure'; but it is hard to accept her suggestion that he chose madness as 'the vehicle through which to describe the moral insanity of sin' (p. 228).

the burning, or 'adustion', of one or other of the body's four natural humours. If, as seems likely, Hoccleve thought that his own dominant humour was black bile or melancholy, he may have identified the 'venom' that drove his brain wild as adust melancholy. According to the chief medical authority on the subject, Constantinus Africanus, such burnt or adust melancholy humours cause *alienatio*, alienation or derangement of the mind, as well as gloomy fears and irrational doubts and suspicions.[110]

THE COPYING OF THE 'SERIES'

Hoccleve may be supposed to have presented a fair copy of the *Series* to Duke Humphrey, either commissioned from a scribe or written out by himself.[111] No such manuscript survives; but there remain two copies in the poet's own hand: *Learn to Die* as included by Hoccleve in his collection of shorter pieces, now MS HM 744, and the Durham copy of the complete *Series*. At an early stage, also, a scribal copy was evidently made; for all surviving scribal copies of the *Series* share many non-authorial variants which must go back to that archetype. Its earliest descendant, the Selden MS, was made during the poet's lifetime, or very shortly therafter. The scribal archetype derived, directly or indirectly, from Hoccleve's working copy at a stage distinct from those represented in the two holographs—the stage that I refer to as VO, the Variant Original. The holographs and VO show no major textual variants, nothing like the 'pre-publication' adding of the post-

[110] 'Quae enim de humoribus est melancholicis in cerebro incensis, nimiam habet alienationem, angustias, tristitias, timores, dubitationes, malas imaginationes, suspiciones et similia', Constantinus Africanus, *Opera*, Vol. II (Basel, 1539), p. 249: from his *Theorica Pantegni*, Book IX, Chapter 8. The passage is cited in R. Klibansky, E. Panofsky, F. Saxl, *Saturn and Melancholy* (London, 1964), p. 87. Their chapter 'Melancholy as an Illness', pp. 75–97, is of fundamental importance. See also S. W. Jackson, *Melancholy and Depression: From Hippocratic Times to Modern Times* (New Haven, Conn., 1986). A standard treatise on melancholy was the *De Melancholia* of Constantinus Africanus. He writes: 'Fumus enim cholerae nigrae cum ad cerebrum saliat & ad locum mentis veniat, lumen eius obscurat, turbat & pessundat, ne quod comprehendere solebat, secundum quod oportet comprehendat. Unde haec suspicio generatur pessima, ut imaginetur non imaginanda & cor timere faciat terribilia', *De Melancholia*, ed. Garbers, p. 88 (Basel *Opera*, I 280–81). According to the *Isagoge* of Johannitius, a medical textbook, black bile when adust 'has in itself a most deadly quality and a pernicious character', trans. H. P. Cholmeley in his *John of Gaddesden and the Rosa Medicinae* (Oxford, 1912), p. 138. On the term 'venom' applied to adust melancholy, see n. to C234.

[111] Hoccleve himself evidently made fair copies of his *Regiment* for John of Lancaster, and of his balades for the Duke of York, though neither has survived: *Thomas Hoccleve*, p. 23.

script stanza (*Dialogue* 134–40); but Hoccleve evidently went on introducing small alterations, probably both in the working copy itself and also in the act of transcribing fair copies from it. The evidence of these variants suggests that VO belongs somewhere between the two holographs, but leaves it hard to determine which of the latter came first. The order was perhaps Huntington—VO—Durham.[112] In that case, the Durham holograph would represent the process of authorial tinkering at the latest stage of which we have knowledge. This copy alone has a final envoy stanza directing it to the Countess of Westmorland, for whom Hoccleve made it perhaps not very long before his death in the spring of 1426.

The *Series* never matched the success of Hoccleve's *Regiment of Princes*, of which no less than forty-three copies survive; but the work was far from passing unnoticed. The relationships of the five scribal copies of the complete work that survive imply the existence of at least three other lost manuscripts: the archetypal ancestor of all five, and the ancestors of BLY and LY. To these may be added the exemplar from which John Stow supplied the missing matter in the Durham holograph. There are also surviving manuscripts which contain parts of the *Series*, not studied here because they contain nothing of the *Complaint* or *Dialogue*. Bodleian Library MS Eng. Poet. d. 4 preserves fragments of what was evidently once a complete copy of the *Series*; and separate items are found in British Library MSS Harley 172 (*Learn to Die*) and Royal 17 D. vi (*Jereslaus, Learn to Die, Jonathas*), and Bodleian Library MS Digby 185 (*Jereslaus, Jonathas*).[113]

TREATMENT OF THE TEXTS

The nature of this edition has required that its three stretches of text should not have uniform treatment.

1. The text of the non-holograph section as it stands in the Selden MS is printed on lefthand pages, facing the edited text on the right for purposes of comparison. Selden's scribal text, including its headings and Latin glosses, is transcribed without alteration. Manuscript punctuation

[112] See Excursus I, pp. 116–18. It is the writing of the first person singular pronoun in Durham which chiefly suggests that that copy was probably made later than Huntington.
[113] See *Thomas Hoccleve*, pp. 51–2. The Royal and Digby MSS also contain the *Regiment of Princes*, as do all five of the copies containing scribal texts of the *Series*. The Durham holograph has only the *Series*.

and word-division are preserved. Initial letters of lines are treated as capitals, representing *ff* as *F*. Expanded abbreviations are italicized and interlinear or marginal insertions indicated by ` ´.

2. The edited text of the non-holograph section, an editorial reconstruction of the Variant Original, is printed on righthand pages, facing the diplomatic Selden text. Capitalization and word-division are editorial, as is punctuation. However, Selden's virgules are retained. These present a problem. Comparison between the practice of Selden and that of Hoccleve himself in the holograph *Dialogue* shows a marked discrepancy in the frequency of virgules. In the latter, 221 out of 574 lines lack virgules (see above, p. liv), but in the corresponding Selden lines only five are without the mark. Selden is equally free with virgules in the non-holograph section, marking them in all but eight of the 665 lines. Comparison with the only scribal copy apart from Selden to employ the mark, that of John Stow, suggests that this very persistent use of virgules goes back to the scribal archetype from which they both derive; but it seems unlikely that the Variant Original itself differed so markedly in this respect from the Durham holograph, whose lighter virgulation is matched in the Huntington holographs. For lack of a better solution, however, I reproduce Selden's virgules in the reconstructed text, except where textual differences require a change (C58, 148, 153), or Stow offers better (C67, 292, 367, 388, 411; D20, 81, 161, 166, 231). All substantive variants from the reconstructed text and glosses, including those in Selden, are recorded in the textual apparatus beneath. Scribal corrections are noted there, together with such spelling variants as are either notable in themselves or indicative of manuscript affiliations. Manuscripts supporting adopted readings are listed only in cases of departure from Selden.

3. The text of the holograph section follows the Durham copy. The few words or letters introduced editorially are enclosed in square brackets (D373, 380, 404, 426, 586, 665, 667), but omissions are not marked (D291, 381, 445). Hoccleve's interlinear insertions are indicated by ` ´. The flourish on final *r* and the bar through final *ll* have been expanded to *-e*. Like all other expansions, these are marked by italics. The poet's virgules and paraphs are preserved, but otherwise punctuation is editorial, as are capitalization (representing *ff* by *F*) and word-division. All substantive variants in the scribal copies are recorded in the textual apparatus beneath. Scribal corrections, including Hoccleve's own, are noted there, together with such spelling variants as are either notable in

themselves or indicative of manuscript affiliations. Manuscript support for adopted readings is given only where the holograph is not followed. Latin glosses in scribal copies which have no equivalent in Durham, most of which probably go back to VO, are recorded in the notes rather than in the apparatus.

BIBLIOGRAPHY

TEXTS AND EDITIONS

Burrow. J. A. (ed.), *English Verse 1300–1500* (London, 1977).

Faral, E. (ed.), *Les Arts Poétiques du XIIe et du XIIIe Siècle* (Paris, 1924).

Fenster, T. S., and M. C. Erler (eds), *Poems of Cupid, God of Love* (Leiden, 1990).

Furnivall, F. J. (ed.), *Hoccleve's Works: I The Minor Poems* (EETS, ES 61, 1892), revised by J. Mitchell and A. I. Doyle, reissued in one volume with Part II (1970).

Furnivall, F. J. (ed.), *Hoccleve's Works: III The Regement of Princes* (EETS, ES 72, 1897).

Garbers, K. (ed.), *Ishaq Ibn Imran, Maqala fi L-Malihuliya (Abhandlung über die Melancholie) und Constantini Africani, Libri Duo de Melancholia* (Hamburg, 1977).

Gollancz, I. (ed.), *Hoccleve's Works: II The Minor Poems* (EETS, ES 73, 1925), revised by J. Mitchell and A. I. Doyle, reissued in one volume with Part I (1970).

Gower, John, *Confessio Amantis*, in *The English Works of John Gower*, ed. G. C. Macaulay, 2 vols (EETS, ES 81, 82, 1900, 1901).

Hammond, E. P. (ed.), *English Verse between Chaucer and Surrey* (Durham, NC, 1927).

Langland, William, *Piers Plowman: The B Version*, ed. G. Kane and E. T. Donaldson (London, 1975).

Lucas, P. J. (ed.), *John Capgrave's Abbreuiacion of Cronicles* (EETS, 285, 1983).

O'Donoghue, B. (ed.), *Thomas Hoccleve: Selected Poems* (Manchester, 1982).

Pryor, M. R. (ed.), 'Thomas Hoccleve's Series: An Edition of MS Durham Cosin V iii 9', Ph. D. Thesis (University of California, Los Angeles, 1968).

Roman de la Rose, ed. F. Lecoy, 3 vols (Paris, 1965–70).

Seymour, M. C. (ed.), *Selections from Hoccleve* (Oxford, 1981).

Suso, Heinrich, *Heinrich Seuses Horologium Sapientiae*, ed. P. Künzle (Freiburg, 1977).

Trevisa, John, *On the Properties of Things: John Trevisa's Translation of Bartholomaeus Anglicus De Proprietatibus Rerum*, ed. M. C. Seymour *et al.*, 3 vols (Oxford, 1975–88).

STUDIES

Blyth, C., 'Editing *The Regiment of Princes*', in *Essays on Thomas Hoccleve*, ed. C. Batt (Westfield Publications in Medieval Studies 10, London, 1996), pp. 11–28.

Bornstein, D., 'Anti-Feminism in Thomas Hoccleve's Translation of Christine de Pizan's *Epistre au dieu d'amours*', *English Language Notes*, 19 (1981–82), 7–14.

Bowers, J. M., 'Hoccleve's Two Copies of *Lerne to Dye*: Implications for Textual Critics', *Papers of the Bibliographical Society of America*, 83 (1989), 437–72.

——, 'Hoccleve's Huntington Holographs: the First "Collected Poems" in English', *Fifteenth-Century Studies*, 15 (1989), 27–51.

Brink, B. ten, *The Language and Metre of Chaucer*, 2nd edn rev. F. Kluge, trans. M. B. Smith (London, 1901).

Brown, A. L., 'The Privy Seal Clerks in the Early Fifteenth Century', in *The Study of Medieval Records: Essays in Honour of Kathleen Major*, ed. D. A. Bullough and R. L. Storey (Oxford, 1971), pp. 260–81.

Brown, C., and R. H. Robbins, *The Index of Middle English Verse* (New York, 1943).

Burrow, J. A., 'Autobiographical Poetry in the Middle Ages: The Case of Thomas Hoccleve', *Proceedings of the British Academy*, 68 (1982), 389–412.

——, 'Hoccleve's *Series*: Experience and Books', in *Fifteenth-Century Studies: Recent Essays*, ed. R. F. Yeager (Hamden, Conn., 1984), pp. 259–73.

——, *Thomas Hoccleve* (Authors of the Middle Ages 4, Aldershot, 1994).

——, 'Thomas Hoccleve: Some Redatings', *Review of English Studies*, NS 46 (1995), 366–72.

——, 'Hoccleve and the Middle French Poets', in *The Long Fifteenth Century: Essays for Douglas Gray*, ed. H. Cooper and S. Mapstone (Oxford, 1997), pp. 35–49.

——, 'Hoccleve's *Complaint* and Isidore of Seville Again', *Speculum*, 73 (1998), 424–28.

Cerquiglini, J., 'Le Clerc et l'écriture: le *Voir Dit* de Guillaume de Machaut et la définition du dit', in *Literatur in der Gesellschaft des Spätmittelalters*, ed. H. U. Gumbrecht (Heidelberg, 1980), pp. 151–68.

Claridge, G., M. R. Pryor, and G. Watkins, *Sounds from the Bell Jar: Ten Psychotic Authors* (London, 1990).

Davis, N., 'Notes on Grammar and Spelling in the Fifteenth Century', in *The Oxford Book of Late Medieval Verse and Prose*, ed. D. Gray (Oxford, 1985), pp. 493–508.

Doob, P. B. R., *Nebuchadnezzar's Children: Conventions of Madness in Middle English Literature* (New Haven, Conn., 1974).

Doyle, A. I., and G. B. Pace, 'A New Chaucer Manuscript', *PMLA*, 83 (1968), 22–34.

Doyle, A. I., and M. B. Parkes, 'The Production of Copies of the *Canterbury Tales* and the *Confessio Amantis* in the Early Fifteenth Century', in *Medieval Scribes, Manuscripts and Libraries: Essays Presented to N. R. Ker*, ed. M. B. Parkes and A. G. Watson (London, 1978), pp. 163–210.

Edwards, A. S. G., 'Medieval Manuscripts Owned by William Browne of Tavistock (1590/1?-1643/5?)', in *Books and Collectors 1200–1700: Essays Presented to Andrew Watson*, ed. J. P. Carley and C. G. C. Tite (London, 1997), pp. 441–49.

Edwards, A. S. G., and J. I. Miller, 'Stow and Lydgate's "St. Edmund"', *Notes and Queries*, 218 (1973), 365–69.

Edwards, A. S. G., and J. Hedley, 'John Stow, *The Craft of Lovers* and T. C. C. R. 13. 19', *Studies in Bibliography*, 28 (1975), 265–68.

Everest-Phillips, L. C. Y., 'The Patronage of Humphrey, Duke of Gloucester: A Re-Evaluation', Ph. D. Thesis (York, 1983).

Fleming, J. V., 'Hoccleve's "Letter of Cupid" and the "Quarrel" over the *Roman de la Rose*', *Medium Aevum*, 40 (1971), 21–40.

Greetham, D. C., 'Normalisation of Accidentals in Middle English Texts: the Paradox of Thomas Hoccleve', *Studies in Bibliography*, 38 (1985), 121–50.

——, 'Challenges of Theory and Practice in the Editing of Hoccleve's *Regement of Princes*', in *Manuscripts and Texts: Editorial Problems in Later Middle English Literature*, ed. D. Pearsall (Cambridge, 1987), pp. 60–86.

——, 'Self-Referential Artifacts: Hoccleve's Persona as a Literary Device', *Modern Philology*, 86 (1989), 242–51.

Greg, W. W., *Collected Papers*, ed. J. C. Maxwell (Oxford, 1966).

Griffiths, J., and D. Pearsall (eds), *Book Production and Publishing in Britain, 1375–1475* (Cambridge, 1989).

Hammond, E. P., 'The Nine-Syllabled Pentameter Line in some Post-Chaucerian Manuscripts', *Modern Philology*, 23 (1925), 129–52.

Hudson, A., 'John Stow (1525?-1605)', in *Editing Chaucer: The Great Tradition*, ed. P. G. Ruggiers (Norman, OK, 1984), pp. 53–70.

Jefferson, J. A., 'The Hoccleve Holographs and Hoccleve's Metrical Practice', in *Manuscripts and Texts: Editorial Problems in Later Middle English Literature*, ed. D. Pearsall (Cambridge, 1987), pp. 95–109.

Kane, G., *Chaucer and Langland: Historical and Textual Approaches* (London, 1989).

Kern, J. H., 'Zum Texte einiger Dichtungen Thomas Hoccleve's', *Anglia*, 39 (1916), 389–494.

——, 'Hoccleve's Verszeile', *Anglia*, 40 (1916), 367–69.

——, 'Die Datierung von Hoccleve's Dialog', *Anglia*, 40 (1916), 370–73.

Killough, G. G., 'Punctuation and Caesura in Chaucer', *Studies in the Age of Chaucer*, 4 (1982), 85–107.

——, 'Middle English Verse Punctuation: A Sample Survey', *Text*, 4 (1988), 163–88.

Klibansky, R., E. Panofsky, and F. Saxl, *Saturn and Melancholy* (London, 1964).

Kurtz, B. P., 'The Source of Occleve's *Lerne to Dye*', *Modern Language Notes*, 38 (1923), 337–40.

Lucas, P. J., 'Consistency and Correctness in the Orthographic Usage of John Capgrave's *Chronicle*', *Studia Neophilologica*, 45 (1973), 323–55.

——, 'An Author as Copyist of his own Work: John Capgrave OSA (1393–1464)', in *New Science out of Old Books: Studies in Manuscripts and Early Printed Books in Honour of A. I. Doyle*, ed. R. Beadle and A. J. Piper (Aldershot, 1995), pp. 227–48.

MacLennan, G., *Lucid Interval: Subjective Writing and Madness in History* (Leicester, 1992).

Mann, J., *Apologies to Women* (Inaugural Lecture, Cambridge, 1991).

Marzec, M. S., 'The Latin Marginalia of the *Regiment of Princes* as an Aid to Stemmatic Analysis', *Text*, 3 (1987), 269–84.

Medcalf, S. (ed.), *The Later Middle Ages* (London, 1981).

Mitchell, J., *Thomas Hoccleve: A Study in Early Fifteenth-Century English Poetic* (Urbana, Ill., 1968).

——'Hoccleve's *Minor Poems*: Addenda and Corrigenda', *Edinburgh Bibliographical Society Transactions*, V 3 (1983), 9–16.

Mustanoja, T. F., *A Middle English Syntax: Part I Parts of Speech* (Helsinki, 1960).

Nolcken, C. von, '"O why ne had y lerned for to die?": *Lerne for to Dye* and the Author's Death in Thomas Hoccleve's *Series*', *Essays in Medieval Studies*, ed. A. J. Frantzen, 10 (1993), 27–51.

Parkes, M. B., *Pause and Effect: An Introduction to the History of Punctuation in the West* (Aldershot, 1992).

Rigg, A. G., 'Hoccleve's *Complaint* and Isidore of Seville', *Speculum*, 45 (1970), 564–74.

Robbins, R. H., and J. L. Cutler, *Supplement to the Index of Middle English Verse* (Lexington, Ky, 1965).

Samuels, M. L., 'Chaucer's Spelling', in *The English of Chaucer and his Contemporaries*, ed. J. J. Smith (Aberdeen, 1988), pp. 23–37.

——, 'The Scribe of the Hengwrt and Ellesmere Manuscripts of *The Canterbury Tales*', in *The English of Chaucer and his Contemporaries*, ed. J. J. Smith (Aberdeen, 1988), pp. 38–50.

Schulz, H. C., 'Thomas Hoccleve, Scribe', *Speculum*, 12 (1937), 71–81.

Shailor, B. A., *Catalogue of Medieval and Renaissance Manuscripts in the Beinecke Rare Book and Manuscript Library, Yale University*, 2 vols (Binghamton, NY, 1984–87).

Simpson, J., 'Madness and Texts: Hoccleve's *Series*', in *Chaucer and Fifteenth-Century Poetry*, ed. J. Boffey and J. Cowan (King's College London Medieval Studies V, London, 1991), pp. 15–29.

Stanley, E. G., 'Chaucer's Metre after Chaucer, I: Chaucer to Hoccleve', *Notes and Queries*, 234 (1989), 11–23.

Tout, T. F., *Chapters in the Administrative History of Mediaeval England*, Vol. V (Manchester, 1930).

Vickers, K. H., *Humphrey, Duke of Gloucester: A Biography* (London, 1907).

Vollmer, E., 'Sprache und Reime des Londoners Hoccleve', *Anglia*, 21 (1899), 201–21.

Whiting, B. J., and H. W. Whiting, *Proverbs, Sentences, and Proverbial Phrases from English Writings Mainly Before 1500* (Cambridge, Mass., 1968).

Youmans, G., 'Reconsidering Chaucer's Prosody', in *English Historical Metrics*, ed. C. B. McCully and J. J. Anderson (Cambridge, 1996), pp. 185–209.

ABBREVIATIONS

AV	Authorised Version of the Bible. [Latin citations from the Vulgate, English from the Douai Version].
CT	Chaucer's *Canterbury Tales*.
EETS (ES)	Early English Text Society (Extra Series).
Furn.	Furnivall (ed.), *Hoccleve's Minor Poems* [cited by item and line number].
Goll.	Gollancz (ed.), *Hoccleve's Minor Poems* [cited by item and line number].
IMEV	Brown-Robbins *Index of Middle English Verse* and Robbins-Cutler *Supplement*.
MED	*Middle English Dictionary*.
OED	*Oxford English Dictionary*.
PL	*Patrologia Latina*.
PMLA	*Publications of the Modern Language Association of America*.
SATF	Société des Anciens Textes Français.
SC	*Summary Catalogue of Western Manuscripts in the Bodleian Library at Oxford* (Oxford, 1895–1953).
VO	Variant Original.
Whiting	Whiting and Whiting, *Proverbs, Sentences, and Proverbial Phrases*.

COMPLAINT AND *DIALOGUE*

SELDEN MS.

Aftir þat heruest Inned had hise sheues.
And that the broun sesoun of Mihelmesse.
Was come / and gan / the trees robbe of her leues.
That grene had ben / and in lusty freisshenesse.
And hem in to colour / of ȝelownesse.   5
Had died / and doun throwen vndir foote.
That chaunge sanke / in to myn herte roote.

For freisshly brouȝte it / to my remembrau*n*ce.
That stablenesse / in this worlde / is ther noon.
Ther is no þing / but chaunge and variau*n*ce.   10
Howe welthi a man be / or wel be goon.
Endure it shal not / he shal it forgoon.
Deeth vndir foote / shal him þriste a doun.
That is eu*er*y wiȝtes conclucioun.

Wiche for to weyue / is in no ma*n*nes myȝt.   15
Howe riche he be / stronge lusty freissh & gay.
And in the ende / of Nouembre vppon a niȝt.
Siȝynge sore / as I in my bed lay.
For this and oþir þouȝtis / wiche many a day.
Byforne I tooke / sleep cam noon in myn ye.   20
So vexid me / the þouȝtful maladie.

I sy wel sithin I / with siknesse last.
Was scourgid / cloudy hath bene þe fauour.
That shoon on me / ful briȝt in times past.
The su*n*ne abated / and þe dirke shour.   25

EDITED TEXT

Aftir þat heruest inned had his sheeues,
And þat the broun sesoun of Mighelmesse
Was come / and gan / the trees robbe of hir leeues
þat greene had been / and in lusty fresshnesse,
And hem into colour / of yelownesse   5
Had died / and doun throwen vndir foote,
þat chaunge sank / into myn herte roote.

For fresshly broghte it / to my remembrance
þat stablenesse / in this world / is ther noon;
There is no thyng / but chaunge and variance.   10
How welthy a man be / or wel begoon,
Endure it shal nat / he shal it forgoon.
Deeth vndir foote / shal him thriste adoun,
þat is euery wightes conclusioun;

Which for to weyue / is in no mannes might,   15
How riche he be / strong, lusty, fressh and gay.
And in thende / of Nouembre vpon a nyght,
Sighynge sore / as I in my bed lay
For this and othir thoght / which many a day
Before I took / sleep cam noon in myn ye,   20
So vexid me / the thoghtful maladie.

I sy wel syn I / with seeknesse last
Was scourgid / cloudy hath been the fauour
þat shoon on me / ful bright in tymes past.
The sonne abated / and the dirke shour   25

C1 þat] þe C   C2 broun] brome CSt   C3 gan] gone B   robbe] rubbe L
C5 yelownesse] *over eras.* L   C6 died] dyen St   doun] do'w'ne L   throwen]
threste C   C7 sank] *corr. from* sange St   myn] my BLY   C8 it] *om.* St
C10 is] 'is' Y   C12 *line om.* C   shal(1)] shall he Y   C13 thriste] thirst
LY   C14 wightes] wites St   C16 he be] be he C   C17 a] *om.* Y
C19 thoght] C, þou3tis SBLYSt   C20 Before] CSt, byforne SBLY   myn]
my BLY   C22 sy] see St   syn] sithin SBLYSt, *om.* C   C24 on] *om.* St
tymes] tyme's' L   C25 abated] *over eras.* C

Hilded doun riȝt on me / and in langour.
Me made swymme / so that my spirite.
To lyue / no lust had / ne `no´ delite.

The greef aboute myn herte / so `sore´ swal.
And bolned euere / to and to so sore.   30
That nedis oute / I muste ther withal.
I thouȝte I nolde / kepe it cloos no more.
Ne lete it in me / for to eelde and hore.
And for to preue / I cam of a womman.
I braste oute / on þe morwe / and þus bigan.   35

Here endith my prolog: and folwith my compleinte:

Almyȝty god / as liketh his goodnesse.
Vesiteþ folke al day / as men may se.
With los of good / and bodily sikenesse.
And amonge othir / he forȝat not me.
Witnesse vppon / the wilde infirmite.   40
Wiche þat I hadde / as many a man wel knewe.
And wiche me oute of my silfe / caste and threwe.

It was so knowen to þe peple / and kouthe.
That counseil was it noon / ne not be miȝt.
Howe it wiþ me stood / was in euery mannes mouþe. 45
And þat ful sore / my frendis affriȝt.
They for myn helþe / pilgimages hiȝt.
And souȝte hem / somme on hors and somme on foote.
God ȝelde it hem / to gete me my boote.

But al þouȝ the substaunce / of my memorie.   50
Wente to pleie / as for a certein space.

Hildid doun right on me / and in langour
Me made swymme / so þat my spiryt
To lyue / no lust hadde / ne delyt.

The greef aboute myn herte / so swal
And bolned euere / to and to so sore   30
þat needes oute / I muste therwithal.
I thoghte I nolde / keepe it cloos no more
Ne lette it in me / for to eelde and hore;
And for to preeue / I cam of a womman
I brast out / on the morwe / and thus began.   35

Heere endith my Prolog, and folwith my Conpleynte.

Almighty God / as lykith his goodnesse,
Visiteth folk al day / as men may see,
With los of good / and bodily seeknesse,
And among othir / he forgat nat me;
Witnesse vpon / the wylde infirmitee   40
Which þat I hadde / as many a man wel kneew,
And which me out of myself / caste and threew.

It was so knowen to the peple / and kowth
þat conseil was it noon / ne nat be mighte.
How it with me stood / was in euery mowth,   45
And þat ful sore / my freendes affrighte.
They for myn helthe / pilgrimages highte
And soghte hem / some on hors and some on foote,
God yilde it hem / to gete me my boote.

But althogh the substance / of my memorie   50
Wente to pleye / as for a certein space,

C26 and] *om.* Y   C27 Me] he St   spiryt] wite St   C28 no] in C   ne] St,
noo C, ne 'no' S, ne nokynnes L Y, nor nokyns B   C29 myn] my BLY St   so] CBY St,
ran so L (ran *canc.*), so 'sore' S   C30 bolned] volued C   so] *om.* C   C32 nolde]
wolde B   keepe it] it kepe St   C33 lette] lett BSt, let CLY, lete S
eelde] olde St   C36 *heading* folwith] biginnith C   C37 folk] folks St
C39 othir] all othir C   C41 þat] *om.* Y   wel kneew] wole knawe B
C42 And which] and me which Y (me *canc.*), that C   C44 nat] none St, *om.* C
C45 euery] euery mannes SCBLSt, euere mans Y   C47 myn] my CBLY   helthe]
hele B   pilgrimages] pilgrimage B   C48 some(1)] *om.* C   some(2)] eke C
C49 it] *om.* C   gete] get gete L (get *canc.*)   my] *om.* St   C50 althogh] though
all C, of althogh Y (of *canc.*)

Ʒit the lorde of vertue / the kyng of glorie.
Of his hiƷe myƷt / and his benigne grace.
Made it for to retourne / in to the place.
Whens it cam / wiche at alle halwemesse.   55
Was fiue Ʒeere / neither more ne lesse.

And euere sithin / thankid be god oure lord.
Of his good and gracious / reconsiliacioun.
My wit and I / haue bene of suche acord.
As we were / or the alteracioun.   60
Of it was / but by my sauacioun.
Sith þat time / haue I be sore sette on fire.
And lyued in greet turment / & martire.

For þouƷ that my wit / were hoom come aƷein.
Men wolde it not so / vndirstonde or take.   65
With me to dele / hadden they disdein.
A rietous persone / I was and forsake.
Min oolde frendshipe / was al ouershake.
No wiƷt with me / list make daliaunce.
The worlde me made / a straunge countinaunce.   70

With þat myn herte / sore gan to tourment.
For ofte whanne I / in Westmynstir halle.
And eke in londoun / amonge the prees went.
I sy the chere / abaten and apalle.
Of hem þat weren wonte / me for to calle.   75
To companie / her heed they caste a wry.
Whanne I hem mette / as they not me sy.

Yit the lord of vertu / the kyng of glorie,
Of his hye might / and benigne grace
Made it for to retourne / into the place
Whens it cam / which was at Alle Halwemesse,   55
Was fiue yeer / neither more ne lesse.

And euere syn / thankid be God our lord
Of his good reconsiliacioun,
My wit and I / han been of swich accord
As we were / or the alteracioun   60
Of it was / but by my sauuacioun,
þat tyme / haue I be sore set on fyre
And lyued in greet torment / and martire.

For thogh þat my wit / were hoom come ageyn,
Men wolde it nat so / vndirstonde or take.   65
With me to delen / hadde they desdeyn;
A riotous persone I was / and forsake;
Myn old frendshipe / was al ouershake;
No wight with me / list make daliance.
The world me made / a straunge contenance,   70

Which þat myn herte / sore gan tormente;
For ofte whan I / in Westmynstre halle
And eek in Londoun / among the prees wente,
I sy the cheere / abaten and apalle
Of hem þat weren wont / me for to calle   75
To conpaignie / Hire heed they caste awry
Whan I hem mette / as they nat me sy.

C53 benigne] CBLYSt, his benigne S   C54 for] *om.* St   the] that C
C55 Whens] thens C   which was] CBLYSt, wiche S (*over eras., altered from* wiche was)
Alle] *om.* C   C56 yeer] yere seth BLY   C57 euere] every St   syn] sithin
SCSt, seth BLY   C58 good] good and gracious SCBLYSt   C61 Of]
or C   C62 þat tyme] CBLYSt, sith þat time S (*over eras.*)   set] 'set' L
C63 greet] *om.* B   C64 thogh] thowgh St (*corr. from* thowght)   C65 nat] no St
C66 delen] dele C (*over eras.*)   C67 forsake] a forsake L   C69 wight] wyte St,
om. B   list] lest to C   make] make me Y   C70 straunge] strong BLY
C71 Which þat] St, with þat SCBL, with 'þat' Y   myn] my BLY   sore gan] sore gan to
SBLYSt, gan sore C   C72 ofte] *om.* L   C74-146 *lacking in* L *through loss of
leaf*   C74 sy] see BYSt   C75 weren] war B, was C   C76 awry] *corr. from*
away B, away C   C77 sy] sey C

¶ Qui videbant me
foras fugierunt a
me. obliuioni datus
sum. sicut mortuus
a corde. ¶ Factus
sum tanquam vas
perditum. quoniam
audiui vituperacio-
nem multorum
commorancium in
circuitu.

As seide is in þe sauter / miȝt I sey.

They þat me sy / fledden a wey fro me.

Forȝeten I was / al oute of mynde a wey.   80

As he þat deed was / from hertis cherte.

To a lost vessel / lickned miȝte I be.

For manie a wiȝt / aboute me dwelling.

Herde I me blame / and putte in dispreisyng.

Thus spake manie oone / and seide by me.   85

Al þouȝ from him / his siiknesse sauage.

Withdrawen and passed / as for a time be.

Resorte it wole / namely in suche age.

As he is of / and thanne my visage.

Bigan to glowe / for the woo and fere.   90

Tho wordis hem vnwar / cam to myn eere.

Whanne passinge hete is quod þei / trustiþ this.

Assaile him wole aȝein / that maladie.

And ȝit parde / thei token hem amis.

Noon effecte at al / took her prophecie.   95

Manie someris bene past / sithen remedie.

Of that / god of his grace me purueide.

Thankid be god / it shoop not as þei seide.

f. 78ʳ ¶ Nota. bene. nota.

What falle shal / what men so deme or gesse.

To him that woot / euery hertis secree.   100

Reserued is / it is a lewidnesse.

Men wiser hem pretende / þan thei be.

And no wiȝt knowith / be it he or she.

Whom / howe / ne whanne / god wole him vesite.

It happith often / whanne men wene it lite.   105

As seid is in the psalter / mighte I seye:

They þat me sy / fledden away fro me;

Foryete I was / al out of mynde aweye   80

As he þat deed was / from hertes cheertee.

To a lost vessel / likned mighte I be;

For many a wight / aboute me dwellynge

Herde I me blame / and putte in dispreisynge.

¶ Qui videbant me foras fugierunt a me. Obliuioni datus sum, sicut mortuus a corde. ¶ Factus sum tanquam vas perditum; quoniam audiui vituperacionem multorum commorancium in circuitu.

Thus spak many oon / and seide by me: 85

'Althogh from him / his seeknesse sauage

Withdrawe and past / as for a tyme be,

Resorte it wole / namly in swich age

As he is of' / and thanne my visage

Began to glowe / for the wo and fere;   90

Tho wordes, hem vnwaar / cam to myn ere.

'Whan passynge hete is,' quod they / 'trustith this,

Assaile him wole ageyn / þat maladie.'

And yit pardee / they token hem amis,

Noon effect at al / took hir prophecie.   95

Many someres been past / syn remedie

Of þat / God of his grace me purueide.

Thankid be God / it shoop nat as they seide.

What falle shal / what men so deeme or gesse,

To him þat woot / euery hertes secree   100

Reserued is / It is a lewdenesse

Men wyser hem pretende / than they be;

And no wight knowith / be it he or she,

Whom / how / ne whanne / God wole him visyte;

It happith often / whan men weene it lyte.   105

C78 *Gloss om.* St   audiui vituperacionem] ad iuuituperacionem C   C79 They] the C   sy] sethe C   C80 aweye] alway YB   C81 he] *om.* Y   C85 spak] speke Y   C86 Althogh] all I thoffe B   from] fro BY   C87 past] passed S (*corr.* from* passed be) CBYSt   C88 namly] and nameli C   C90 Began] gan C   for the] than for C   C93 him wole ageyn] wole hym agayne St, ayenne wolle hym C   maladie] *rubbed* B   C94 they] they they B   token hem] tolden her tale C   amis] *rubbed* B   C96 syn] sithen SCBYSt   C97 St *writes after 98*   C98 St *writes before 97*   C99 What] that BY   men so] so men CBY   C100 euery] euere Y   hertes] mans BSt   secree] seree Y, secrete B   C102 hem] they B   C103 wight] withgt Y   C105 often] ofte CBYSt   weene it] weneth C

Somtime I wende / as lite as any man.
For to han falle / in to that wildenesse.
But god / whaɴne him liste / may wole & can.
Helthe withdrawe / and sende a wiȝt siiknesse.
Thouȝ man be wel this day / no sikernesse.   110
To hym bihiȝte is / that it shal endure.
God hurte nowe can / and nowe hele and cure.

¶ Nota. bene. nota.

He suffrith longe / but at the laste he smit.
Whaɴne þat a man is / in prosperite.
To drede a falle comynge / it is a wit.   115
Who so that taketh hede / ofte may se.
This worldis chauɴge / and mutabilite.
In sondry wise / howe nedith not expresse.
To my mater / streite wole I me dresse.

Men seiden I loked / as a wilde steer.   120
And so my looke / aboute I gan to throwe.
Min heed to hie / anothir seide I beer.
Ful bukkissh is his brayn / wel may I trowe.
And seide the thridde / and apt is in þe rowe.
To site of hem / that a resounles reed.   125
Can 'he' ȝeue / no sadnesse is in his heed.

f. 78ᵛ

Chaunged had I me pas / soɴme seiden eke.
For here and there / forþe stirte I as a roo.
Noon abood / noon areest / but al brainseke.
Another spake / and of me seide also.   130
My feet weren ay / wauynge to and fro.
Whaɴne þat I stonde shulde / and wiþ meɴ talke.
And þat myn yen / souȝten euery halke.

Sumtyme I wende / as lyte as any man
For to han falle / into þat wyldenesse;
But God / whan him liste / may, wole and can
Helthe withdrawe / and sende a wight seeknesse.
Thogh man be wel this day / no sikirnesse   110
To him behight is / þat it shal endure;
God hurte now can / and now hele and cure.

He suffrith longe / but at the laste he smit.
Whan þat a man is / in prosperitee
To dreede a fal comynge / it is a wit.   115
Whoso þat takith heede / ofte may see
This worldes chaunge / and mutabilitee
In sundry wyse / how needith nat expresse.
To my mateere / streight wole I me dresse.

Men seide I lookid / as a wylde steer   120
And so my look / aboute I gan to throwe.
Myn heed to hye / anothir seide I beer.
'Ful bukkissh is his brayn / wel may I trowe,'
Seide the thridde / 'and apt is in the rowe
To sitte of hem / þat a resounlees reed   125
Can yeue / no sadnesse is in his heed.'

Changed had I my paas / some seide eek,
For heere and ther / forth stirte I as a ro,
Noon abood / noon areest / but al braynseek.
Anothir spak / and of me seide also   130
My feet were ay / wauynge to and fro
Whan þat I stonde sholde / and with men talke,
And þat myn yen / soghten euery halke.

C106 lyte] litill Y   C107 þat] what C   C109 a wight] hem C   seeknesse] sekenes Y (*corr. from* sekernes)   C110 man] men C   sikirnesse] sekernes Y (*corr. from* sekeenes)   C111 To] so BY   C113 but] *om.* St   C115 a(2)] *om.* Y   C116 þat] *om.* C   C118 sundry] sundyr B   how] it C   expresse] to expresse C   C119 streight] CY, stright B, streite S, streit St   C120 steer] starre B   C121 look] booke Y   gan] began B   throwe] thowe B   C122 anothir] men C   C124 Seide] and seide SCBYSt   C125 a] *om.* C   C126 yeue] CSt, 'he' ȝeue S, he yeue BY   is] *om.* BY   C127 I] *om.* Y   my] CBYSt, me S   C129 abood noon areest] areste none abode C   C130 Anothir spak and] and anoþer C   C131 wauynge] wawynge C, wadyng BY   C132 þat] 'þat' Y   C133 euery] ever B

I leide an eere ay to / as I by wente.
And herde al / and þus in myn herte I caste.   135
Of longe abidinge here / I may me repente.
Lest that of hastinesse / I at the laste.
Answere amys / beste is / hens hie faste.
For if I in þis prees / amys me gye.
To harme wole it me turne / and to folie.   140

And this I demed wel / and knewe wel eke.
What so þat euere / I shulde answere or seie.
They wolden not / han holde it worth a leke.
For why / as I had lost my tunges keie.
Kepte I me cloos / and trussid me my weie.   145
Droupinge and heuy / and al woo bistaad.
Smal cause hadde I / me þouȝte to be glad.

My spirites labouriden / euere ful bisily.
To peinte countenaunce / chere & look.
For þat men spake of me / so wondringly.   150
And for the verry shame / and feer I qwook.
Thouȝ myn herte hadde be / dippid in þe brook.
It weet and moist was / `ynow' of my swoot.
Wiche was nowe frosty colde / nowe firy hoot.

f. 79ʳ   And in my chaumbre at home / whanne þat I was.   155
My silfe aloone / I in þis wise wrouȝt.
I streite vnto my mirrour / and my glas.
To loke howe þat me / of my chere þouȝt.

I leide an ere ay to / as I by wente
And herde al / and thus in myn herte I caste: 135
'Of long abydynge heere / I may repente;
Lest þat of hastinesse / I at the laste
Answere amis / best is / hens hie faste,
For if I in this prees / amis me gye
To harm wole it me torne / and to folie.'   140

And this I deemed wel / and kneew wel eek,
Whatso þat euere / I sholde answere or seye
They wolden nat / han holde it worth a leek;
Forwhy / as I had lost my tonges keye
Kepte I me cloos / and trussid me my weye   145
Droupynge and heuy / and al wo bistad;
Smal cause hadde I / me thoghte, to be glad.

My spirites / laboured bisily
To peynte contenance / cheere and look
For þat men speke of me / so wondryngly;   150
And for the verray shame / and fere I qwook.
Thogh myn herte had be / dippid in the brook
It weet and moist ynow was / of my swoot,
Which was now frosty cold / now fyry hoot.

And in my chambre at hoom / whan þat I was   155
Myself allone / I in this wyse wroghte:
I streighte vnto my mirour / and my glas
To looke how þat me / of my cheere thoghte,

C134 ay to] to ay C   I(2)] 'I' B   by] be CBYSt   C135 and(2)] *om.* B   myn]
my BY   C136 repente] BYSt, me repente SC   C137 Lest] loste B   þat] it BY,
om. St   hastinesse] hardinesse C   C138 amis] of mys B   is] I C   hens hie] hie
hens CB   C140 To] tho Y   C141 this] þus C   kneew] knowe B
C142 þat] *om.* St   I] *corr. from* I seyde St   C143 nat] *om.* C   worth] nat
worþe C   C144 lost] lesst C   C145 I] *om.* C   my weye] a way B
C146 al] 'al' Y   C148 L *adds whole line later*   laboured bisily] CSt, labouriden
euere ful bisily S (*altered by eras. from* labourid bisily), hem labured þen full
besely BLY   C149 and] ad Y   C150 speke] C, spake SBLYSt
wondryngly] wondirly CBLY   C151 the] *om.* C   fere] woo C   C152 Thogh]
that C   myn] my BLY   the] a L, *om.* Y   C153 moist ynow was] CSt, moste
enogh was B, mo'ï'st I'now' was L, mosty now was Y, moist was 'ynow' S
C154 now(2)] & nowe C   fyry] fire CBL   C155 þat] *om.* CBSt
C156 allone] along Y   C157 streighte] streight C, streite SSt, sterte BLY
C158 how] on C   thoghte] me thoght BLY

If any othir were it / than it ouȝt.
For fain wolde I / if it not had bene riȝt.   160
Amendid it / to my kunnynge and myȝt.

Many a saute made I / to this mirrour.
Thinking / if þat I looke / in þis manere.
Amonge folke / as I nowe do / noon errour.
Of suspecte look / may in my face appere.   165
This countinaunce / I am sure / and þis chere.
If I it forthe vse / is no thing repreuable.
To hem þat han / conceitis resonable.

And ther with al / I þouȝte þus anoon.
Men in her owne cas / bene blinde alday.   170
As I haue herde seie / manie a day a goon.
And in that same plite / I stonde may.
Howe shal I do / wiche is the beste way.
My troublid spirit / for to bringe in rest.
If I wiste howe / fain wolde I do the best.   175

Sithen I recouered was / haue I ful ofte.
Cause had of anger / and Inpacience.
Where I borne haue it / esily and softe.
Suffringe wronge be done / to me & offence.
And not answerid aȝen / but kepte scilence.   180
Leste þat men of me / deme wolde and sein.
Se howe this man / is fallen in aȝein.

f. 79ᵛ
As that I oones / fro westminstir cam.
Vexid ful greuously / with þouȝtful hete.
Thus thouȝte I / a greet fool I am.   185
This pauyment / a daies thus to bete.

If any othir were it / than it oghte;
For fayn wolde I / if it had nat been right,   160
Amendid it / to my konnynge and might.

Many a saut made I / to this mirour
Thynkynge / 'If þat I looke / in this maneere
Among folk / as I now do / noon errour
Of suspect look / may in my face appeere.   165
This contenance / I am seur / and this cheere
If I foorth vse / is no thyng repreeuable
To hem þat han / conceites resonable.'

And therwithal / I thoghte thus anoon:
'Men in hire owne cas / been blynde alday,   170
As I haue herd seyn / many a day agoon,
And in þat same plyt / I stonde may.
How shal I do / which is the beste way
My troublid spirit / for to brynge in reste?
If I wiste how / fayn wolde I do the beste.'   175

Syn I recouered was / haue I ful ofte
Cause had of anger / and inpacience,
Where I born haue it / esily and softe,
Suffryng wrong be doon / to me and offense
And nat answerd ageyn / but kept silence,   180
Lest þat men of me / deeme wolde and seyn
'See how this man / is fallen in ageyn.'

As þat I ones / fro Westmynstre cam
Vexid ful greuously / with thoghtful hete,
Thus thoghte I / 'A greet fool I am   185
This pauyment / adayes thus to bete,

C159 othir] *om.* St   it(1)] *om.* C   oghte] oglit B (*corr. from* thoght)   C160 had
not] CBLYSt, not had S   right] ariht C   C161 Amendid] amende C   and]
a`n´d Y   C162 a saut] assaute CB (*and* LY?)   this] þat C   C163 Thynkynge]
thyn`k´gyng Y   C164 now do] do nowe C   C166 seur] sore St
C167 foorth vse] CBLYSt, it forthe vse S   C168 resonable] re`so´nable Y
C171 a day] days BLY   C172 same] *om.* St   C174 troublid] troublie C   in]
at St   C175 the] for þe C   C176 Syn] sithen SCBLYSt
C177 inpacience] inpaciencie L, paciencie Y   C180 nat] nowght St   C183 I]
`I´ B   Westmynstre] Westmester C   C185 a] *om.* BLY   fool] foly L
C186 pauyment] pament C   adayes] aday`s´s´ L

And in and oute / laboure faste and swete.
Wondringe / and heuinesse to purchace.
Sithen I stonde out / of al fauour & grace.

And thanne þouȝte I / on þat othir side.   190
If that I not be sen / amonge þe prees.
Men deme wole / that I myn heed hide.
And am werse than I am / it is no lees.
O. lorde so my spirit / was restelees.
I souȝte reste / and I not it fonde.   195
But ay was trouble / redy at myn honde.

I may not lette / a man to ymagine.
Fer aboue þe mone / if þat him liste.
Ther by the sothe / he may `not´ determine.
But by the preef / ben thingis knowen & wiste.   200
Many a doom / is wrappid in the myste.

¶ A fructibus eorum
congnoscetis eos

Man bi hise dedis / and not by hise lookes.
Shal knowen be / as it is writen in bookes.

Bi taaste of fruit / men may wel wite and knowe.
What that it is / othir preef is ther noon.   205
Euery man woote wel that / as þat I trowe.
Riȝt so thei / that deemen my wit is goon.
As ȝit this day / ther deemeth many oon.
I am not wel / may as I by hem goo.
Taaste and assay / if it be so or noo.   210

f. 80ʳ ¶ Nota. bene. nota.

Vppon a look / is harde men hem to grounde.
What a man is / ther by the sothe is hid.
Whethir hise wittis / seek bene or sounde.
By countynaunce / is it not wist ne kid.

And in and out / laboure faste and swete
Wondrynge / and heuynesse to purchace,
Syn I stonde out / of al fauour and grace.'

And thanne thoghte I / on þat othir syde: 190
'If þat I nat be seen / among the prees
Men deeme wole / þat I myn heed hyde
And am wers than I am / it is no lees.'
O lord, so my spirit / was restelees;
I soghte reste / and I nat it fond, 195
But ay was trouble / redy at myn hond.

I may nat lette / a man to ymagyne
Ferre aboue the moone / if þat him list;
Therby the soothe / he may nat determyne,
But by the preef / been thynges knowe and wist. 200
Many a doom / is wrappid in the mist;
Man by his deedes / and nat by his lookes
Shal knowen be / as it is write in bookes.

¶ A fructibus eorum cognoscetis eos.

By taast of fruyt / men may wel wite and knowe
What þat it is / othir preef is ther noon, 205
Euery man woot wel þat / as þat I trowe;
Right so they / þat deemen my wit is goon,
As yit this day / ther deemeth many oon
I am nat wel / may as I by hem go
Taaste and assaye / if it be so or no. 210

Vpon a look / is hard men hem to grownde
What a man is / therby the soothe is hid;
Whethir his wittes / seeke been or sownde
By contenance / is it nat wist ne kid.

C188 Wondrynge] wondring Y (*corr. from* womdring), wonderyng BSt   C189 Syn]
sithen SCBLYSt   C190 thanne] 'than' Y   C191 þat I nat be seen] I am nat
seyn C   C192 wole] wele St   C193 than] and Y   C196 myn]
my BLY   C198 Ferre] CSt, ferrer BLY, fer S   aboue] about C   þat]
om. C   C199 nat] 'not' S   C200 been] 'be' B, by C   knowe] *followed by*
'be' *canc.* B   C201 *line add. in margin* B   C202 *Gloss om.* CSt   L *adds*
nota   C203 it] *om.* B   C204 wel] *om.* C   C206 man] 'man' B   þat(1)]
om. C   þat(2)] *om.* C   C208 many] many a St   C209 may] many C   go]
gone B   C210 it] *om.* Y   no] none B   C212 is therby] þerby is B
C213 Whethir] whither St, where C   C214 is it] is 'it' Y, it is St   ne] nor B, or C

Thouȝ a man harde / haue oones ben bitid.   215
God shilde it shulde / on him contynue alway.
By commvnynge / is the beste assay.

I mene to commvne / of thingis mene.
For I am but riȝt lewide / douteles.
And Ignoraunt / my kunnynge is ful lene.   220
Ȝit homely resoun / knowe I neuerethelees.
Not hope I founden be / so resounlees.
As men deemen / Marie crist forbede.
I can no more / preue may the dede.

¶ Nota bene nota. If a man oones / falle in drunkenesse.   225
Shal he contynue / therynne euere mo.
Nay / þouȝ a man do / in drinking excesse.
So ferforþe / þat not speke / he ne can ne goo.
And hise wittis / welny bene refte him fro.
And buried in the cuppe / he aftirward.   230
Cometh to hym silfe aȝein / ellis were it hard.

Riȝt so / þouȝ þat my witte / were a pilgrim.
And wente fer from home. he cam a ȝain.
God me deuoide`d' / of the greuous venim.
That had enfectid / and wildid my brain.   235
See howe the curteise leche / moost souerain.
Vnto the seke / ȝeueth medicine.
In nede / and hym releueth / of his greuous pine.

f. 80ᵛ ¶ Nota. bene. nota. Nowe lat this passe / god woot many a man.
Semeth ful wiis / by countenaunce and chere.   240
Wiche and he tastid were / what he can.

Thogh a man harde / haue ones been betid   215
God sheelde it sholde / on him continue alway.
By communynge / is the beste assay.

I meene to commune / of thynges mene,
For I am but right lewde / doutelees,
And ignorant / my konnynge is ful lene.   220
Yit hoomly resoun / knowe I nathelees;
Nat hope I fownden be / so resounlees
As men deemen / Marie, Cryst forbeede!
I can no more / preeue may the deede.

If a man ones / falle in dronkenesse   225
Shal he continue / therin euere mo?
Nay / thogh a man do / in drynkynge excesse
So ferfoorth / þat nat speke / he can ne go,
And his wittes / wel ny been reft him fro
And biried in the cuppe / he aftirward   230
Comth to himself ageyn / elles were hard.

Right so / thogh þat my wit / were a pilgrym
And wente fer from hoom / he cam agayn.
God me voidid / of the greuous venym
þat had infectid / and wyldid my brayn.   235
See how the curteys leche / souerain
Vnto the seeke / yeueth medecyne
In neede / and him releeueth / of his pyne.

Now let this passe / God woot, many a man
Seemeth ful wys / by contenance and cheere   240
Which, and he taastid were / what he can,

C215 Thogh] tohoh Y   harde haue ones been] harde haue once B, ones harde
be C   C216 on him continue] contynu on hym B   C217 communynge] good
commynyng LY, gode connyng B   C219 right] `right' St   C221 nathelees]
neueretheleees SCBLYSt   C222 hope . . .resounlees] I hope to be founden so
recheles C   C223 As] os C   C224 may] may men BLY   C225 ones falle]
falle ones C   C227 thogh] thoght Y   C228 nat speke he can] not speke he ne can
SBLYSt, he nat speke can C   C231 were] were it SCBLYSt   C232 þat] *om.*
St   C233 from] fro BLYSt   he] it C   C234 voidid] CBLYSt, deuoide`d' S
the] this St   C235 wyldid] wildud Y, weldid L, wilkyd B   C236 souerain]
moost souerain SCBLYSt   C238 pyne] C, peyne St, greuous pine S (*altered by eras.
from* pine), grevos payn BLY

Men miȝten licken him / to a fooles peere.
And somman lokeþ / in foltisshe manere.
As to þe outwarde doom / and Iugement.
That at þe preef / discreet is and prudent.   245

But algatis howe so be / my countinaunce.
Debaat is nowe noon / bitwixe me and my wit.
As þouȝ þat ther were / a disseueraunce.
As for a time / bitwixe me and it.
The gretter harme is myn / þat neuere ȝit.   250
Was I wel lettrid / prudent and discreet.
Ther neuere stood ȝit / wiis man on my feet.

The sothe is this / suche conceit as I had.
And vndirstonding / al were it but smal.
Bifore þat my wittis / weren vnsad.   255
Thanked be / oure lorde ihesu crist of al.
Suche haue I nowe / but blowe is ny oueral.
The reuerse / wherþoruȝ moche is my mornynge.
Wiche causeth me thus / syȝe in compleinynge.

Sithen my good fortune / hath chaungid hir chere.   260
Hie tyme is me / to crepe in to my graue.
To lyue Ioielees / what do I here.
I in myn herte / can no gladnesse haue.
I may but smal seie / but if men deme I raue.
Sithen oþir þing þan woo / may I noon gripe.   265
Vn to my sepulcre / am I nowe ripe.

f. 81ʳ   My wele a dieu / farwel my good fortune.
Oute of ȝoure tables / me planed han ȝe.

Men mighte likne him / to a fooles peere;
And sum man lookith / in foltissh maneere
As to the outward doom / and iugement
þat at the preef / discreet is and prudent.   245

But algate how so be / my contenance,
Debat is now noon / twixt me and my wit,
Althogh þat ther were / a disseuerance
As for a tyme / betwixt me and it.
The gretter harm is myn / þat neuere yit   250
Was I wel lettrid / prudent and discreet;
Ther neuere stood yit / wys man on my feet.

The soothe is this / swich conceit as I hadde
And vndirstondyng / al were it but smal,
Before þat my wittes / were vnsadde,   255
Thankid be / our lord Ihesu Cryst of al,
Swiche haue I now / but blowe is ny oueral
The reuers / wherthurgh moche is my mournynge,
Which causith me thus / sighe in conpleynynge.

Syn my good fortune / hath changed hir cheere   260
Hy tyme is me / to creepe into my graue.
To lyue ioielees / what do I heere?
I in myn herte / can no gladnesse haue;
I may but smal seyn / but men deeme I raue.
Syn othir thyng than wo / may I noon grype   265
Vnto my sepulture / am I now rype.

My wele adieu / farwel my good fortune!
Out of your tables / me planed han yee.

C243 foltissh] a foltissh C   C245 prudent] right prudente BLY
C246 algate] algates CSBLYSt   C247 now] 'now' L   twixt] bitwixt CSt, bitwixe
SBLY   C248 Althogh] CBLYSt, as þou3 S   þat] *om.* CSt   C249 As for]
afore C   betwixt] CSt, bitwixe SBLY   C257 *marked as the stanza's last line by B,*
with disruption of stanza-division and rhyme brackets up to C273   C258 wherthurgh]
where for C   moche] *om.* St, mygch Y   my] the St   C259 sighe] say BLY, here C
C260 Syn] sithen SCBLYSt   C261 me] to me C   C262 ioielees] *corr. from*
ioyele y B   C263 myn] my BLY   C264 but(2)] C, but if SBLYSt   deeme]
deme þat C, *om.* Y   C265 C *writes after 266*   Syn] sithen SCBLYSt   than] the St
C266 C *writes* For ioie is ther none yit vnto me ripe *before 265*   sepulture] St, sepultre Y,
sepulcre SBL   C267 my(2)] *om.* C   C268 planed] playned BLYSt

Sithen welny eny wiȝt / for to commvne.
With me / loth is / farwel prosperite.   270
I am no lenger / of ȝoure liuere.
Ȝe haue me putte / oute of ȝoure retenaunce.
A dieu my good auenture / and good chaunce.

And aswithe aftir / thus biþouȝte I me.
If þat I / in this wise / me dispeire.   275
It is purchas / of more aduersite.
What nedith it / my feble wit appeire.
Sith god hath made / myn helþe home repeire.
Blessid be he / and what men deme and speke.
Suffre it þenke I / and me not on me wreke.   280

But somdel had I / reioisinge amonge.
And a gladnesse also / in my spirite.
That þouȝ þe peple / took hem mis & wronge.
Me deemyng of my siiknesse not quite.
Ȝit for they / compleined / the heuy plite.   285
That they had seen me in / wiþ tendirnesse.
Of hertis cherte / my greef was the lesse.

In hem putte I / no defaute but oon.
That I was hool / þei not ne deme kowde.
And day by day / þei sye me bi hem goon.   290
In hete and coolde / and neiþer stille or lowde.
Knewe þei me do / suspectly a dirke clowde.
Hir siȝt obscurid / withynne and wiþ oute.
And for al þat / were ay in suche a doute.

f. 81ᵛ   Axide han they / ful ofte sithe and freined.   295
                      Of my felawis / of the priue seel.

Syn wel ny any wight / for to commune
With me / looth is / farwel prosperitee!   270
I am no lenger / of your liueree;
Yee han me put / out of your retenance.
Adieu my good auenture / and good chance!

And as swythe aftir / thus bethoghte I me:
'If þat I / in this wyse / me despeire   275
It is purchas / of more aduersitee.
What needith it / my feeble wit appeire
Syn God hath maad / myn helthe hoom repeire?
Blessid be he / and what men deeme or speke
Suffre it thynke I / and me nat on me wreke.'   280

But sumdel had I / reioisynge among
And a gladnesse also / in my spiryt
þat thogh the peple / took hem mis and wrong,
Me deemynge of my seeknesse nat qwyt,
Yit for they / conpleyned / the heuy plyt   285
þat they had seen me in / with tendrenesse
Of hertes cheertee / my greef was the lesse.

In hem putte I / no deffaute but oon:
þat I was hool / they nat ne deeme kowde,
And day by day / they sy me by hem goon   290
In hete and cold / and neithir stille or lowde
Kneew they me do suspectly / a dirk clowde
Hir sighte obscured / withynne and withoute,
And for al þat / were ay in swich a doute.

Axid han they / ful ofte sythe and freyned   295
Of my felawes / of the priuee seel

C269 Syn] sithen SCBLYSt   C271 lenger] longar B   C272 retenance]
remembraunce St   C273 and] ad Y, and my C   C275 me] thus B
C276 purchas] pu'r'chas Y   C277 appeire] to appere B   C278 Syn] sith SSt,
sithen CBLY   myn] my BLY   helthe] helpe BLY   hoom] to C
C279 or] CBLYSt, and S   C280 it] *om.* Y   C282 a] *om.* St   also]
'also' Y   C283 thogh] thoght Y   took hem] hem toke C   mis] *om.* Y
C284 Me] mo BLY   C285 heuy] 'hevy' B   C286 me in] me 'in' B, in
me C   C289 ne] me CBLY   C290 sy] se St   C291 or] nor St,
ne CBLY   C293 and] and eke CBLY   C294 ay] thay CSt
C295 sythe and] sythes and BLY, and sethen C

And preied hem to telle hem / wiþ herte vnfeined.
Howe it stood with me / wethir yuel or wel.
And they the sothe / tolde hem euerydel.
But þei helden / her wordis not but lees.   300
Thei miȝten as wel / haue holden her pees.

This troubly liif / hath al to longe endurid.
Not haue I wist / hou in my skyn to tourne.
But nowe my silfe / to my silfe haue ensurid.
For no suche wondringe / aftir this to mourne.   305
As longe as my liif / shal in me soiourne.
Of suche ymaginynge / I not ne recche.
Lat hem deeme as hem list / & speke & drecche.

¶ Hic est lamentacio
hominis dolentis.

This othir day / a lamentacioun.
Of a wooful man / in a book I sy.   310

¶ Resoun.

To whom wordis / of consolacioun.
Resoun ȝaf / spekynge effectuelly.
And wel esid / myn herte was therby.
For whanne I had a while / in þe book reed.
With the speche of resoun / was I wel feed.   315

¶ Anima mea in
angustiis est. cor
meum fluctuat /
vbicunque fugero.
mala mea sequitur
me sicut vmbra
persequitur corpus.
et non possum ea
fugere etc

The heuy man / wooful and angwisshous.
Compleined in þis wise / and þus seide he.
My liif is vn to me / ful encomborus.
For whidre / or vn to what place I flee.
My wickidnessis / euere folowen me.   320
As men may se / the shadwe a body sue.
And in no manere / I may hem eschewe.

And preide hem to telle hem / with herte vnfeyned
How it stood with me / whethir euele or weel;
And they the soothe / tolde hem euerydeel,
But they heelden / hir wordes nat but lees;   300
They mighten as wel / haue holden hir pees.

This troubly lyf / hath al to longe endurid;
Nat haue I wist / how in my skyn to tourne.
But now myself / to myself haue ensurid
For no swich wondrynge / aftir this to mourne   305
As longe as my lyf / shal in me soiourne.
Of swich ymagynynge / I nat ne recche;
Let hem dreeme as hem list / and speke and drecche.

This othir day / a lamentacioun   ¶ Hic est lamentacio
Of a woful man / in a book I sy,   310   hominis dolentis.
To whom wordes / of consolacioun
Resoun yaf / spekynge effectuelly;
And wel esid / myn herte was therby,
For whan I had a whyle / in the book red
With the speeche of Resoun / was I wel fed.   315

The heuy man / woful and angwisshous,   ¶ Anima mea in
Conpleyned in this wyse / and thus seide he: angustiis est, cor
'My lyf is vnto me / ful encombrous,   meum fluctuat. Vbi-
                                                            cunque fugero, mala
For whidir / or vnto what place I flee,   mea sequntur me,
My wikkidnesses / euere folwen me,   320   sicut vmbra perse-
                                                            quitur corpus, et
As men may see / the shadwe a body sue;   non possum ea
And in no manere / I may hem eschue.   fugere etc.

C297 hem(2)] *om.* C   C298 whethir] whither St, where C   euele] yll St,
goode B   weel] eville B   C299 euerydeel] euere dele Y   C300 heelden]
holden B   C302 troubly] trubbelos B   C304 to] haue to BLY   haue] *om.*
BLY, is C   C307 ne] `ne' C   C308 dreeme] St, deeme SCBLY   list] list
best L   C309 *Gloss om.* St   BLY *add* Reson   C310 sy] sye L (*corr. from* see) YSt,
sey C, see B   C311 consolacioun] *corr. from* Reason consolation St   C313 myn]
my BLY   C314 red] St, redde B, radde C, ired LY, reed S   C315 fed]
feed S   C316 angwisshous] angwysshiows St   *Gloss om.* St   fugero] fugo L,
fugio Y   sequntur] BLY, sequitur SC   persequitur] prosequitur BLY   etc] *om.* C
BLY *add* Homo   C319 whidir] whedir CB   vnto] into C, on vnto LY   flee] flye
St   C320 wikkidnesses] wickidnesse CB   folwen] foloweth C   C322 hem]
hym C

f. 82^r

Vexacioun of spirit / and turment.
Lacke I riȝt noon / I haue of hem plente.
Wondirly bittir / is my taast and sent.   325
Woo be be time / of my natiuite.
Vnhappi man / þat euere shulde I be.

¶ O. mors q*uam*
dulcis es male
viuentibus.

O. deeth thi strook / a salue is of swetnesse.
To hem þat lyuen / in suche wrecchidnesse.

¶ Melius est me
mori. q*uam* infeli-
citer viuere.

Gretter plesaunce / were it me to die.   330
By manie foolde / than for to lyue so.
Sorwes so manie / in me multiplie.
That my liif is / to me a verre foo.
Comforted may I not / be of my woo.
Of my distresse / see noon ende I can.   335
No force howe soone / I stinte to be a man.

¶ Racio / Quare
tantu*m* fra*n*geris in
adu*er*sis *om*mitte
tristiciam repelle
dolore*m* a corde
¶ Homo / Qual*iter*
quom*odo* qua
racione quo
co*n*silio i*n*genio

Thanne spake Resoun / what meneth al this fare.
Thouȝ welþe be not frendly to thee / ȝit.
Oute of thin herte / voide woo and care.
By what skile / howe / and by what reed & wit.   340
Seide this wooful man / miȝte I doon it.
Wrastle quod Resoun / a ȝein heuynesse.
Of þe worlde / troublis suffringe & duresses.

¶ Racio / Sume
luctame*n* co*n*tra
tristicias tempor-
ales. Respice sile*n*s
euent*us* etc

Biholde howe many a man / suffrith dissese.
As greet as þou / and al away grettere.   345
And þouȝ it hem pinche / sharply and sese.
Ȝit paciently / thei it suffre and bere.
Thinke here on / and the lesse it shal þe dere.

'Vexacioun of spirit / and torment
Lakke I right noon / I haue of hem plentee;
Wondirly bittir / is my taast and sent.   325
Wo be the tyme / of my natiuitee,
Vnhappy man / þat euere sholde it be!
O deeth, thy strook / a salue is of swetnesse   ¶ O mors, quam
To hem þat lyuen / in swich wrecchidnesse.   dulcis es male
                                                        viuentibus.

'Gretter plesance / were it me to die   330 ¶ Melius est me mori
By many fold / than for to lyue so.   quam infeliciter
Sorwes so many / in me multiplie   viuere.
þat my lyf is / to me a verray fo;
Conforted may I nat / be of my wo.
Of my distresse / see noon ende I can;   335
No force how soone / I stynte to be a man.'

Than spak Resoun / 'What meeneth al this fare?   ¶ Racio: Quare
Thogh welthe be nat freendly to thee / yit   tantum frangeris in
Out of thyn herte / voide wo and care.'   aduersis? Omitte
'By what skile / how / and by what reed and wit,' 340 tristiciam, repelle
Seide this woful man / 'mighte I doon it?'   dolorem a corde.
'Wrastle,' quod Resoun / 'ageyn heuynesses'   ¶ Homo: Qualiter?
Of the world / troubles, suffrynge and duresses.   quomodo? qua
                                                     racione? quo
'Beholde how many a man / suffrith disese   consilio, ingenio?
As greet as thow / and al away grettere,   345 ¶ Racio: Sume
And thogh it hem pynche / sharply and sese   luctamen contra
Yit paciently / they it suffre and bere.   tristicias temporales.
Thynke heeron / and the lesse it shal thee dere;   Respice similes
                                                    euentus etc.

C323 spirit and] `spirits´ B   C324 *line add. in margin* L, *marking omission with*
defectus   right] *om.* C   C325 taast] taat St, state B   C326 *line om.* BLY (LY
mark omission with defectus, Y *after C327*)   the] be S   C327 it] CBLYSt, I S
C328 *Gloss om.* St   es] *om.* C   C329 lyuen] leueth C   C330 *Gloss*
om. CSt   C333 verray] CB, verre S, verry LY, wery St   C334 *line add. in*
margin Y   I] *om.* B   nat] no`t´ Y   C335 see noon ende I] none eende see I
ne C   C337 *Gloss om.* St   tantum] *om.* BLY   corde] corde tuo B
C340 *Gloss om.* St   C341 mighte I] I myght B   C342 ageyn] ayne B,
ayens C   heuynesses] St, heuynesse SCBLY (*altered from* heuenes Y)   *Gloss om.* St
contra] qua B   Respice similes euentus etc] *om.* LY, modificare valeas B   similes] silens
SC   C343 world] worldis C   troubles suffrynge] trouble suffringe C, sufferyng
trowbils BLY   duresses] duresse CBL   C345 al away] all way BY   C346 it
hem] hym it C   pynche] punsshe C   C347 Yit] they BLY

Suche suffrau*n*ce is / of ma*n*nes gilte clensinge.
And hem enableth / to Ioie eu*er*e lastinge. 350

f. 82ᵛ ¶ Dolor & tristicia
co*m*munia sunt
omnibus.
¶ Hic deus vuln*er*at
eos q*uo*s rep*ar*at ad
et*er*nam salut*em*

Woo / heuinesse / and tribulacioun.
Comen aren to me alle / and profitable.
Thou3 greuous be / ma*n*nes temptaciou*n*.
It sleeth man not / to hem þat ben suffrable.
And to whom goddis strook / is acceptable. 355
Purueied ioie is / for god woundith tho.
That he ordeined hath / to blis to goo.

¶ Auru*m* dequoqui-
tur purga*tur* in
fornace vt purius
fiat.

Golde purgid is / thou seest in þe furneis.
For þe finer and clenner / it shal be.
Of þi dissese / the wei3te and þe peis. 360
Bere li3tly / for god to prove þe.
Scourgid þe hath / wiþ sharpe adu*er*site.
Not grucche and seie / whi susteine I this.
For 'if' þou do / thou the takist amis.

But þus þou shuldist / þinke in þin herte. 365
And seie / to þee lorde god / I haue a gilte.
So sore / I moot / for myn offensis smerte.
As I am worthi / O. lorde I am spilte.
But þou to me / þi mercy grau*n*te wilte.
I am ful sure / þou maist it not denie. 370
Lorde I me repente / and I the m*er*cy crie.

Lenger I þou3te / reed haue in þis book.
But so it shope / þat I ne mi3te nau3t.
He þat it ou3te / a 3en it to him took.

Swich souffrance is / of mannes gilt clensynge
And hem enablith / to ioie aylastynge.   350

'Wo / heuynesse / and tribulacioun
Commune arn to men alle / and profitable.
Thogh greuous be / mannes temptacioun
It sleeth man nat / to hem þat been souffrable;
And to whom Goddes strook / is acceptable   355
Purueied ioie is / for God wowndith tho
þat he ordeyned hath / to blisse go.

'Gold pourged is / thow seest, in the fourneys
For the fyner and clenner / it shal be.
Of thy disese / the weighte and the peys   360
Bere lightly / for God to preeue thee
Scourgid thee hath / with sharp aduersitee;
Nat grucche and seye / "Why susteene I this?"
For if thow do / thow thee takist amis.

'But thus thow sholdest / thynken in thyn herte   365
And seyn / "To thee, lord God / I haue agilt;
So sore I moot / for myn offenses smerte
As I am worthy / O lord, I am spilt,
But thow to me / thy mercy graunte wilt –
I am ful seur / thow maist it nat denye.   370
Lord, I repente / and I thee mercy crye."'

Lenger I thoghte / red haue in this book
But so it shoop / þat I ne mighte naght;
He þat it oghte / ageyn it to him took,

Marginal glosses:

¶ Dolor et tristicia communia sunt omnibus.

¶ Hic Deus vulnerat eos quos preparat ad eternam salutem.

¶ Aurum dequoquitur, purgatur in fornace, vt purius fiat.

C349 Swich] such Y (*corr. from* ouch)   C350 hem] hym CBLY   enablith]
avales B   aylastynge] euere lastinge SCLYSt, every lastyng B   C351 *Gloss om.*
St   et] *om.* C   C352 Commune] comon St, commen B, comen SLY, come C
men] St, me SCBLY   and profitable] vnprofitabill B   C354 sleeth] fleth Y   hem]
corr. from hym Y   C356 Purueied] purved B   wowndith] wo`u´ndith Y   *Gloss*
om. St   preparat] reparat S   BLY *add* Quem (quos L) diligo castigo   C357 go] to
goo SCBLYSt   C358 is] as B   seest] seyst St   *Gloss om.* St   C *adds* etc
C359 fyner] fayrrer B   shal] shulde BLY   C360 and] and eke C   C364 if] `if´
S   thee takist] takest the C   C365 thyn] þi BLY   C367 I] that I C   moot]
not BLY   offenses] offence CB   C368 spilt] *corr. from* sel L   C369 thy] the
St   C370 maist] wolt C   C371 repente] me repente SCBLYSt
C372 red haue] to haue radde C   C373 naght] no aghte B, noaght LY
C374 it to] to to St, to C   took] *corr. from* I toke Y

Me of his hast vnwar / ȝit haue I cauȝt.   375
Sum of the doctrine / by resoun tauȝt.
To þe man / as a bove haue I said.
Wel þerof I holde me / ful wel apaid.

f. 83ʳ ¶ No*ta. bene. no*ta. For eu*ere* sithen / sett haue I the lesse.
By the peples / ymaginacioun.   380
Talkinge this and þat / of my siknesse.
Wich cam / of goddis visitacioun.
Miȝte I haue be fou*n*de / in probaciou*n*.
Not grucching / but han take it in souffrau*n*ce.
Holsum and wiis / had be my gou*er*nau*n*ce.   385

Farwel my sorowe / I caste it to the cok.
With pacience / I hens forþe thinke vnpike.
Of suche þouȝtful dissese and woo the lok.
And lete hem out / þat han me made to sike.
Here after / oure lorde god may if him like.   390
Make al myn oolde / affeccioun resorte.
And in hope of þat / wole I me comforte.

¶ No*ta. bene. no*ta. Thoruȝ goddis iust doom / and his iugement.
And for my best / nowe I take and deeme.
Ȝaf þat good lorde / me my punischement.   395
In welthe I tooke of him / noon hede or ȝeme.
Him for to plese / and him honoure and queme.
And he me ȝaf aboon / on for to gnawe.
Me to correcte / and of him to have awe.

He ȝaf me wit / and he tooke it a way.   400
Wha*n*ne that he sy / that I it mis dispente.
And ȝaf aȝein / wha*n*ne it was to his pay.
He gr*a*untide me / my giltis to repente.

Me of his haaste vnwaar / Yit haue I caght   375
Sum of the doctrine / by Resoun taght
To the man / as aboue haue I said,
Whereof I holde me / ful wel apaid.

For euere sythen / set haue I the lesse
By the peples / ymaginacioun,   380
Talkynge this and þat / of my seeknesse,
Which cam / of Goddes visitacioun.
Mighte I han be fownde / in probacioun
Nat grucchyng / but han take it in souffrance,
Holsum and wys / had be my gouernance.   385

Farwel my sorwe / I caste it to the cok!
With pacience / I hens foorth thynke vnpyke
Of swich thoghtful disese and wo / the lok,
And lete hem out / þat han me maad to syke.
Heeraftir / our lord God may, if him lyke,   390
Make al myn olde / affeccioun resorte,
And in hope of þat / wole I me conforte.

Thurgh Goddes iust doom / and his iugement
And for my beste / now I take and deeme,
Yaf þat good lord / me my punysshement.   395
In welthe I took of him / noon heede or yeeme
Him for to plese / and him honure and qweeme,
And he me yaf a boon / on for to gnawe
Me to correcte / and of him to haue awe.

He yaf me wit / and he took it away   400
Whan þat he sy / þat I it mis despente,
And yaf ageyn / whan it was to his pay.
He grauntid me / my giltes to repente

C377 as] *om.* C   C378 Whereof] CBLYSt, wel þerof S (þerof *add. in different ink over
eras.*)   C379 euere] every B   C380 peples] *corr. from* pleples L
C387 pacience] paciencie L   I hens foorth] hensforthe I C   C388 lok] looke BLY
(*altered from* booke Y)   C389 han me maad] hath made me C, me have made BL, have
made Y   C391 affeccioun] effeccioun C   C394 I take] take I C   C395 Yaf]
of C   C396 In] and 'in' B   C397 him(2)] 'hym' Y   C398 for] *corr. from*
to Y   gnawe] knaw St   C401 sy] se St   it] 'it' B   mis despente]
mys'dis'pente Y   C402 yaf] yafe it C   his] hym C

And hens forwarde / to sette myn entente.
Vn to his deitee / to do plesaunce.   405
And to amende / my sinful gouernaunce.

Laude and honour / and þanke vnto þee be.
Lorde god / that salue art / to al heuinesse.
Thanke of my welthe / and myn aduersitee.
Thanke of myn elde / and of my seeknesse.   410
And thanke be to thin / infinit goodnesse.
And thi ȝiftis / and benefices alle.
And vn to thi mercy / and grace I calle.

And endid my compleinte / in this manere.
Oon knockid / at my chaumbre dore sore.
And criede a lowde / howe hoccleue art þou here.
Open thi dore / me thinketh ful ȝore.
Sithen I the sy / what man for goddis ore.   5
Come oute / for this quarter / I not the sy.
By ouȝt I woote / and oute to hym cam I.

This man was my good frende / of fern a goon.
That I speke of / and þus he to me seide.
Thomas / as thou me louest / telle anoon.   10
What didist þou / whanne I knockede and leide.
So faste vppon þi dore / and I obeide.
Vn to his wil / come in quod I and see.
And so he dide / he streit wente in wiþ me.

And hens forward / to sette myn entente
Vnto his deitee / to do plesance   405
And tamende / my synful gouernance.

Laude and honour / and thank vnto thee be,
Lord God / þat salue art / to al heuynesse:
Thank of my welthe / and myn aduersitee,
Thank of myn elde / and of my seeknesse;   410
And thank be / to thyn infynyt goodnesse
For thy yiftes / and benefices alle;
And vnto thy mercy / and grace I calle.

Heere endith my Conpleynte and begynneth a Dialog.

And, endid my conpleynte / in this maneere,
Oon knokkid / at my chambre dore sore
And cryde alowde / 'How, Hoccleue, art thow heere?
Opne thy dore / Me thynkith ful yore
Syn I thee sy / What, man, for Goddes ore   5
Come out / for this quarter / I nat thee sy
By aght I woot' / and out to him cam I.

This man was my good freend / of fern agoon
þat I speek of / and thus he to me seide:
'Thomas / as thow me louest / telle anoon,   10
What didest thow / whan I knokkid and leide
So faste vpon thy dore?' / And I obeide
Vnto his wil / 'Come in,' quod I, 'and see.'
And so he dide / he streight wente in with me.

C404 hens forward] hensforth C   C405 deitee] dignete C   do] doo hym C
C406 tamende] to amende SCBLYSt   C409 and] and of C   C410 Thank] *corr.*
from thand Y   myn] my BLY   elde] hele C   C411 to] *om.* L   thyn]
his C   C412 For] CBLYSt, and S   benefices] þi benefices LY, thy benefaces B,
thi benefites C   C413 St *writes* for thy g *above and cancels*   *Heading* BLY, *blank
space for heading unfilled* S, Hic finit questus siue planctus Thome Occleue. Et incipit quidam
Dialogus inter eundem Thomam & quemdam amicum suum etc C, Thomas Hoccleve St
(Dialogus cum Amico *add. below in hand of George Davenport*)   D1 endid]
endith B   D3 Hoccleue] Occleve CL   heere] þere C   D5 Syn] sithen
SCBLYSt   sy] se St   D6 nat thee] the ne C   D7 aght] oght BLY,
ought C   D9 speek] speke SBYSt, spek L, spak C   he] 'he' Y
D10 anoon] me anone Y, on C   D14 he(1)] *corr. from* hed L   streight wente
in] BLYSt, streit wente in S, went in streite C

To my good frende / not þouȝte I to make it queinte.
Ne my labour / from him to hide or leine.   16
And riȝt anoon / I redde hym my compleinte.
And that done / þus he seide / sin we tweine.
Ben here / and no mo folke / for goddis peine.
Thomas. suffre me speke and be not wrooth.   20
For the to offende / were me ful looth.

That I shal seie / shal be of good entente.
Hast þou maad þis compleint / forth to goo.
Amonge þe peple / ȝe frende so I mente.
What ellis / nay Thomas war / do not so.   25
If þou be wiis / of that mater ho.
Reherse þou it not / ne it a wake.
Kepe al that cloos / for thin honours sake.

Howe it stood with thee / leide is al a slepe.
Men han forȝete it / it is oute of mynde.   30
That þou touche ther of / I not ne kepe.
Lat be þat reede I / for I can not finde.
O. man to speke of it / in as good a kinde.
As þou hast stonde / amonge men or þis day.
Stondist þou nowe / A nay quod I. nay. nay.   35

Thouȝ I be lewide / I not so ferforthe dote.
I woote what men han seide / and seien of me.
Her wordis haue I not / as ȝit forgote.
But greet meruaile haue I / of ȝow that ȝe.
No bet of my compleint / avisid be.   40
Sithen mafey / I not redde it vn to ȝow.
So longe a goon / for it was but riȝt now.

To my good freend / nat thoghte I make it qweynte
Ne my labour / from him to hyde or leyne,   16
And right anoon / I redde him my conpleynte;
And that doon / thus he seide / 'Syn we tweyne
Been heere / and no mo folk / for Goddes peyne,
Thomas / suffre me speke / and be nat wrooth,   20
For thee toffende / were me ful looth.

'þat I shal seyn / shal be of good entente;
Hast thow maad this conpleynte / foorth to go
Among the peple?' / 'Yee, freend, so I mente,
What elles?' / 'Nay, Thomas, waar / do nat so.   25
If thow be wys / of þat mateere ho!
Reherce thow it nat / ne it awake;
Keepe al þat cloos / for thyn honoures sake.

'How it stood with thee / leid is al asleepe,
Men han foryete it / it is out of mynde.   30
þat thow touche therof / I nat ne keepe;
Let be, þat rede I / for I can nat fynde
O man speke of it / In as good a kynde
As thow hast stonde / among men or this day
Stondist thow now' / 'A nay,' quod I, 'nay, nay!   35

'Thogh I be lewde / I nat so ferfoorth dote.
I woot what men han seid / and seyn of me;
Hir wordes haue I nat / as yit forgote.
But greet meruaille haue I / of yow þat yee
No bet of my conpleynte / auysed be,   40
Syn, mafey / I nat redde it vnto yow
So longe agoon / for it was but right now.

D15 make] CBLY, to make SSt   it] *om.* B   D16 from] fro CBLY
D17 my] *om.* C   D21 toffende] to offende SCBLYSt   D23 Hast] has B
D25 waar] *om.* CBLY   D27 awake] not awake BLY   D28 thyn] thy LY
honoures] honor BLY   D30 it is] 'it' is Y, it 'is' B   D31 touche] to'u'che L
keepe] *corr. from* slepe kepe B, lepe C   D32 þat] þi B, it C   rede I] red I C (*over
eras.*) Y   D33 speke] to speke SCBLYSt   as] so C   D35 Stondist]
stondeth B   nay nay] a nay B   D36 dote] doote LY, dowte B   D37 han
seid and seyn] seyn and han seid C, have saide and seen B   of] on LY   D38 as yit]
om. C   D41 Syn] sithen SCLYSt, sethe B   D42 it] þat C   but] *om.* BLY

If ȝe took hede / it maketh mencioun.
That men of me speke / in myn audience.
Ful heuily / of ȝoure entencioun.   45
I thanke ȝou / for of beneuolence.
Woote I ful wel / procedeþ ȝoure sentence.
But certis good frende / þat þing þat I heere.
Can I witnesse / and vn to it refeere.

And where as that ȝe / me counseile & rede.   50
That for myn honour / shulde I by no weie.
Any þing mynge / or touche of my wildhede.
I vn to þat / answere thus and seie.
Of goddis strook / howe so it peise or weie.
Ouȝt no man to þinke / repreef or shame.   55
His chastisinge / hurtiþ no mannes name.

Anothir þing / ther meueþ me also.
Sithen my seeknesse / sprad was so wide.
That men knewe wel / howe it stood with me þo.
So wolde I nowe / vppon þat othir side.   60
Wist were / howe oure lorde ihesu / wich is gide.
To al releef / and may alle hertis cure.
Releued hath / me sinful creature.

Had I be / for an homicide I knowe.
Or an extorcioner / or a robbour.   65
Or for a coin clipper / as wide yblowe.
As was my seeknesse / or a werriour.
A ȝein þe feith / or a false maintenour.
Of causes / þouȝ I had amendid me.
Hem to han mynged / had ben nicite.   70

'If yee took heede / it makith mencioun
þat men of me speke / in myn audience
Ful heuily / Of your entencioun   45
I thanke yow / for of beneuolence,
Woot I ful wel / procedith your sentence;
But certes, good freend / þat thyng þat I heere
Can I witnesse / and vnto it refeere.

'And whereas þat yee / me conseille and rede   50
þat for myn honour / sholde I by no weye
Any thyng mynge / or touche of my wyldhede,
I vnto þat / answere thus and seye:
Of Goddes strook / how so it peise or weye,
Oghte no man thynke / repreef or shame;   55
His chastisynge / hurtith no mannes name.

'Anothir thyng / ther meeueth me also:
Syn þat my seeknesse / spred was so wyde
þat men kneew wel / how it stood with me tho,
So wolde I now / vppon þat othir syde,   60
Wist were / how our lord Ihesu / which is gyde
To al releef / and may alle hertes cure,
Releeued hath / me synful creature.

'Had I be / for an homicide yknowe,
Or an extorcioner / or a robbour,   65
Or for a coyn clippere / as wyde yblowe
As was my seeknesse / or a werreyour
Ageyn the feith / or a fals maintenour
Of causes / thogh I had amendid me,
Hem to han mynged / had been nycetee.   70

D44 myn] my B   D46 for of] of your C   D49 vnto] to CL
D52 mynge or touche] touche or meve C   D53 answere thus] thus aunswere C
D54 or] *corr. from* & or Y   D55 thynke] to þinke SCBLYSt   or] *corr. from* no mann
or Y   D58 Syn þat] sithen SCSt, seth BLY   D59 kneew] knowe CB
D61 were] wher CBL   which] þat C   D62 releef] releve B   D63 hath me]
me hath C   D66 coyn] comon St   D67 my] myne B   a] *om.* Y
werreyour] merrure B   D69 thogh] ȝyff C (*over eras.*)   me] be C
D70 mynged] avengid C   had] have St

And whi / for þo proceden of freelte.
Of man hym silfe / he brewith alle þo.
For siþen god to man / ȝoue hath liberte.
Wiche chese may / for to do wel or no.
If he mys chese / he is his owene foo.   75
And to reherse his gilte / wich him accusiþ.
Honour seith nay / there he scilence excusiþ.

But this is / al another caas sothly.
This was the strook of god / he ȝaf me þis.
And sithen he hath / withdrawe it curteisly.   80
Am I not holden / it out / O. ȝis.
But if god had þis þanke / it were amis.
In feith frende / make I thenke an open shrifte.
And hide not / what I had of his ȝifte.

If that a leeche / curid had me so.   85
As they lacken alle / þat science & miȝt.
A name he shulde / han had for euere mo.
What cure he had doon / to so seek a wiȝt.
And ȝit my purs / he wolde haue made ful liȝt.
But curteis ihesu / of his grace pacient.   90
Axith not / but of gilte amendement.

The benefice of god / not hid be sholde.
Sithen of myn heele / he ȝaf me þe triacle.
It to confesse / and þanke hym am I holde.
For he in me / hath shewid his miracle.   95
His visitacioun / is a spectacle.
In wiche that I / biholde may and se.
Bet þan I dide / howe greet a lord is he.

'And why / for tho proceden of freeltee
Of man himself / he breewith alle tho;
For syn God to man / yeue hath libertee
Which cheese may / for to do wel or no,
If he mischeese / he is his owne fo;   75
And to reherce his gilt / which him accusith,
Honour seith nay / there he silence excusith.

'But this is / al anothir cas soothly,
This was the strook of God / he yaf me this;
And syn he hath / withdrawe it curteisly   80
Am I nat holden it oute? / O yis;
But if God had this thank / it were amis.
In feith, freend / make I thynke an open shrifte
And hyde nat / what I had of his yifte.

'If þat a leche / curid had me so –   85
As they lakke alle / þat science and might –
A name he sholde / han had for euere mo
What cure he had doon / to so seek a wight,
And yit my purs / he wolde han maad ful light;
But Ihesu / of his grace pacient,   90
Axith nat / but of gilt amendement.

'The benefice of God / nat hid be sholde;
Syn of myn hele / he yaf me the triacle
It to confesse / and thanke him am I holde,
For he in me / hath shewid his miracle.   95
His visitacioun / is a spectacle
In which þat I / beholde may and see
Bet than I dide / how greet a lord is he.

    D71 for] *om.* C   proceden] procedeth B   D73 syn] siþen SCBLYSt   to man
yeue hath] to man hath yoven C, hath man yeven B   D74 for] *om.* BLY   no]
woo C   D77 seith] say B   D78 soothly] truly CBLY   D80 syn] sithen
SCBLY, sythe St   D81 it] to telle it BLY   D82 amis] o mysse B, anyse
St   D83 I thynke] *om.* St   D84 his] *over eras.* C   D86 and]
of BLY   D87 B *writes after 89, followed by 88, and reverses order of 89 and 87 by
corr.*   D90 Ihesu] curteis Ihesu SCBLYSt   his] 'his' B   D92 hid be] hide
he BLY   D93 Syn] sithen SCSt, seth BLY   myn] my BLY   me] *om.* B   the]
om. St   D94 am I] 'am' I C, I am B, as I St   D97 which] þe which B

But freend / amonge þe vicis þat riȝt now.
Rehercid I / oone of hem dar I seie.   100
Hath hurte me sore / and I woote wel y now.
So hath it mo / wiche is feble moneie.
Manie a man þis day / but þei golde weie.
Of men / not wole it take ne resceiue.
And if it lacke his peis / þei wole it weiue.   105

Howe may it holde his peis / whanne it is wasshe.
So that it lacke / sumwhat in thiknesse.
The false peple / no thing hem abaisshe.
To clippe it eke / it in brede and roundenesse.
Is than it shulde be / alweie the lesse.   110
The pore man / amonge alle othir is.
Ful sore anoied / and greued in this.

If it be golde and hool / that men him profre.
For his laboure / or his chaffre lent.
Take it if him list / and putte it in his cofre.   115
For waisshinge or clipping / holde him content
Or leue / he gete noon othir paiement.
It semeth but smal / othir is ther.
Trouþe is absent / but falsheed is not fer.

Howe shal þe pore do / if in his holde.   120
No more moneie / he ne haue at al.
Parcas but a noble / or halpenie of golde.
And it so thynne is / and so narowe & smal.
That men the eschaunge / eschewen oueral.
Not wil it goo / but miche he theronne leese.   125
He moot do so / he may noon other chese.

'But, freend / among the vices þat right now
Reherced I / oon of hem, dar I seye,   100
Hath hurt me sore / and I woot wel ynow
So hath it mo / which is feeble moneye.
Many a man this day / but they gold weye,
Of men / nat wole it take ne receyue,
And if it lakke his peys / they wole it weyue.   105

'How may it holde his peys / whan it is wasshe
So þat it lakkith / sumwhat in thiknesse?
The false peple / nothyng hem abasshe
To clippe it eek / in brede and in rowndnesse,
†Is than it sholde be / alway the lesse.   110
The poore man / among alle othir is
Ful sore annoyed / and greeued in this.

'If it be gold and hool / þat men him profre
For his labour / or his chaffare lent,
Take if him list / and putte it in his cofre;   115
For wasshynge or clippynge / holde him content
Or leue / he get noon othir paiement;
†It seemeth but smal / othir is ther.
Trouthe is absent / but falshede is nat fer.

'How shal the poore do / if in his hold   120
No more moneye / he ne haue at al
Parcas but a noble / or halpeny of gold,
And it so thynne is / and so narw and smal
þat men theschaunge / eschuen oueral?
Nat wole it go / but moche he theron leese;   125
He moot do so / he may noon othir cheese.

D100 oon] on L, one Y (*corr. from* none)   dar I] I dar wel C   D102 feeble] feole
St, felle BLY   D103 but] but if L   they] þe BLY   D104 nat] þat L, þat
not Y   D105 they] ȝe Y   wole] wich L   D107 lakkith] CBLYSt,
lacke S   sumwhat] sumphat L   D109 in(1)] CBLYSt, it in S   in(2)] BLYSt, *om.*
SC   D110 Is than] is that St   sholde] holde B   alway] all away CBLY
D112 Ful sore] for sore Y, for soith B   D114 lent] bent L   D115 Take] take it
SCBLYSt   D117 get] BLYSt, gete SC   D118 othir] þat oþer
coyne BLY   D119 falshede] falsed C   D120 if] *corr. from* if he St,
and C   D122 halpeny] an halpeny C   D123 smal] so small C
D124 theschaunge] BLY, the eschaunge SCSt   D125 moche he theron] he theron
moche C   D126 moot] muste B   noon] non L, no Y

I my silfe in þis caas / ben haue or this.
Wherfore I knowe it / a greet dele þe bet.
He that in falsing of coyn / gilty is.
Hath greet wronge / þat he nere on þe gebet.   130
It is pitee / that he ther from is let.
Sithen he ther to hath / so greet title and riȝt.
Regne Iustice / and preue on him thi myȝt.

Whanne I this wroot / many men dide amis.
Thei weied gold / vnhad auctorite.   135
No statute made was þanne / as þat nowe is.
But sithen gold to weie / charged nowe ben we.
Resoun axeth / that it obeied be.
Nowe time it is / vn to weiȝtes vs drawe.
Sithen that the parlement / hath maad it a lawe.   140

Ȝit othir shrewis / doon a werse gyn.
And tho bene they / þat þe coyn countirfete.
And thei that with golde / copir clothe and tyn.
To make al seme golde / þei swinke and swete.
In helle for to purchace / hem a sete.   145
If thidre lede hem / her false couetise.
That purchas maad was / in a fooltisch wise.

What causith trowen ȝe / al this mischaunce.
What coumforte ȝouen is / to this vntrouþe.
In feith men sein / it is the maintinaunce.   150
Of grete folke / wich is a greet harme & rouþe.
God graunte herafter / that ther be no slouþe.
Of this tresoun / punischement to do.
Riȝt suche as that is / partinent ther to.

'I myself in this cas / been haue or this,
Wherfore I knowe it / a greet deel the bet.
He þat in falsynge of coyn / gilty is
Hath greet wrong / þat he nere on the gibet;   130
It is pitee / þat he therfrom is let
Syn he therto hath / so greet title and right.
Regne iustice / and preeue on him thy might!

'Whan I this wroot / many men dide amis,
They weyed gold / vnhad auctoritee;   135
No statut maad was thanne / as now is.
But syn gold to weye / charged now been we
Resoun axith / þat it obeied be;
Now tyme it is / vnto weightes vs drawe
Syn þat the parlement / hath maad it a lawe.   140

'Yit othir shrewes / doon a werse gyn,
And tho been they / þat the coyn countrefete
And they þat with gold / copir clothe and tyn.
To make al seeme gold / they swynke and swete
In helle for to purchace / hem a sete.   145
If thidir lede hem / hir fals couetyse
þat purchas maad was / in a foltissh wyse.

'What causith, trowen yee / al this mischaunce?
What confort yeuen is / to this vntrouthe?
In feith, men seyn / it is the maintenaunce   150
Of grete folk / which is greet harm and routhe.
God graunte heeraftir / þat ther be no slouthe
Of this tresoun / punisshement to do
Right swich as þat is / pertinent therto.

D127 been haue] haue ben CBLY   D129 coyn] þe coyne C   D130 the] a
St   D132 Syn] sen C, sithen SBLYSt   so] *om.* BLY   D133 him] hem C, them
St   D134 men] med St, a man B   D135 They] the`i´ S   D136 maad] *om.*
St   as] CBLYSt, as þat S   D137 syn] sithen SCBLYSt   charged now] nowe
chargid C, charged BLY   D139 vnto] to C   D140 Syn] sithen SCBLYSt
þat] *om.* C   a] *om.* C   D142 countrefete] confrete B   D143 with] *om.* Y
copir clothe] clothe copir BLY   D145 for] *om.* C   D146 If] it L
D148 trowen yee] `trow ȝe´ Y   D149 to] vnto B   D150 feith] feyte B
D151 greet] CBLYSt, a greet S   D152 slouthe] showþe St   D154 þat] *om.* C

Thei þat consenten / to that falsehede.   155
As wel as the werkers / wiþ peine egal.
Punischid ouȝten be / as þat I rede.
Nowe maintenours / bi war nowe of a fal.
I speke of no persone / in special.
In countrees diuerse / is ther many oon.   160
Of ȝow / and hath be many a day a goon.

Allas / that to oure kingis preiudice.
And harme to alle / hise lege peple trewe.
Contynue shal / þis foule and cursid vice.
Of falsing of coyn / not bigonne of newe.   165
Wiche and it forþe goo / many oon shal it rewe.
God and oure kyng / remedie al this greef.
For to þe peple / it is / a foule mischeef.

Bi comoun harme / is not smal to sett.
That venym / ouere wide and brood spredith.   170
Greet merite were it / suche þing stoppe & lett.
As þat þe comoun / in to mischef leedith.
¶ Vox popoli vox dei The vois of þe peple / veniaunce on ȝow gredith.
ȝe cursid men / ȝe false moneyours.
And on ȝoure outereris / & ȝoure maintenours.   175

O this I drede alweie / this heuieþ me.
Many a sithe / that punischement.
Noon falle shal / on this cursid meine.
Howe trewe so be / her enditement.
Oure lige lorde / shal be so Innocent.   180

'They þat consenten / to þat falsehede,   155
As wel as the werkers / with peyne egal
Punisshid oghten be / as þat I rede.
Now maintenours / be waar now of a fal!
I speke of no persone / in special;
In contrees dyuerse / is ther many oon   160
Of yow / and hath be / many a day agoon.

'Allas / þat to our kynges preiudice
And harm to al / his lige peple treewe
Continue shal / this foule and cursid vice
Of falsynge of coyn / nat begonne of neewe,   165
Which / and it foorth go / many oon shal it reewe.
God and our kyng / remedie al this greef,
For to the peple / it is / a foul mescheef.

'By commune harm / is nat smal to sette;
þat venym / ouer wyde and brode spredith.   170
Greet merit were it / swich thyng stoppe and lette
As þat the commune / into mescheef ledith.
The vois of the peple / vengeance on yow gredith,   ¶ Vox populi vox
Yee cursid men / yee false moneyours,   Dei.
And on your outrers / and your maintenours.   175

'O, this I dreede alway / this heuieth me
Many a sythe / þat punisshement
Noon falle shal / on this cursid meynee.
How treewe so be / hire enditement,
Our lige lord / shal be so innocent   180

D155 to] to do St   D156 with] þat L   D157 oghten] oght to BLYSt
D158 waar] *corr. from* was Y   D159 special] especiall St   D160 contrees]
cun'c'tres L, cunctres Y   ther] *om.* Y   D161 a day] days BLY   agoon]
goone BLY   D164 foule and] *om.* C   D166 oon] men BLY, *om.* C
D167 al] *om.* C   D168 foul] grete C   D169 is] it is C   D170 and]
om. C   brode] CB, brod St, brood SLY   D172 mescheef] þis mischefe BLY
D173 gredith] gretith BL   *Gloss om.* CSt   D174 Yee] the BLY   yee]
þe BLY   D175 outrers] BLY, outereris S, outeris St, actores C   and(2)] and
on C   D177 Many a] *corr. from* many þat L, many Y   D178 Noon] nowe C
falle shal] shall fall B (*line add. in margin*)   D179 *line add. in margin* B   treewe]
om. C   enditement] BLY, *corr. by eras. from* entendement S, *preceded by canc.* d Y,
entendement CSt

That vn to him / shal hid be þe notice.
Vnwaisshen gold / shal waisshe a wey þat vice.

Enformed shal be / his hie excellence.
By menes / whom þat þe lady moneye.
Hath rowned with / and shewid euidence.   185
In plate / þat al wronge is þat men seie.
Of þat false folke / my soule dar I leie.
Tho meenes shullen haue / no deffectif plate.
Her receit shal be / good and fin algate.

Nowe in good feith / I drede ther shal be.   190
Suche multitude / of þat false secte.
Wiþynne þis twoo ȝeere / or ellis thre.
But if þis stinking errour / be correcte.
That so moche of this land / shal be infecte.
Ther wiþ / þat trouþe shal a doun be þrowe.   195
And that cursid falsheed / it ouere growe.

Lo frende / nowe haue I myn entent vnreke.
Of my longe tale / displese ȝow nouȝt.
Nay Thomas nay / but lat me to the speke.
Whanne þi compleinte / was to the ende ybrouȝt.   200
Cam it ouȝt in þi purpos / and þi thouȝt.
Ouȝt ellis ther with / to han maad þan that.
Ȝee certein frende / O. nowe good Thomas what.

Frende þat I shal telle / as blyue y wys.
In latyn haue I seen / a smal tretice.
Wiche lerne for to die / callid is.   205

þat vnto him / shal hid be the notice;
Vnwasshen gold / shal wasshe away þat vice.

'Enformed shal be / his hye excellence
By menes / whom þat the lady moneye
Hath rowned with / and shewid euidence   185
In plate / þat al wrong is þat men seye
Of þat fals folk / My soule dar I leye,
Tho menes shuln han / no deffectif plate;
Hir receit shal be / good and fyn algate.

'Now in good feith / I dreede ther shal be   190
Swich multitude / of þat false secte
Withynne this two yeer / or elles three,
But if this stynkyng errour / be correct,
þat so moche of this land / shal be infect
Therwith / þat trouthe shal adoun be throwe   195
And þat cursid falshede / it ouergrowe.

'Lo freend / now haue I myn entente vnreke;
Of my long tale / displese yow noght.'
'Nay, Thomas, nay / but lat me to thee speke.
Whan thy conpleynte / was to thende ybroght,   200
Cam it aght in thy purpos / and thy thoght
Aght elles therwith / to han maad than that?'
'Yee, certein, freend' / 'O now, good Thomas, what?'

'Freend, þat I shal yow telle / as blyue ywis.
In Latyn haue I seen / a smal tretice   205
Which Lerne for to Die / callid is.

D181 shal hid be] shall hit be Y, hid be shall B, hidde shal be C, be so *canc. after* shall St
the] *om.* Y   D182 wasshe] vanyshe St   þat] þe CBL   D184 *marked as the
stanza's last line by* B, *after omission of 178–79, with disruption of stanza-division and rhyme
brackets up to* D203   D188 menes] meneys B, mens St   D189 good]
golde B   D190 feith] feyte B   D192 Withynne] with'in' Y
D194 infect] effecte C   D195 Therwith] *corr. from* with þer B   adoun]
doun C   D196 falshede] falsed L, and falsed Y   it] is St   D199 thee]
you C   D200 thende] the ende SCBLYSt   ybroght] ib'r'oght L
D201 aght] oght BLY, ou3t S, owght St, out C   D202 Aght] oght BLY, ou3t S, owght
St, out C   than] but C   D204 I shal] shall I CBLY   yow telle as blyue] CSt, telle
as blyue S, as blive yow telle BLY   D205 C *rewrites*: Haue I seene a smal tretice in Latyn
or this   D206 callid] *corr. from* is callyd St, calles C

A bettir restreint / knowe I noon fro vice.
For whanne þat deeth / shal man from hennes trice.
But he þat lessoun / lerned haue or thanne.
War that / for deeth comeþ / woot þere no wiȝt whanne. 209

And that haue I / purposid to translate.
If god his grace / list ther to me lene.
Siþen he of helþe / hath opened me þe ȝate.
For where my soule is / of vertu al lene.
And þoruȝ my bodies gilte / foule & vnclene. 215
To clense it / sumwhat by translacioun.
Of it shal be / myn occupacioun.

For I not oonly / but as that I hope.
Many another wiȝt / eke ther by shal.
His conscience / tendirly groope. 220
And wiþ him silfe acounte / and recken of al.
That he hath in this liif / wrouȝt greet or smal.
While he tyme hath / and freissh witt and vigour.
And not abide / vn to his deeþis hour.

Man may in þis tretiis / here aftirward. 225
If þat hym like / rede and biholde.
Considre and see wel / þat it is ful hard.
Delaie acountis / til liif bigynne to colde.
Shorte tyme is þanne / of hise offensis oolde.
To make a iust / and trewe reckenynge. 230
Sharpnesse of peine is ther / to greet hinderinge.

A bettre restreynt / knowe I noon fro vice;
For whan þat deeth / shal man from hennes tryce,
But he þat lessoun / lerned haue or thanne,   209
Waar that / and deeth comth / woot ther no wight whanne.

'And þat haue I / purposid to translate,
If God his grace / list therto me lene,
Syn he of helthe / hath opned me the yate;
For wher my soule is / of vertu al lene
And thurgh my bodyes gilt / foul and vnclene,   215
To clense it / sumwhat by translacioun
Of it shal be / myn occupacioun.

'For I nat oonly / but, as þat I hope,
Many anothir wight / eek therby shal
His conscience / tendreliche grope,   220
And with himself acounte / and rekne of al
þat he hath in this lyf / wroght greet or smal,
While he tyme hath / and fressh wit and vigour,
And nat abyde / vnto his deethes hour.

'Man may in this tretice / heere aftirward,   225
If þat him lyke / reden and beholde,
Considere and see wel / þat it is ful hard
Delaye acountes / til lyf gynne colde.
Short tyme is thanne / of his offenses olde
To make a iust / and treewe rekenynge;   230
Sharpnesse of peyne / is therto greet hyndrynge.

D208 þat] *om.* C   man] men St   from] fro BLY   D209 he] *om.* Y   haue]
hath C   thanne] tane BLY   D210 Waar] whare B   and] BLYSt, for S (*over eras.*),
whan C   D211 haue I purposid] purpos I C   D212 God his] Goddes his Y,
Godis C   D213 Syn] siþen SCBLYSt   he] me L   helthe] his helth Y, helpe C
the] þat BLY   D214 is of vertu] of vertue is C   al] *corr from* full al L   lene]
clene C   D215 foul] & fowle St   D221 al] *preceded by canc.* h Y
D222 this] his CSt, *om.* Y   or] & LSt   D223 fressh wit] wit helth B
D224 abyde vnto] to habide to B   hour] oure BLY   D225 this] `this' Y,
þe C   D228 til] to B   gynne] bigynne to SCBLYSt   D229 his] thine C
offenses] offence BLY   D230 treewe] a true B

Not hath me stirid / my deuociou*n*.
To do this labour / ȝe shullen vnderstonde.
But at þe excitinge / and mocioun.
Of a deuoute man / take I here on honde.   235
This labour / and as I can / wole I fonde.
His reed þoruȝ goddis grace / to parforme.
Thouȝ I be bare / of Intellecte and forme.

And wha*nn*e that endid is / I neu*ere* þinke.
More in englissh / after be occupied.   240
I may not labour / as I dide and swinke.
Mi lust is not ther to / so wel applied.
As it hath ben / it is ny mortified.
Wherfore I cesse þinke / be þis doon.
The niȝt approcheþ / it is fer past noon.   245

Of age am I. fifty wintir and three.
Ripenesse of deeth / faste vppon me now hastiþ.
My lymes sumdel / now vnweldy be.
Also my siȝt / appeiriþ faste and wastiþ.
And my conceit / adaies nowe not tastiþ.   250
As it hath doon / in ȝeeris precedent.
Nowe al a nother / is my sentement.

'Nat hath me stired / my deuocioun
To do this labour / yee shuln vndirstonde;
But at thexcitynge / and monicioun
Of a deuout man / take I heere on honde   235
This labour / and as I can / wole I fonde
His reed thurgh Goddes grace / to parfourme,
Thogh I be bare / of intellect and fourme.

'And whan þat endid is / I neuere thynke
More in Englissh / aftir be occupied.   240
I may nat laboure / as I dide and swynke;
My lust is nat therto / so wel applied
As it hath been / it is ny mortified;
Wherfore I cesse thynke / be this doon;
The nyght approchith / it is fer past noon.   245

'Of age am I / fifty wyntir and three.
Ripnesse of deeth / faste vpon me haastith;
My lymes sumdel / now vnweeldy be,
Also my sighte / appeirith faste and waastith,
And my conceit / adayes now nat taastith   250
As it hath doon / in yeeres precedent;
Now al anothir / is my sentement.

D232 hath] *corr. from* have I St   D234 at thexcitynge] at þe excitinge SBLYSt,
atte excitinge C   monicioun] St, mocioun SCBLY   D235 on] an BY
D236 fonde] founde L   .   D237 thurgh] thorowe B (*canc. in red*), and through C
D240 aftir be] to ben C   D246 am I] I am BLY   D247 faste] now faste BLY
haastith] CBLYSt, now hastiþ S   D248 sumdel now] nowe somdel C
D249 Also] all St   appeirith] appereth BLYSt   faste and] and fast C   D250 taas-
tith] attastith BLY   D251 As] *corr. from* and my St   D252 sentement] discent C

f.13^r

'More am I heuy now vpon a day
Than I sumtyme was in dayes fyue;
Thyng þat or this me thoghte game & play   255
Is ernest now / the hony fro the hyue
Of my spirit withdrawith wondir blyue.
Whan al is doon / al this worldes swetnesse
At ende torneth into bittirnesse.

¶ Fallit*ur* insipiens
vite pres*entis*
amore etc.

'The fool thurgh loue of this lyf present   260
Deceyued is / but the wys man woot weel
How ful this world of sorwe is and torment,
Wherfore in it / he trustith nat a deel.
Thogh a man this day / sitte hye on the wheel
Tomorwe he may be tryced from his sete;   265
This hath be seen often / among the grete.

'How fair thyng / or how precious it be
þat in the world is / it is lyk a flour
To whom / nature yeuen hath beautee
Of fressh heewe / and of ful plesant colour,   270
With soote smellynge also and odour;
But as soone as it is bicomen drye,
Farwel colour / and the smel gynneth dye.

f.13^v

'Rial might and eerthely magestee,
Welthe of the world / and longe & fair*e* dayes   275
Passen / as dooth the shadwe of a tree;

D253 heuy] 'heuy' B (*in margin, marked for insertion after* now)   D254 dayes]
dayd L   fyue] seven B   D255 or this me thoghte] me thought or þis C
D256 now] now 'then' H (then *add. in a later hand*)   fro] from SCBLY   D257 spirit]
spirites C   withdrawith] withdrawe C   blyue] swythe C   D258 al(2)] *om.*
SCBLY   worldes] worlde B   D259 At] atte CY, at þe B   into] 'in' to L
D260 this] his LY   *Gloss* De mundi contemptu fallitur insipiens SCBLY
D262 this world of sorwe is] this world 'is' of sorow B (*line add. in margin*), of sorowe þis worlde
is C   D263 Wherfore] wher B   he] *om.* B (*line add. in margin*)   nat] neuer
CBLY   D264 this day sitte] sytte this day C (*line add. by* B *in margin, with disruption of
stanza-division and rhyme brackets up to D280 and 287 respectively*)   D266 often] ofte
SCBLY   D267 thyng] thyngh B, thinges L   D269 yeuen] *corr. from* youen H
D270 of(2)] *om.* C   D271 soote] swete BY, so L   also and] and also L
odour] colour (*canc.*) odour Y   D272 it is bicomen] hit bicome is C, þat it bicome is S, þat
it becommys BLY   D273 gynneth] bigynnyth CB, 'be'gynneth 'to' H (*add. by later
hand, probably Stow's*)   D274 and] and al SCBLY   D276 Passen] passeth B

Whan deeth is come / ther be no delayes.
The worldes trust / is brotil at assayes;
The wyse men / wel knowen this is sooth,
They knowen / what deceit to man it dooth.   280

'Lond / rente / catel / gold / honour / richesse,
þat for a tyme lent been to been ouris,
Forgo we shole / sonner than we gesse.
Paleses / maners / castels grete & touris
Shul vs bireft be / by deeth þat ful sour is;   285
Shee is the rogh besom / which shal vs all*e*
Sweepe out of this world / whan God list it fall*e*.

'And syn þat shee shal of vs make an ende
Holsum is hir*e* haue 'ofte' in remembrance
Or shee hir messager seeknesse vs sende.   290
¶ Now, my freend / so God yeue yow good chaunce,
Is it nat good to make a purueance
Ageyn the comynge of þat messageer
That we may stande in conscience cleer?'

¶ 'Yis, Thomas, yis / thow hast a good entente,   295   f.14ʳ
But thy werk hard is to parfo*u*rme, I dreede.
Thy brayn parcas / therto nat wole assente,
And wel thow woost / it moot assente neede
Or thow aboute brynge swich a deede.
Now in good feith / I rede as for the beste,   300
þat purpos caste out of thy myndes cheste.

D278 brotil] *corr. from* bretil H, bretil S, brucull B, brotull LY   D279 wyse] wyse
knaw L (knaw *canc.*)   knowen] knowen þat SCBLY   D280 to man] to to man H (to(2)
canc.), to a man BLY, to men C   it] is L   D281 catel] castell Y   richesse] and
ricchesse SCLY, and ricchenesse B   D282 lent been] ben lente vs SCBLY
D283 Forgo] for good C   D284 Paleses] *corr. from* ?palases H, paleis SCBL,
payles Y   grete &] and grete C   touris] tovnes C   D285 Shul] *altered to* shal *by
a later hand* H   D286 rogh besom] rowe bosome C   D287 Sweepe]
swope C   D288 syn] siþen SCBY, lethen L   D289 hire haue 'ofte'] her to
haue offte C, here hir haue ofte S, here hir ofte have BLY   D291 God] SCBLY,
good H   D292 Y *writes after 293 and corr.*   nat] *om.* C   D293 Y *writes before
292 and corr.*   Ageyn] apon L   D297 Thy] thyne BLY   D298 thow]
yow Y   it moot] thou must C   C300 feith] fey C   as] 'as' Y   the] þi S
D301 caste] þat thou cast C   thy myndes cheste] þine hert C

'Thy bisy studie aboute swich mateere
Hath causid thee / to stirte into the plyt
That thow wer*e* in / as fer as I can heere;
And thogh thow deeme / thow be there*of* qwyt,   305
Abyde / and thy purpos putte in respyt
Til þat right wel stablisshid be thy brayn,
And therto thanne / I wole assente fayn.

'Thogh a strong fyr / þat was in an herth late,
Withdrawen be / and swept away ful cleene,   310
Yit aftirward / bothe the herth and plate
Been of the fyr warm / thogh no fyr be seene
There as þat it was / and right so I meene:
Althogh past be the grete of thy seeknesse,
Yit lurke in thee may sum of hir warmnesse.'   315

f.14ᵛ

¶ 'O what is yow, freend / benedicitee?
Right now, whan I yow redde my conpleynte,
Made it nat mynde / it standith wel with me?
Myn herte with your speeche gynneth feynte.
Shuln we be now / al neewe to aqweynte   320
þat han so wel aqweynted be ful yore?
What / han yee now lerned a neewe lore?

'Han yee lerned / your freend for to mistruste
And to his wordes / yeue no credence?
If your frendshipe cancre so and ruste   325
Sore wole it trouble myn innocence,
þat ay yow holden haue in existence
A verray freend / Certes, sore am I greeued
That yee nat leeue / how God me hath releeued.

D302 swich] such a Y (a *canc.*)   D303 stirte] *corr. from* ?starte H   the]
þat C   D304 were] was B   D305 thow be thereof] þat þou þere of be C
qwyt]whittB   D306 thy]`þi´B          purpos]pu`r´posL   D307 Til]toB   wel]
willY,*om.*L   D308 Iwole]wolIC   D310 swept]swopeC   D311 herth]
erthe L   D313 þat] `þat´ Y, *om.* C   D314 past] passid SCBLY
D315 hir]þeC   D316 yow]*corr.from*ȝowrY   D317 whanIyowredde]whanI
red yow B, haue I radde C   D319 Myn] my BLY   gynneth]bigynneth to SCBLY
D320 Shuln] *altered to* shuld *by a later hand* H   neewe]nowB   D322 nowlerned]
lerned nowe C   D323 Han] whan C   for]*om.* C   D324 yeue] to yeue C
D325 cancre so] so cankir B   D326 trouble myn] trouble nowe myn SBLY, nowe
trouble myn C   D327 ay] euere SCBLY   D328 Certes] cretes BLY
D329 me hath] hath me SCBLY

'Whoso nat leeueth / what þat a man seith 330
Is signe þat he trustith him but lyte;
A verray freend yeueth credence & feith
Vnto his freend / whatso he speke & wryte.
Frendshipes lawe / nat worth were a myte
If þat vntrust / vnto it were annexid; 335
Vntrust hath many a wight ful sore vexid.

'I with myseluen made foreward, f.15ʳ
Whan with the knotte of frendshipe I me knytte
Vnto yow, þat I neuere aftirward
Fro þat hy bond departe wolde or flitte, 340
Which keepe I wole ay / O, your wordes sitte
Ny to myn herte / and thogh yee me nat loue,
My loue fro yow / shal ther no wight shoue.

¶ 'Tullius seith / þat frendshipe verray
Endurith euere / how so men it assaille. 345
Frendshipe is noon / to loue wel this day
Or yeeres outhir / and aftirward faille;
A freend to freend / his peyne & his trauaille
Dooth ay, frendshipe to keepe & conserue
Til dethes strook þat bond asondir kerue. 350

'To this matire accordith Salomon –
Yee knowe it bet than I by many fold:
Ones freend / and holde euere therupon.
In your frendshipe were a slipir hold
If it abate wolde and wexe cold, 355
þat vnto now hath been bothe hoot & warm;
To yow were it repreef / and to me harm.

D330 Whoso] tho so S   D331 C *has whole line over eras.*   signe] a signe
SCBLY   þat] *om.* S   trustith] truste BLY   lyte] a lite SCBLY
D332 yeueth] yeue I C   D333 freend] frendis Y   &] or SCBLY   D335 vnto]
to BLY   D336 vexid] avexed CY   D337 I with myseluen] I with my silfe haue
SBLY, with myself haue I C   D338 with] that C   D339 neuere] no
more C   D340 bond] bounde BLY   D342 Ny] so ny BLY   myn] my BLY
and] *om.* L   loue] leve L   D343 fro] from SBLY   D345 men it] it
men C   D346 this] 'þis' B   D347 Or] ?si B   aftirward] aftirwardes
BLY   D348 his(1)] dothe his C   his(2)] *om.* C   D349 Dooth] do þer YBL,
and C   D350 Til] to B   dethes] deth BLY   bond] knotte SCBLY
D351 *see note for VO gloss*   D352 fold] a fold Y   D353 and] an Y   euere]
om. C   D355 wolde] wole LY   D356 been] 'be' B, *om.* LY

f.15^v

'If þat me list in this mateere dwelle
And it along / for to drawe and dilate,
Auctoritees an heep kowde I yow telle   360
Of frendshipe / but stynte I moot algate
Or elles wole it be ful longe & late
Or I haue endid my purposid werk,
For feeble is my conceit & dul & derk.

'But as þat I seide eer / and sooth it is,   365
My sclendre wit feele I as sad and stable
As euere it was at any tyme or this,
Thankid be our lord Ihesu merciable.'
¶ 'Yit Thomas, herkne a word and be souffrable
And take nat my speeche in displesance;   370
In me shalt thow fynde no variance.

'I am thy freend / as þat I haue ay been
And euere wole / doute it nat [at] al;
But truste wel, it is but seelden seen
þat any wight / þat caght hath swich a fal   375
As thy seeknesse was, þat aftir shal
Be of swich disposicioun and might
As he was erst / and so seith euery wight.

f.16^r

'Of studie was engendred thy seeknesse,
And þat was hard / Woldest [thow] now agayn   380
Entre into þat laborous bisynesse,
Syn it thy mynde and eek thy wit had slayn?
Thy conceit is nat worth a payndemayn.
Let be / let be / bisye thee so no more
Lest thee repente / and reewe it ouer sore.   385

D358 dwelle] to dwelle SCBLY   D359 it along for to drawe] for to drawe it alonge SCLY, forto drawe alonge B   dilate] to dilate BLY   D360 yow] *om.* C
D361 moot]moste B   D362 Or]and SCBLY   it]I t' L   D364 & dul & derk]
'&' ful dul and derke S, ful dull and derke C, and full darke BLY   D365 þat] *om.* SCBLY
and] full BLY   D366 sclendre] skelende C, sklandir B   stable] feble C
D368 our lord Ihesu] god lorde ihesu criste C   D371 shalt]shall BLY   fynde]nowe
finde SC, not fynde BLY   D372 ay] euere SCBLY   D373 at al] SBLY, al
HC   D375 þat(2)]*om.* C   D378 he]*corr. from* we Y   erst]affter C   euery]
euere LY   D379 engendred] 'en'gendrid L   D380 thow] SCBLY, *om.* H
now] not B   D381 into] in Y   laborous] laborus SCLY, laborious HB
D382 Syn] sen C, sithen SBLY   it...wit] my mynde and my witte eke C   and]*om.* Y
had] hath BLY   D384 so] not so BLY   D385 ouer sore] euere sore LY, ever
sore B (sore *corr. from* more)

'My reed procedith nat of froward wil,
But it is seid of verray freendlyhede;
For if so causid seeknesse on me fil
As dide on thee, right euene as I thee rede
So wolde I do myself / it is no drede;   390
And Salomon bit / aftir conseil do,
And good is it / conforme thee therto.

'He þat hath ones in swich plyt yfalle,
But he wel rule him / may in slippen eft.
This rede I thee / for aght þat may befalle: 395
Syn þat seeknesse God hath thee byreft,
The cause eschue / for it is good left;
Namely thyng of thoghtful studie kaght
Perillous is / as þat hath me been taght.

¶ 'Right as a theef þat hath eschapid ones   400   f.16ᵛ
The roop / no dreede hath eft his art to vse
Til þat the trees him weye vp, body and bones,
So looth is him / his sory craft refuse,
S[o] farest thow / ioie hastow for to muse
Vpon thy book / and there in stare & poure   405
Til þat it thy wit / consume and deuoure.

'I can no more / the lattere errour
Wers is, rede I / than þat þat was beforn.
The smert of studie / oghte be mirour
To thee / let yit thy studie be forborn.   410
Haue of my wordes / no desdeyn or scorn,
For þat I seye, of freendly tendrenesse
I seye it al / as wisly God me blesse.

D386 froward] a froward C, forward LY   *see note to D391 for VO gloss*
D389 right] ryght as L (as *canc.*)   D392 is it] it is SBLY   conforme] to confourme
BLY   thee] *om.* B   D393 hath] is C   D394 wel] wolle C   D395 aght]
oght BLY, ought C   D396 Syn] siþen SCBLY   D397 is] were C
D398 Namely] nam ly Y (*corr. from* nam by)   D399 is] it is SCBLY   þat] it
SCBLY   me been] be me C   D400–551 *lacking in B through loss of leaves*
D400 eschapid] a scapyd L, a scape Y   *see note for VO gloss*   D403 sory]
sore L   D404 So] SCLY, sa H   D406 it] *om.* SCLY   D407 the] but
þat the SCL, but at þe Y   *see note for VO gloss*   D408 rede I] *om.* C   þat þat] þat
SCLY   D409 smert] *corr. from* swert Y   oghte] ough C, of L   be] be a SCL, by
a Y   D411 or] ne C   D413 al as] a'l's L, als Y

'If thee nat list vpon thyself to reewe,
Thomas / who shal reewe vpon thee, I preye?   415
Now do foorth / let see / and thyn harm reneewe;
And heuyere / shal it peise and weye
Than it dide eer / therto my lyf I leye,
Which thee wolde ouer mochil harme & greeue.'
¶ 'Freend, as to þat / answere I shal by leeue.   420

f.17ʳ

'Where as þat yee deemen of me and trowe
That y of studie my disese took,
Which conceit eek / among the peple is sowe,
Trustith right wel / þat neuere studie in book
Was cause / why my mynde me forsook,   425
But i[t] was causid of my long seeknesse
And othir wyse nat / in soothfastnesse.

'And forthy neuere aftir this / preye y yow,
Deemeth no more so / ne nat it mynge.
That men kneew I had seeknesse, is ynow,   430
Thogh they make of the cause no serchynge;
Ther cometh but smal fruyt of swich deemynge.
To yow told haue I treewely the cause;
Now let vs stynten heere / & make a pause.

'In this keepe I no replicacioun,   435
It is nat worth / the labour is in veyn;
Shal no stirynge or excitacioun
Lette me of this labour, in certeyn.
Trustith wel this purpos is nat sodeyn;
Vpon my wittes stithie hath it be bete   440
Many a day / of this no lenger trete.

D415 reewe vpon thee] vpon þe rewe LY, on þe rewe SC   preye] þe preie S
D418 therto] and þereto C   D419 Which thee] and þat SCLY   wolde] wol C
mochil] moche þe SC, mych þe LY   D420 shal by leeue] shal bileue S (*add. later in
darker ink*) C   D425 why] þat C   mynde] frend mynd L (frend *canc.*)
D426 it] SCLY, is H   D430 kneew] knowe C   is] *om.* C   D431 Thogh]
thogh þat LY   D432 smal] litile SCLY   D434 Now] no Y   D435 keepe]
`kepe´ Y   D437 or] nor C   D439 is] *om.* L   D440 stithie] stefly C   it]
þis LY   D441 of] or C

'I haue a tyme resonable abide f.17ᵛ
Or that I thoghte in this laboure me,
And al to preeue myself I so dide.
A man in his conceit / may serche & see 445
In [fyue] yeer / what he do may, pardee,
And aftir þat take vpon him and do
Or leue / reson accordith heerto.'

¶ 'O Thomas, holdist thow it a prudence
Reed weyue and wirke aftir thyn owne wit? 450
Seide y nat eer / þat Salomons sentence
To do by reed / and by conseil men bit?
And thow desdeynest / for to folwen it.
What, art thow now / presumptuous become
And list nat of thy mis / been vndirnome?' 455

¶ 'Nay, freend / nat so / Yee woot wel, elleswhere
Salomon bit / oon be thy conseillour   ¶ Vnus sit tibi consi-
Among a [thowsand]; and if þat yee were   liarius inter mille.
As constant as yee han been or this hour,
By yow wolde I be red / but swich errour 460
In your conceit I feele now, sanz faille,
That in this cas yee can nat wel consaille.

'For God woot / a blynd counseillour is he f.18ʳ
Which þat conseille shal in a mateere,
If of a soothe / him list nat lerned be, 465
And euene swich oon / fynde I yow now heere.
I pleynly told yow haue the maneere
How þat it with me standen hath / and stant,
But of your trust to me-ward / be yee scant.

443 laboure] to laboure SCLY   D444 myself] my life C   D445 serche]
serchee H   D446 fyue].vᵉ. H   do may] may do LY   D448 heerto] ther to SC
D449 O Thomas]E Thomas S, Thomas C   thow it]it nat C   D450 weyue]wyiue L,
swyth C   wit] witt L (*corr. from* will)   D451 eer] or C   D452 To] *corr. from*
do C   D455 thy mis] þis vice C   been] to be SC   D457 *Gloss* consiliarius]
consiliarius Thomas LY   D458 thowsand] .ml. H (*corr. from* a)   D463 is]
om. Y   D466 euene] euere SCLY   D467 told yow haue] told have ȝow Y, ȝow
have told L   D468 þat] *om.* C   standen] stoode C

'Han yee aght herd of me in co*m*munynge   470
Wherthurgh yee oghten deeme of me amis?
Haue I nat seid reson / to your thynkynge?'
¶ 'For soothe, Thomas / to my conceit / yis.
But euere I am agast & dreede this:
Thy wit is nat so mighty to susteene   475
That labour / as thow thyself woldest weene.'

¶ 'Freend, as to þ*at*, he lyueth nat þ*at* can
Knowe / how it standith with anothir wight
So wel as himself / Althogh many a man
Take on him more / than lyth in his might   480
To knowe / þ*at* man is nat ruled right
þ*at* so presumeth in his iugement.
Beforn the doom, good wer*e* auisament.'

f.18ᵛ   ¶ 'Now Thomas / by the feith I to God owe,
Had I nat taastid thee / as þ*at* I now   485
Doon haue, it had been hard / maad me to trowe
The good plyt / which I feele wel þ*at* thow
Art in / I woot wel thow art wel ynow,
Whatso men of thee ymagyne or clappe.
Now haue I God, me thynkith, by the lappe.   490

'But also hertly / as I can or may,
Syn þ*at* thow wilt to þ*at* labour thee dresse,
I preye thee / in al maneere way
Thy wittes to conserue / in hir fresshnesse;
Whan thow therto goost / take of hem the lesse.   495
To muse longe / in an hard mateere
The wit of man abieth it ful deere.'

    D470 aght herd] herde ought C   D471 Wherthurgh] wher`thurgh' L   yee] þe
S   oghten] oght can Y (can *canc.*)   of me amis] `of' me amys Y, me of mys L
D474 I am] am I LY   D475 so] *om.* Y   D476 That] this LY   thow] that C
D479 a] `a' L   D480 lyth] is SCLY   D481 man] a man LY   right]
aright C   D483 Beforn] bifore SCLY   D484 I] þat I SCLY
D487 thow] ȝow LY   D488 thow] ȝow LY   D490 thynkith] þinke S
D491 also] as SCLY   or] and LY   D492 Syn þat] siþen þat SC, sithen `þat' Y,
sithen L   D493 in] by SCLY   way] a way LY   D495 hem] it SCLY
D497 abieth] abyith Y (*corr. from* abydith), beieth C

¶ 'Freend / I nat medle of matires grete,
Therto nat strecche may myn intellect.
I neu*ere* yit was brent with studies hete,   500
Let no man holde me therin suspect.
If I lightly / nat cacche may theffect
Of thyng / in which / laboure I me purpose,
Adieu my studie / anoon my book I close.

'By stirtes / whan þat a fressh lust me takith,   505   f.19ʳ
Wole I me bisye now and now a lyte,
But whan þat my lust dullith and asslakith,
I stynte wole / and no lenger*e* wryte;
And pardee, freend / þat may nat hyndre a myte,
As þat it seemeth to my symple auys.   510
Iugeth yourself / yee been prudent and wys.'

¶ 'Sikir, Thomas / if thow do in swich wyse
As þat thow seist / I am ful wel content
þat thow vpon thee take þat empryse
Which þat thow hast purposed and yment;   515
Vnto þat ende / yeue y myn assent.
Go now therto / in Ih*esu* Crystes name,
And as thow haast me seid, do thow þat same.

'I am seur þat thy disposicioun
Is swich / þat thow maist more take on hoonde   520
Than I first wende in myn oppinioun,
By many fold / thankid be Goddes soonde.
Do foorth in Goddes name / & nat ne woonde
To make and wryte / what thyng þat thee list.
þat I nat eer kneew, now is to me wist.   525

'And of o thyng / now wel I me remembre,   f.19ᵛ
Why thow purposist in this book trauaill*e*.

D502 lightly nat] not liȝtly SCLY   cacche may] may cacche SC, may kecche LY
theffect] þe effecte SCLY   D503 in] 'in' Y   D506 and] *om.* C
D507 whan þat] whanne S, whan CLY   D512 thow] ȝow LY   D513 As þat] as
SCLY   thow] ȝow LY   D517 Go] soo L   now] þou SCY, ȝow L
D518 thow(1)] ȝow LY   þat] the SCLY   D521 myn] my LY   D522 By] in
SCLY   thankid] thankyng L, tankyng Y   D524 þat thee] þat ȝe L, ȝe Y, þe C
D525 eer kneew] knewe or C   now is] is nowe SCLY   D526 now] *om.* C   me] me
'now' C   wel] will L, wol C   D527 trauaille] to trauaile SCLY

I trowe þat in the monthe of Septembre
Now last, or nat fer from / it is no faille –
No force of the tyme / it shal nat auaille   530
To my mateere / ne it hyndre or lette –
Thow seidist / of a book thow were in dette

'Vnto my lord / þat now is lieutenant,
My lord of Gloucestre / is it nat so?'
¶ 'Yis soothly, freend / and as by couenant   535
He sholde han had it many a day ago;
But seeknesse and vnlust / and othir mo
Han be the causes of impediment.'
¶ 'Thomas / than this book haast thow to him ment?'

¶ 'Yee sikir, freend, ful treewe is your deemynge;   540
For him it is / þat I this book shal make.
As blyue as þat I herde of his comynge
¶ *Scilicet de secundo*   Fro France, I penne and ynke gan to take,
reditu suo de
Francia.   And my spirit I made to awake,
þat longe lurkid hath in ydilnesse   545
For any swich labour or bisynesse.

f.20ʳ

'But of sum othir thyng fayn trete I wolde
My noble lordes herte / with / to glade,
As therto bownden am I deepe & holde.
On swich mateere / by God þat me made,   550
Wolde I bestowe many a balade,
Wiste I what / Good freend / telle on what is best
Me for to make / and folwe it am I prest.

'Next our lord lige / our kyng victorious,
In al this wyde world / lord is ther noon   555

D529 nat] *om.* C   from it] from it it S, from þat C   D530 tyme] *corr. from*
thine H   D531 ne] *or* C   it] *om.* SCLY   or] ne LY   D532 þow] 30w Y
D533 now is] is nowe C   D534 is] was SCLY   D535 and] *om.* C
D536 a] *om.* LY   D537 othir] many anoþer C   D538 impediment] my
impediment LY   D540 Yee sikir freend] siker freend 3e SL, syker 3e frend 3e Y
(3e(1) *canc.*), sekirli frende yee C   ful] *om.* LY   D543 *Gloss om.* SCLY
D544 And] *corr. from* off *in margin* Y   D546 For] fro C   or] and SCLY
D548 My] myne C   with] therwith SCLY   D549 As] and S   bownden am I
deepe] deepe I bounden am SCLY   & holde] iholde C   D550 God] him
SCLY   D552 what(1)] 'what' Y, *om.* C   D553 it] *om.* SCBLY   am I] I am B
D554 lord lige] lege lorde SCBLY   our(2)] *om.* BY, þe C   D555 lord] *om.* C

Vnto me so good ne so gracious,
And haath been swich / yeeres ful many oon.
God yilde it him / as sad as any stoon
His herte set is / and nat change can
Fro me, his humble seruant & his man.   560

'For him I thoghte han translated Vegece
Which tretith of the art of chiualrie;
But I see his knyghthode so encrece
þat no thyng my labour sholde edifie,
For he þat art / wel can for the maistrie.   565
Beyonde he preeued hath his worthynesse,
And among othre / Chirburgh to witnesse.

'This worthy prynce lay beforn þat hold   f.20^v
Which was ful strong / at seege many a day,
And thens for to departe hath he nat wold,   570
But knyghtly there abood / vpon his pray
Til he by force it wan / it is no nay.
Duc Henri, þat so worthy was and good,
Folwith this prince / as wel in deede as blood.

¶ 'Or he to Chirburgh cam / in iourneyynge,   575
Of Constantyn / he wan the cloos and yle,
For which / laude and honur and hy preysynge
Rewarden him / and qwyten him his whyle.
Thogh he beforn þat had a worthy style,
Yit of noble renoun / is þat encrees.   580
He is a famous prince / doutelees.

'For to reherce or telle in special
Euery act þat his swerd / in steel wroot there

D556 ne]no B   D557 swich]sethen B, seth LY   ful]om. CBLY   D559 set
is]is sette S   D560 Fro]from C   D561 translated]translate B   Vegece]*added
after line-stop* S, *added later* BLY, om. C   D564 labour]'labour' B   D565 þat]
'þat' Y   D568 beforn] bifore SCBLY   þat] þi Y   D569 at] atte CLY
D570 thens] hens B   for to] to BLY   hath] om. C   D572 wan] whan Y
D573 Henri] herry SCBLY   D574 blood] in blood C   D575 Chirburgh]
repeated in margin by Stow in H   cam] com B, come LY   D576 Constantyn]
Constantin S   D577 hy] bi SC   D578 qwyten] whiten B   whyle] wyle S,
qwhyle LY   D580 of] a BLY   D581 doutelees] and þat is doutelees
SCBLY   D583 swerd] *corr. from* swedd Y   wroot] wroght BLY

And many a place elles, I woot nat al;
And thogh euery act come had to myn ere –   585
To e[x]presse hem / my spirit wolde han fere,
Lest I his thank parchaunce mighte abregge
Thurgh vnkonnynge / if I hem sholde allegge.

'But this I seye / he callid is Humfrey
Conueniently / as þat it seemeth me,   590
For this conceit is in myn herte alwey:
Bataillous Mars / in his natiuitee
Vnto þat name / of verray specialtee
Titled him / makynge him therby promesse
þat strecche he sholde / into hy worthynesse.   595

'For Humfrey / as vnto myn intellect,
"Man make I shal" / in Englissh is to seye;
And þat byheeste / hath taken treewe effect,
As the commune fame / can bywreye.
Whoso his worthy knyghthode / can weye   600
Duely in his conceites balaunce,
Ynow hath / wherof his renoun enhaunce.

'To cronicle his actes / were a good deede,
For they ensaumple mighte and encorage
Ful many a man / for to taken heede   605
How for to gouerne hem in the vsage
Of armes / It is a greet auauntage
A man before him / to haue a mirour,
Therin to see the path vnto honour.

'O lord / whan he cam to the seege of Roon   610
Fro Chirburgh / whethir fere or cowardyse

D584 many a] many another SCBL, anoþer Y   elles] *om.* SCBLY   D585 euery]
ouery C   come had] had come C   D586 expresse] SCBLY, yepresse H
D588 sholde] shulde have B   D589 B *incorrectly marks as the last line of the previous
stanza, with disruption of stanza-division and rhyme brackets to the end of the Dialogue*   this]
thus C   D591 in] 'in' S   myn] my B   D593 specialtee] specialite BLY
D595 into] vnto SCBLY   worthynesse] prowesse SC, provesse LYB   D596 vnto]
to C   D597 is] it is C   D598 þat] by þat Y (by *canc.*)   D599 commune]
common B, comine LY, comen C   D600 his] is CBLY   D602 his] *corr. from*
is L   D603 were] hit were C   D604 encorage] *corr. from* corage Y
D606 vsage] *corr. from* vsase L   D608 before] biforne C   D610 cam] com BL,
come Y   D611 Chirburgh] Chirborough C, Chirborwe S   whethir] where BLY

So ny the walles / made him for to goon
Of the town / as he dide? I nat souffyse
To telle yow / in how knyghtly a wyse
He logged him ther*e* / and how worthyly   615
He baar him / What / he is al knyght soothly.

¶ 'Now good freend / shoue at the cart, I yow preye.
What thyng may I make vnto his plesance?
Withouten your reed / noot I what to seye.'
¶ 'O / no, pardee, Thomas / O no, ascau*n*ce.'   620
¶ 'No, certein, freend / As now no cheuissance
Can I. Your conseil is to me holsum;
As I truste in yow / mynystreth me sum.'

¶ 'Wel, Thomas / trowest thow his hy noblesse
Nat rekke / what mateere *þat* it be   625
þat thow shalt make of?' ¶ 'No, freend, as I gesse,
So *þat* it be mateere of honestee.'
¶ 'Thomas, and thanne I wole auyse me;
For whoso reed / & conseil yeue shal
May nat on heed / foorth renne therw*i*t*h*al.   630

'And *þat* so noble a prince, namely
So excellent / worthy and honurable,
Shal haue / needith good auys soothly,
þat it may be plesant and agreable
To his noblesse / it is nat couenable   635
To wryte to a prince so famous
But it be good mateer*e* and vertuous.

'Thow woost wel / who shal an hous edifie
Gooth nat therto withoute auisament
If he be wys / for w*i*t*h* his mental ye   640

f.22ʳ

¶ Si quis ha*b*et
fundar*e* domu*m*,
non currit ad actu*m*
¶ Impetuosa manus
etc.

D613 the] *om.* L   D614 wyse] wysye Y   D616 al knyght] alknyght
LY   D617 yow] *þe* C   D619 Withouten] withoute BLY   noot I] not I not
BLY   D620 O no ascaunce] parde escaunce C   D622 conseil] councell Y (*corr.*
from coucell)   D623 me] to me C   D624 Thomas trowest] Throwist B
noblesse] nobilnes B   D626 shalt] shall BLY   D628 I wole] wol I C
D630 foorth renne] renne forth C   therwithal] with all CBLY   D631 *þat*] *þat* `to' S,
þat to BL, *þer* to Y   D633 needith] nede B   auys] `a'visement C
D635 noblesse] nobilnes B   it] that C   D637 be] `be' Y   D638 who] how B,
ho LY   *Gloss* fundare domum] domum fundare L   etc.] *om.* SC   D639 Gooth]
couth C   withoute] withouten C   auisament] visement B

First is it seen / purposid / cast & ment,
How it shal wroght been / elles al is shent.
Certes / for the deffaute of good forsighte
Mistyden thynges / þat wel tyde mighte.

'This may been vnto thee / in thy makynge   645
A good mirour / Thow wilt nat haaste, I trowe,
Vnto thy penne / and therwith wirke heedlynge
Or thow auysed be wel / and wel knowe
What thow shalt wryte / O Thomas / many a throwe
Smertith the fool / for lak of good auys;   650
But no wight hath it smerted þat is wys,

'For wel is he waar / or he wryte or speke,
What is to do or leue / Who by prudence
Rule him shal, no thyng shal out from him breke
Hastily ne of rakil negligence.'   655
¶ 'Freend, þat is sooth / O now your assistence
And help / what I shal make, I yow byseeche.
In your wys conceit / serche yee & seeche.'

¶ He a long tyme in a studie stood,
And aftir `þat' thus tolde he his entente: 660
¶ 'Thomas, sauf bettre auys, I holde it good,
Syn now the holy seson is of Lente,
In which it sit euery man him repente
Of his offense / and of his wikkidnesse,
Be heuy of thy gilt / and the[e] confesse,   665

'And satisfaccion do thow for it.
Thow woost wel / on wommen greet wyt[e] & lak
Ofte haast thow put / Be waar / lest thow be qwit.

D642 wroght] wroth Y   D643 the] *om.* SCBLY   forsighte] oure sight B
D644 tyde] bitiden SCBLY   D645 vnto] to C   D647 thy] þe C   wirke]
w`i'rche L   D648 wel(1)] *om.* BLY   knowe] iknowe C   D649 many]
may C   D652 is he] he is BLY   D653 by] but C   D654 out] *om.*
BLY   from] fro CLY   D655 ne] nor B   of] of of C   D658 yee]
you C   D659 tyme] while SCBLY   D660 aftir `þat'] aftirwarde SCBLY
tolde he] he tolde SCBLY   D661 sauf] savinge C   D662 Syn] siþin
SCBLY   D663 man] wiȝt SCBLY   D665 thy] þer Y   thee] S, the HCBL,
þei Y   D666 thow]ȝow LY   D667 wyte] SCBLY, wyt H   D668 haast]
has B   Be] bi S

Thy wordes fille wolde a quarter sak
Which thow in whyt / depeynted haast with blak. 670
In hir repreef / mochil thyng haast thow write
That they nat foryeue haue / ne foryite.

'Sumwhat now wryte in honour & preysynge   f.23ʳ
Of hem / so maist thow do correccioun
Sumdel of thyn offense and misberynge.   675
Thow art cleene out of hire affeccioun.
Now, syn it is in thyn eleccioun
Whethir thee list / hir loue ageyn purchace
Or stonde as thow doost / out of loue & grace,

'Bewar, rede I / cheese the bettre part.   680
Truste wel this / wommen been felle and wyse;
Hem for to plese / lyth greet craft & art.
Wher no fyr maad is / may no smoke aryse,
But thow haast ofte / if thow thee wel auyse,
Maad smoky brondes / and for al þat gilt   685
Yit maist thow stonde in grace / if þat thow wilt.

'By buxum herte & by submissioun
To hir graces / yildynge thee coupable,
Thow pardon maist haue & remissioun
And do vnto hem plesance greable.   690
To make partie / art thow nothyng able.
Humble thy goost / be nat sturdy of herte;
Bettre than thow art / han they maad to smerte.

'The Wyf of Bathe take I for auctrice   f.23ᵛ
þat wommen han no ioie ne deyntee   695
þat men sholde vpon hem putte any vice;

D670 Which] that SCBLY   depeynted] depayntest LYB   haast] hath B
D671 mochil] moche SC, mych BLY   D672 That] which CSBLY   nat foryeue
haue] foryeue not haue BL, forþe forȝeve not have Y (forþe *canc.*)   D674 maist]
maste B   D675 misberynge] mys heering SC   D677 syn] sithen SCBLY
D678 hir loue ageyn] ayeyne here luff B   D680 Bewar] be wys SCBLY   rede I] I
reede C   D681 this] thes C, þees B   D683 Wher] were Y   maad] is maad Y (is
canc.)   aryse] ryse B   D684 thee wel] well þe C   D685 smoky]
smoke Y   D686 þat] *om.* S   D688 graces] grace C   D690 vnto]
to C   D692 thy] *om.* L   D694 auctrice] auctorice L auctorite CBY
D696 vpon] on L, vp Y

I woot wel so / or lyk to þat seith shee.
By wordes writen / Thomas, yilde thee.
Euene as thow by scripture hem haast offendid,
Right so / let it be by wrytynge amendid.'   700

¶ 'Freend / thogh I do so / what lust or pleisir
Shal my lord haue in þat? / Noon / thynkith me.'
¶ 'Yis Thomas, yis / his lust and his desir
Is / as it wel sit / to his hy degree,
For his desport / & mirthe in honestee   705
With ladyes / to haue daliance;
And this book / wole he shewen hem parchance.

'And syn he thy good lord is, he be may
For thee swich mene / þat the lightlyere
Shuln they foryeue thee / Putte in assay   710
My conseil / let see / nat shal it thee dere;
So wolde I doon / if in thy plyt I were.
Leye hond on thy breest / if thow wilt so do,
Or leue / I can no more seyn therto.

f.24ʳ   ¶ 'But thogh to wommen thow thyn herte bowe   715
Axynge hir graces / with greet repentance
For thy giltes, thee wole I nat allowe
To take on thee swich rule and gouernance
As they thee rede wolde / for greuance
So greet / ther folwe mighte of it parcas   720
That thow repente it sholdest ay, Thomas.

¶ 'Adam begyled was with Eeues reed
And sikir so was shee by the serpent,
To whom God seide / "This womman thyn heed.
Breke shal / for thurgh thyn enticement   725

¶ Genesis: Ait Dominus ad serpentem / Ipsa conteret caput tuum etc.

D698 yilde] yolde C   D699 hem haast] hast hem SCBLY   D701 thogh] if B   do so] so do C   D702 haue in þat] haue þere in CB, þerynne haue SLY   D706 to] for to SCBLY   D707 shewen hem] hem shewe SCBLY   D708 syn] siþen SCBLY   D709 mene] a meene SCBLY   D710 Shuln] shuld Y   Putte] putte it SCBL   D712 in thy plyt I] in þi plite 'I' S, I in thi plite C   D713 wilt] will LY   D715 thogh] þou B   thow] will B   D716 graces] grace C   D717 thy] þou B   giltes] corr. from geltes Y, giltees S   allowe] a low L, a law Y   D721 ay] euere SCBLY   D722 with] þoruȝ SCBLY   D723 Gloss Genesis] Genesis iiiᵒ SCBLY   etc.] om. SCBLY

Shee þath ybroken my commandement."
Now syn womman had of the feend swich might,
To breke a mannes heed / it seemeth light.

'Forwhy, let noon housbonde / thynke it shame
Ne repreef vnto him / ne vilenye,   730
Thogh his wyf do to him þat selue same.
Hir reson axith haue of men maistrie;
Thogh holy writ witnesse and testifie
Men sholde of hem han dominacioun,
It is the reuers in probacioun.   735

¶ Eodem capitulo /
Sub viri potestate
eris / & ipse domi-
nabitur tui etc.

'Hange vp his hachet / & sette him adoun,   f.24ᵛ
For wommen wole assente in no maneere
Vnto þat poynt / ne þat conclusioun.
¶ Thomas / how is it twixt thee & thy feere?'
¶ 'Wel, wel', quod I / 'What list yow thereof heere?
My wyf mighte haue hokir & greet desdeyn   741
If I sholde in swich cas / pleye a soleyn.'

¶ 'Now Thomas / if thee list to lyue in ese,
Prolle aftir wommennes beneuolence.
Thogh it be dangerous / good is hem plese,   745
For hard is it / to renne in hire offense.
Whatso they seyn / take al in pacience.
Bettre art thow nat / than thy fadres before,
Thomas, han been / be right wel waar therfore.'

¶ 'Freend, hard it is / wommen to greeue, I grante;
But what haue I agilt / for him þat dyde?   751

D727 Now] O SCBLY   syn] sithen SCBLY   womman] women C, wymmen B
of] on SCBLY   D731 Thogh] that SCBLY   wyf do to him] wiif dooth to him SLY,
wife to hym 'do' B (wife corr. from doth)   D732 reson] ax reson Y (ax canc.)   haue] to
haue SCBLY   men] hem C   maistrie] þe maistrie SCBLY   D733 witnesse]
witnesse it SCBLY   Gloss Eodem] in eodem B   etc.] om. SBLY   D734 Men] man
SCBLY   D735 the] om. C   D736 his] þine C   D737 wommen]
womman SLY   D738 ne] and B   D739 twixt] bitwixt C, bitwixe
SBLY   D740 yow] corr. from 3owr Y   heere] to here SC
D741 haue hokir] hoker haue SBLY, grete hoker haue C   greet] om. C   D742 a]
om. Y   D743 thee] þou SCBLY   to] om. B   D744 wommennes] wommans
BLY   D745 is] is it C   plese] to plese BLY   D746 it] om. S   D748 before]
beforne B   D749 Thomas han been] han ben Thomas SCBY, haue Thomas L   right
wel waar] war right wel C   D751 agilt] gilt B

Nat haue I doon why / dar I me auante,
Out of wommennes graces slippe or slyde.'
¶ 'Yis, Thomas, yis / in thepistle of Cupyde
Thow haast of hem / so largeliche said   755
That they been swart wrooth / & ful euele apaid.'

f.25ʳ

¶ 'Freend / doutelees sumwhat ther is therin
þat sowneth but right smal to hir honour.
But as to þat / now, for your fadir kyn,
Considereth / therof / was I noon auctour.   760
I nas in þat cas / but a reportour
Of folkes tales / as they seide, I wroot:
I nat affermed it on hem / God woot.

'Whoso þat shal reherce a mannes sawe
As þat he seith / moot he seyn & nat varie;   765
For, and he do / he dooth ageyn the lawe
Of trouthe / he may tho wordes nat contrarie.
Whoso þat seith I am hire aduersarie
And dispreise hir condicions and port,
For þat I made of hem swich a report,   770

'He misauysed is / and eek to blame.
Whan I it spak / I spak conpleynyngly;
I to hem thoghte no repreef ne shame.
What world is this / how vndirstande am I?
Looke in the same book / What stikith by?   775
Whoso lookith aright / there in may see
þat they me oghten haue in greet cheertee;

D752 dar I] dar ʒe S (ʒe *over* I *erased*), I C   D753 wommennes] wommans B
graces] grace C   slyde] slyd LY   D754 thepistle] þe epistle SBLY, þe
pistill C   D755 said] yseide C   D756 swart wrooth] blak wrooþ SCBL (L
corr. wrogh *to* wroth), blak wroght Y   ful] *om.* C   D757 ther] *om.* SCBLY
D758 sowneth] soundeth B   right] *om.* C   D759 þat] þat cas BLY   for] be B
D760 Considereth] considre SCBLY   therof was I] I was þer of SCBLY
D761 nas] was B   D762 as] and as B (I *del. after* as) LY, and þat SC   D763 God
woot] god it woote SCBLY   D764 þat] *om.* B   D765 þat] *om.* B   moot]
muste B   D766 ageyn] ayns B, ayenst C   D767 tho wordes nat] nat þe
wordes C   D770 swich a] suche S   D771 *see note for VO gloss*   D772 con-
pleynyngly] complenynge C   D773 ne] nor LY   D774 I] *om.* C
D776 aright] þere in C   there in may] þerynne may þei SBY, þer in may he L, may
þere C   D777 haue] 'haue' C, to have B

'And elles / woot I neu*er*e what is what.   f.25ᵛ
The book concludith for hem / is no nay,
Vertuously / my good freend / dooth it nat?'   780
¶ 'Thomas, I noot / for neu*er*e it yit I say.'
¶ 'No, freend?' ¶ 'No, Thomas' / ¶ 'Wel trowe I, `in´ fay;
For had yee red it fully to the ende,
Yee wolde seyn / it is nat as yee wende.'

¶ 'Thomas / how so it be / do as I seide: 785
Syn it displesith hem, amendes make.
If þat some of hem thee therof vpbreide,
Thow shalt be bisy ynow, I vndirtake,
Thy kut to keepe / Now I thee bytake
To God / for I moot needes fro thee weende.   790
The loue and thank of wo*m*men / God thee seende.

'Among, I thynke thee for to visyte
Or þat thy book fully finisshid be,
For looth me wer*e* / thow sholdest aght wryte
Wherthurgh / thow mightest gete any maugree,   795
And for þat cause / I wole it ouersee.
And, Thomas / now adieu & fare weel;
Thow fynde me shalt / also treewe as steel.'

¶ Whan he was goon / I in myn herte dredde   f.26ʳ
Stonde out of wo*m*mennes beneuolence;   800
And to fulfille þat / þat he me redde,
I shoop me do my peyne and diligence
To wynne hir loue by obedience.
Thogh I my wordes can nat wel portreye,
Lo heer the fourme / how I hem obeye.   805

D778 I] `I´ Y   neuere] not SCBLY   D779 is] it is SCBLY   D781 neuere it
yit I] зit I neuere it SCBLY   D783 fully] ful C   D784 nat] nat fulli C
D786 Syn] siþen SCBLY   D787 thee] ther BLY   therof] *corr. from* þerfor L
D788 shalt] shall Y   D789 Now] and nowe SCBLY   D790 moot] mote B (*corr.
from* wote)   needes fro thee] fro þe nedeth B   D791 God] nowe god S
D792 for] *om.* C   D794 aght] oght BLY, ought C   D795 thow] *om.* L
mightest] might B   D797 adieu] a deye B   D798 shalt] shall B   also] as CB
steel] any stele C   D799 myn herte] my hert BLY, my C   D800 Stonde] to
stonde SCBLY   D802 do] to do SCBLY   D804 wordes] woorde C

¶ My ladyes all*e* / as wisly God me blesse,
Why þat yee meeued been / can I nat knowe;
My gilt cam neu*ere* yit / to the ripnesse.
Althogh yee for your fo / me deeme & trowe,
But I your freend be / byte me the crowe!   810
I am al othir to yow / than yee weene;
By my wrytynge / hath it, & shal, be seene.

But nathelees / I lowly me submitte
To your bontees / as fer as they han place
In yow / Vnto me, wrecche, it may wel sitte   815
To axe p*a*rdoun / thogh I nat trespace.
Leuer is me / with pitous cheere & face
And meek spirit, do so / than open werre
Yee make me / & me putte atte werre.

f.26ᵛ

A tale eek / which I in the Romayn Deedis   820
Now late sy / in honur & plesance
Of yow, my ladyes / as I moot needis,
Or take my way / for fer*e* into France –
Thogh I nat shapen be / to prike or prau*n*ce –
Wole I translate / and þat shal pourge, I hope,   825
My gilt / as cleene / as keuerchiefs dooth sope.

D808 the] his SCBLY   D809 Althogh] all þ`o′gh L   me] *om.* C
D813 lowly me] me lowely C   D816 I] *canc.* S   D817 pitous] pituous C,
petyvos B   D818 spirit] spreite C   werre] *corr. from* warre Y   D819 &]
ad L   me putte] put me CBLY   atte] at þe SBLY   D820 Romayn]
Romans B   D821 late] lat B   D822 moot] muste B   needis] *corr. from*
needes H   D824 or] and SCBLY   D825 shal pourge] my gilte
SCBLY   D826 My gilt] shal pourge SCBLY   as(2)] *om.* L   keuerchiefs]
kerchefes LYB, kerchief C

NOTES

C1 The *Series* is the first item in MSS B, L and Y, beginning in each without heading. John Stow headed the text which he supplied in the Durham holograph with 'Thomas Hocclive', to which a seventeenth-century reader, identified by Doyle as George Davenport, added a genitive *-s* and the word 'Complaint'. In MSS S and C the *Series* follows the *Regiment*. S leaves a gap after the explicit to the latter, but no heading is supplied. MS C has the rubric 'Explicit liber de Regimine principum. Et incipit prologus de Incendio Amoris'. The incipit, referring evidently to Richard Rolle's *Incendium Amoris*, appears to be a rubricator's error. See Doyle, *PMLA*, 83 (1968), 24–25.

C1–14 The autumn setting contrasts with the spring opening of Chaucer's *Canterbury Tales*. In autumn, the melancholy humour was thought to prevail: 'heruest is coolde and drie and brediþ humour melancolik þat is coolde and drie', Trevisa, *Properties*, p. 526. Machaut's *Jugement dou Roy de Navarre* opens similarly, in autumn when 'ce qu'estre soloit tout vert | Estoit mué en autre teint', with the narrator alone in his chamber on 9 November suffering from melancholy and pondering the injustices of the world: *Œuvres de Guillaume de Machaut*, ed. E. Hoepffner (SATF, Paris, 1908–21), ll. 13–38. Cf. *Dial.* 2n. On autumnal melancholia in the Middle French poets, see J. Cerquiglini-Toulet, *La Couleur de la Mélancolie* (Paris, 1993). The opening of George Ashby's poem *A Prisoner's Reflections* (1463) describes the poet deserted by his friends 'At the ende of Somer, when wynter began | And trees, herbes and flowres dyd fade': *George Ashby's Poems*, ed. M. Bateson (EETS, ES 76, 1899), ll. 1–2. Cf. also the opening of Skelton's *Bowge of Courte*.

C10 *There*: 'Anticipatory and existential *there*' (Mustanoja, p. 337) is always written *ther* in the holographs, e.g. D277, 343, and hence C9 here. The same form is used for 'in that place', but only in non-eliding contexts where a monosyllable is needed, e.g. Furn. III 195 and C128 here; but otherwise the word in that sense is always *there*, disyllabic or elided, e.g. D571, 583. The form selected here must therefore mean 'in that place', i.e. the world.

C17 *thende of Nouembre*: In *Dialogue* 542–3 Hoccleve claims to have started 'this book' immediately after hearing of Duke Humphrey's return from France, an event which occurred probably in late November 1419: see Introduction, pp. lvii–lviii. All manuscripts read *the ende* as separate words, but the syllable-count requires *thende*. Compare D502 (*theffect*) and 754 (*thepistle*). Comparison of the two holograph copies of *Learn to Die* shows Hoccleve himself inconsistent in writing such elisions: see Excursus I, p. 116

C19 *thoght*: Kern, 'Zum Texte', p. 419, conjectured the singular form (found in the Coventry MS) on metrical grounds. Hoccleve commonly has *thoght* in the sense 'mental suffering, anxiety': *MED thought* n. 5(b), citing *Promptorium Parvulorum* 'Thowhte; or hevynesse yn herte: Mesticia, molestia, tristicia'. Cf. *Jonathas* 582, *Regiment* 7, 13, 245, etc.; also *thoghtful maladie* C21 and *thoghtful hete* C184. Constantinus Africanus speaks of 'nimia cogitatio' in melancholics: *De Melancholia*, ed. Garbers, p. 103 (Basel *Opera* I 283).

C20 *Before*: Hoccleve uses *beforn* only in rhyme, or where *before* would give an unwanted syllable: compare D608 with D483 and 568.

C22 *syn*: Here, as elsewhere, replacing the manuscripts' form *sithin* with Hoccleve's regular *syn* restores the syllable-count (Introduction, p. xlvii). On the poet's *seeknesse* see Introduction, pp. lx–lxii.

C23 The favourable regard in question is implicitly that of Fortune: cf. C260 and Chaucer's 'favour of Fortune' (*CT* I 2682, IV 69). The image of the cloud goes back to Boethius' *De Consolatione*, Bk I, m. 1, 19: Fortune 'fallacem mutavit nubila vultum' ('cloudy, changed her treacherous face'). In Chaucer's Monk's Tale, she is said to 'covere hire brighte face with a clowde' (*CT* VII 2766).

C28 *ne delyt*: a reading found only in St. S adds *no* interlineally in a blacker ink after *ne*, while BLY add *nokynnes*. These variants fail to recognise disyllabic *hadde*, a regular alternative to *had* in the holographs.

C29 *so swal*: S adds *sore* interlineally in a blacker ink after *so* (cf. *so sore* at C30), evidently for metrical reasons.

C31 *oute*: a stressed form of the adverb *out*, as in *Learn to Die* 532: 'so I absolutely had to come out with it'. See *OED out* adv. 13, 'with ellipsis of intr. vb. (*go*, *come*, etc.); hence functioning as a verb without inflexion'; and 13b, 'so *Out with* = have out, bring out', citing only one instance before 1548.

C33 *lette*: The holographs consistently distinguish between *letten* 'hinder' and *leten* 'allow'. Either may be meant here. I assume the former verb, in the sense 'confine': *MED letten* v. 3(a).

C36 All six manuscripts have versions of the same sentence as heading before this line. On the genre complaint and its varieties, see W. A. Davenport, *Chaucer: Complaint and Narrative* (Cambridge, 1988), and R. Deschaux, in *La Littérature Française aux XIVe et XVe Siècles*, ed. D. Poirion (Heidelberg, 1988), pp. 77–83.

C37 On the sickness as a visitation of God, compare C382 and D96, and see Introduction, p. lxi.

C45 The line as it stands in all copies would have two syllables too many. I presume that a word was added in the scribal archetype to make the line more emphatic. Kern, 'Zum Texte', p. 420, proposes omitting *euery*; but omission of *mannes* gives better sense.

C47 Doob, p. 221, compares the pilgrimages undertaken by the queen of Charles VI of France in the hope of remedying his madness. On visiting shrines in cases of mental illness, see B. Clarke, *Mental Disorder in Earlier Britain* (Cardiff, 1975), pp. 120–24.

C50 *memorie*: always a three-syllable word in the holographs, with stress on the second syllable and the final *-e* unpronounced (as in *glorie* C52). Adust melancholy could attack the memory: *Saturn and Melancholy*, pp. 91–2, and Introduction, p. lxii.

C53 S adds a second *his* before *benigne*, failing to recognise the disyllabic form of the weak adjective *hye*.

C55–6 Hoccleve dates his recovery precisely. It occurred on the All Saints' Day (1 November) five years before what at the time of writing was the latest celebration of that feast. If the latest celebration was that in 1419, recovery occurred on 1 November 1414: see Introduction, pp. lx–lxi. Later in the *Series* he appends to his *Learn to Die* a lesson on the joys of heaven from the All Saints liturgy. At C55, the Selden scribe originally wrote *was*, but then deleted it, evidently prompted by the *was* in the following line; but *was fiue yeer* there means 'five years ago'.

C58 All six copies have *and gracious* after *good*; but this makes the line too long by three syllables. *Reconsiliacioun* has seven syllables in its single holograph occurrence: 'In exyl / reconsiliacioun', Goll. V 96. The addition in the archetype would be explained by pious enthusiasm (cf. C236 and D90); but the line may also have seemed too short.

C62 *þat tyme*: 'during that period', i.e. the more than five years since recovery in 1414. S writes *Sith þ¹ time* over an erasure.

C63 *martire*: Hoccleve's holographs distinguish between the forms *martir* 'martyr' and *martire* 'anguish'. For the latter, see *MED martir(e* n.

C67 The virgule after *was* follows Stow.

C69–70 'No one wished to hold any friendly conversation with me. Everyone treated me like a stranger.'

C71 The text is uncertain at two points. SCBLY read *With þat*; but this implies an intransitive use of *tormente*, 'suffer torment', not recorded in the dictionaries. Since Hoccleve does occasionally start a stanza with a relative pronoun linking it to what has gone before (C15 and Furn. I 155), I adopt St's *Which* here, despite the difficulty of explaining how Stow could have it: see Introduction, p. xxxix. Again, the *to* before *tormente* in all copies except Coventry is suspect. Addition of *to* occurs elsewhere in the archetype, producing an extrametrical syllable as here: Introduction, p. xlvii.

C72 *Westmynstre halle*: the great hall in Westminster Palace, on which see R. Allen Brown, H. M. Colvin, A. J. Taylor, *The History of the King's Works,*

Vol. I, The Middle Ages (London, 1963), pp. 491–552 and Plate III. The chief business of the crowds (*prees*) there would be with the courts of law (*King's Works*, pp. 543–45). The Privy Seal may occasionally have done business there; but Hoccleve's regular place of work was probably a little to the NE of the hall, adjacent to the Star Chamber where the king's council met: *King's Works*, pp. 545–46; Tout, *Chapters*, V 72–73.

C73 *Londoun*: In his *Regiment*, l. 5, Hoccleve speaks of himself living in the 'hospicium' or hostel of the Privy Seal, at 'Chestre Ynne, right fast be the Stronde', in the western suburbs of London on the road leading to Westminster. On the hostel, see Tout, *Chapters*, V 68–74, and Brown, 'Privy Seal Clerks', pp. 265–66. In his *Male Regle* (1405 × 1406), Hoccleve locates his ill-regulated doings in both London and Westminster.

C74 The Laud MS lacks ll. 74–146 through loss of one leaf.

C77 The *-e* of *mette* fails to elide before the break marked by the virgule: see Introduction, pp. xxx and xlviii.

C78–84 The gloss gives the source, Psalm 30 (AV 31) 12–14: 'They that saw me without fled from me. I am forgotten as one dead from the heart. I am become as a vessel that is destroyed. For I have heard the blame of many that dwell round about'. Rigg, *Speculum*, 45 (1970), 571, compares a passage from Isidore's *Synonyma*; but this was probably not present in the abbreviated version used by Hoccleve: see Excursus II.

C79 *fro*: The holographs show this to be the most common form of the preposition; but before words beginning with a vowel or ⟨h⟩ *from* is always used, to avoid hiatus: compare D256 and 340 with D265.

C80 *aweye*: Hoccleve's normal form is *away*; but he uses *aweye* where required by the rhyme as here: cf. e.g. Furn. VIII 36.

C81 The line renders 'sicut mortuus a corde', understood to mean 'as one no longer alive in the affections of others'.

C87 *Withdrawe and past*: so Kern, 'Zum Texte', p. 420. The fuller form *withdrawen* is elsewhere trisyllabic (as at D310). *Past* is the poet's usual form of the past participle of *passen* (as at D314).

C88 Hoccleve gives his age at D246 as fifty-three. According to some medical authorities, the third of the four ages of man lasted until the fifty-fifth or sixtieth year and was marked, like its corresponding season autumn (C1–14n), by dominance of the cold and dry melancholy humour: J. A. Burrow, *The Ages of Man* (Oxford, 1988), pp. 12–36, on four-age schemes. Hence, melancholy madness might recur during that age.

    namly: Hoccleve's usual form *namely* would leave an extrametrical syllable; I therefore adopt the form *namly*, used for metrical convenience once in the holographs, Goll. VIII 135.

C91 *hem vnwaar*: 'without their knowing'. An absolute construction; cf. C375, D1, 135.

C92–3 This prognosis conflicts with that at C88, implying, not melancholy madness, but the frenzy to which choleric people were prone: 'þis passioun [frenesy] comeþ to hote men and drie in somer, and al þese haueþ comparisoun to colera', Trevisa, *Properties*, p. 348.

C95 *hir*: Where only one syllable is required in non-eliding position, this word ('her' or 'their') is so written. In eliding contexts *hire* is preferred (e.g. D676).

C96 *Many someres*: cf. C55–6 above. *Someres* is disyllabic.

C99 *what men so*: 'whatever men'. The word-order of S and St is preferred as the more difficult reading. S writes 'Nota. bene. nota' against this passage, alone among the MSS, as also at C113, 211, 225, 239, 379, 393, and D253, 309.

C100 God 'knoweth the secrets of the heart', Psalm 43 (AV 44) 22.

C104 On ignorance of the 'tempus visitationis', see Luke 19.44.

Whom: Syntax and sense would be improved by emending to *Where*, as proposed by Kern, 'Zum Texte', p. 420.

whanne: The word is monosyllabic *whan* as a conjunction (e.g. C105), but disyllabic as an interrogative adverb: 'Whanne ne whidir I sholde hennes sterte', Furn. XVIII 8.

C108 *liste*: a deferential subjunctive, 'when it may please him'. The present indicative form is *list*, e.g. D414.

C113 Proverbial: Whiting G264. Since adverbial *longe* always has -*e* in the holographs, the line is metrically irregular: Introduction, p. xlix. Kern, 'Zum Texte', p. 420, supports the Stow reading without *but*.

C115 MS Bodley has a gloss, shared with Yale (Laud lacks the leaf) and therefore going back at least to their common ancestor β: 'Bernardus. Si omnis timenda est fortuna [omnis fortuna timenda est Y] magis tamen prospera quam aduersa' ('Every kind of fortune is to be feared, but the good even more than the bad'). The absence of this gloss in S and C casts doubt on its authorial origin. The nearest parallel in *PL* occurs in a treatise by Peter of Blois: 'Unde dicit Gregorius: "Etsi omnis fortuna timenda est, magis tamen timenda est prospera quam adversa"', *PL* 207 col. 989C. Gregory says something similar in his *Moralia in Iob*: 'sancti vires magis in hoc mundo prospera quam adversa formident', *PL* 75 cols 679D-680A. The *PL* Database, which Malcolm Godden has kindly consulted, shows no Bernardine parallel.

C120 *steer*: 'young ox'. Cf. Whiting B593: 'As wood (mad) as a wild bullock'. Wild movements of the eyes (C121, 133) are listed by Bartholomaeus Anglicus among the symptoms of 'frenesy', Trevisa, *Properties*, p. 348.

C123 *bukkissh*: This epithet, from *bukke* 'male deer', is recorded only here in *MED*, glossing it 'haughty, overbearing'. But the speaker's following references to mental confusion and instability suggest rather a meaning such as 'disturbed': cf. *Roman de la Rose*, l. 4779, 'plus cornairs qu'un cers ramez' ('more crazed than an antlered stag'). The remark follows directly from the previous speaker's observation that Hoccleve carries his head too high: Christine de Pizan advises ladies to be restrained in demeanour, not jumping about or carrying 'la teste levee comme cers ramages' ('the head lifted like an antlered stag'), *Le Livre des Trois Vertus*, ed. C. C. Willard and E. Hicks (Paris, 1989), p. 73.

C124 The line begins with *And* in all MSS, but this is unmetrical and awkward. Kern, 'Zum Texte', p. 421, rightly proposes to omit it. The archetype evidently failed to see that the third speaker's comments begin with C123.

C126 The interlinear addition by S of *he* before ȝeue is a clear example of erroneous correction, perhaps from a source here sharing a reading with β.

C127–33 Among the signs of 'frenesy', according to Bartholomaeus, are 'strecchinge and castinge of hondes, meuynge and wagynge of hede', Trevisa, *Properties*, p. 348. Cf. notes to C92–3 and 120 above. Medieval opinion valued 'moderatio' in bodily movements and disapproved of 'gesticulatio': J.-C. Schmitt, *La Raison des Gestes* (Paris, 1990).

C128 *ro*: The roe deer was proverbially swift-footed (e.g. 2 Samuel 2.18): see *MED ro* n.(1) (c). The three successive animal comparisons suggest Hoccleve's degradation, in the eyes of others, into a bestial state, like that of mad Nebuchadnezzar: Doob, Chap. 2.

C136 *repente*: The verb is commonly reflexive, as at D385, 663; but *me repente* gives a superfluous syllable both here (where it is the reading of S and C) and at C371 (all MSS). Kern, 'Zum Texte', p. 422, rightly preferred the reading of St (also β) here. Cf. D721.

C143 *leek*: a proverbial type of worthlessness: Whiting L185.

C144 *tonges keye*: Moralists advised locking the teeth and lips on an unruly tongue: see *MED louken* v.(1) 1(c).

C147 The Laud MS resumes with this line after its loss of a leaf.

C148 *laboured bisily*: Metrical considerations favour the reading of C and St. S and β evidently thought the line too short and padded it out. L has the whole line added by the original scribe but in a much paler ink. S has *-en euere ful* after *laboured* over an erasure whose length suggests that the scribe first wrote the line in its authorial form, subsequently 'correcting' it from another copy somehow related to β: see Introduction, p. xxxvii.

C150 *speke*: The majority MS reading supports *spak*, third person singular, past tense. This is possible, because *men* can represent the unstressed form of singular *man* (as at D452). However, Hoccleve's form for the past plural is *speke*, as at Furn. III 158; and I suppose that the scribes, rightly requiring a past tense but mistaking *speke* as present, substituted *spak*.

wondryngly: The reading of S and St, 'with wonderment', is preferred as giving stronger sense than *wondirly*, 'in wonderful fashion', in C and β.

C152–3 That is, 'even if my heart had been dipped in the brook, it would have been no wetter than it already was with my sweat.'

C154 In Furn. I 221, the Virgin Mary addresses herself in her sorrow: 'Now thow art frosty cold / now fyry hoot'.

C157 *streighte*: The forms *streight* in C and *streite* in S and St evidently represent the adverb *streight* 'immediately' (cf. variants at C119), implying omission of the verb of motion: 'I immediately [went] to my mirror'. *Sterte* in β looks like a guess. I conjecture *streighte*, past tense of *strecchen*. *Strecchen to* (cf. D499, 595) is recorded once in the sense 'reach for': 'Sone þenne he starte vp and streiȝte to his hache [axe]', *MED strecchen* v. 5(c). The glass in question is a hand-mirror for which Hoccleve reaches out: cf. Arcite in the Knight's Tale, who 'caughte a greet mirour' to judge his changed appearance, *CT* I 1399. Quintilian, discussing the need for appropriate gesture and facial expression in an orator, reports that Demosthenes 'used to practise his delivery in front of a large mirror' in order to check the effect produced: *Institutio Oratoria*, ed. and trans. H. E. Butler, 4 Vols (Cambridge, Mass., 1920–22), XI iii 68.

C160 *had nat*: The word-order of S might be preferred as more difficult.

C161 'Have improved it, so far as I knew how or was able.' The omission of *have* before the past participle (Kern, 'Zum Texte', p. 422, compares D486) is parallelled in *Confessio Amantis*: '..if that he hadde wolde | His time kept' (IV 248–9, and see Macaulay's note).

C162 *saut*: *MED saut* n.(1) takes this as the shortened form of *assaut*, 'assault', creating a separate entry for the purpose. The use is better referred to *MED saut* n.(2), 'a leap, jump': 'I often rushed to this mirror'.

C163 *maneere*: Hoccleve always writes the word thus in rhyme, where stress is on the second syllable.

C167 Selden has *it* before *forth*, referring to the nearly synonymous *contenance* and *cheere*: 'if I go on using it'. This may improve the syntax of the sentence, but it adds an unmetrical syllable (unless *I* can be slurred with the following vowel).

C169 75 This soliloquy puts the other side of the case stated in 163–8. Another pair of opposed soliloquys follows, C185–9 and 190–3. Chaucer's Criseyde reasons similarly, *sic* and *non*, *Troilus* II 703–63 and 771–805.

C170 Proverbial: Whiting M205, and cf. M244.

C174 *troublid*: a reading challenged by *troublie* in Coventry MS. Cf. C302.

C180 Rigg, *Speculum*, 45 (1970), 572, compares a passage in Isidore's *Synonyma*, *PL* 83 para. 13; but this is omitted from the abridged version used by Hoccleve, the *Tractatus* (see Excursus II), along with the whole section, paragraphs 7–15.

C183 Hoccleve is returning from work at the Privy Seal to his lodgings, along the paved road (*pauyment* 186) between Westminster and London. See notes to C72 and 73.

C184 *thoghtful hete*: Unpleasant sensations such as anxiety (*thoght*, cf. C19n) could, when severe, be considered 'hot'. Cf. *Pearl* l. 388, and *MED hot* adj. 4(b): 'of pain, hunger, misery, distress: burning, sharp, keen'.

C185 The line is unmetrical as it stands, lacking two syllables. See Introduction, p. xlix. Kern, 'Zum Texte', p. 422, proposes adding *thanne*, perhaps before *thoghte* as at C190.

C187 *in and out*: 'indoors and outdoors': *MED in* adv. 1a (b).

C188 *Wondrynge*: The sense 'wondering' (cf. *Jonathas* 288) is possible here: by going to work, Hoccleve invites speculation about his mental state, as at C150. But the collocation with *heuynesse* points rather to a form of ME *wandreth*, 'distress', a word commonly coupled with *wo*. It occurs in the form *wandrynge* in *The Parlement of the Thre Ages*, ed. M. Y. Offord (EETS, 246, 1959), l. 257: see Offord's note. The form *wondering* collocates with *woe* in the *Death and Life*, ed. I. Gollancz (London, 1930), ll. 250 and 440. Hoccleve's use may owe something to confusion with *wonder* in its sense 'great distress or grief': *OED wonder* sb. 5c. *Wondrynge* occurs again at C305, probably also as a form of *wandreth*; but the sense 'wondering, speculation' cannot be excluded there either, given the following reference to people's *ymagynynge* (C307).

C194–5 Hoccleve recalls Matthew 12.43: 'And when an unclean spirit is gone out of a man, he walketh through dry places seeking rest and findeth none'. The whole *Complaint* depicts such a restless condition, following recovery from mental illness.

C195 The *-e* of *reste* fails to elide before the mid-line break: see Introduction, pp. xxx and xlviii.

C198 Proverbial: Whiting M657. The comparative form *ferre* in C and St is supported by *ferrer* in β.

C200 Cited as a proverb by Whiting P412, but with no other examples.

C202 The gloss cites Matthew 7.16: 'By their fruits you shall know them'. Matthew's twelfth chapter, on which Hoccleve drew in C194–5, has a similar verse, 12.33. The image of fruit is introduced into the poem at C204.

C211–12 'It is hard when men base their opinion of what a man is like upon a glance . . .'

C217 *communynge*: The *-e* is unelided before the mid-line break. Here as at D470 the word means 'conversation'. So *commune* 'hold a conversation', C218, 269.

C221 *nathelees*: All MSS read forms of Selden's *neuerethelees*; but the holographs always have *nathelees*, which restores the syllable-count here. So Kern, 'Zum Texte', p. 423, comparing D813.

C224 *preeue may the deede*: i.e. 'may my future conduct provide a demonstration'.

C225-31 Doob, p. 22, cites Chaucer's Pardoner on the kinship between drunkenness and madness: *CT* VI 492-7. Cf. Whiting M60: 'A drunken man is likened to a wood (mad) man'.

C228 All MSS except Coventry have an extra *ne* before *can*. Its omission, as by Kern, 'Zum Texte', p. 423, restores the syllable-count.

C231 The line as it stands in the MSS has two syllables too many. Adoption of Hoccleve's regular alternative form *comth* removes one, and omission of *it* after *were* removes the other. Archetypal addition of *it* occurs five times in the holograph *Dialogue*: D399, 710, 733, 763, 779. Absence of the word here is idiomatic: cf. C211 above, and see Mustanoja, p. 143. So: 'it would be hard if it were not so'.

C234 *venym*: perhaps adust melancholy. See Introduction, p. lxii. A passage in the Middle English translation of Guy of Chauliac's surgical treatise speaks of 'venenosity' as one consequence of the burning or adustion of melancholic material (cited in *MED* s.v. *adustioun* n.). Hoccleve refers to *venim* in a similar context in *Regiment* 270-3: 'Vnwise is he þat besy þoght ne dredeþ. | In whom þat he his mortel venym schedeþ, | But if a vomyt after folwe blyue, | At þe port of despeir he may arryue.' *Voide* is the technical term for such discharging, as in *CT* I 2751: see *OED void* v. 7.

C236 Here, as at C58 and D90, pious enthusiasm produced an unmetrical line in the scribal archetype. I assume an original *leche souerain;* cf. Furn. XVIII 61.

C238 BLY and S have *greuous* before *pyne*, an unmetrical scribal expansion, prompted by C234. S has the word by 'correction', over an erasure whose length suggests its original absence there. See Introduction, p. xxxvii.

C241 *and . . .can*: 'if he were tested to see what he is capable of'.

C242 *fooles peere*: 'fool's peer', i.e. no better than a fool. A pun on *pere* 'pear' is possible, given *taastid* at 241 (cf. 204, 210). Pears often seem good when rotten. They were a proverbial type of worthlessness: see *Regiment* 103, and Whiting P78-85.

C246 *algate*: All MSS have forms of *algates*. Kern, 'Zum Texte', p. 423, rightly conjectured Hoccleve's more frequent form *algate*, which can lose its third syllable here by elision, as the metre requires.

C247 *twixt*: 'between', conjectured by Kern, 'Zum Texte', p. 424, comparing D739. There as here the scribal copies have *bitwixt* or *bitwixe* for an original *twixt*.

C253–5 All copies have the rhyme forms *had* and *vnsad*, except Y (*hade, vnsade*). But the holographs never show past-tense *had* in rhyming position, preferring *hadde* there. This implies the plural form *vnsadde* (cf. plural *sadde*, *Jereslaus* 402).

C260 See C23n.

C264 'I can say very little without men thinking that I am raving.' Kern, 'Zum Texte', p. 424, proposed omission of *if*, found in all copies except Coventry after the second *but*. The omission, together with substitution of *seyn* for *seye*, restores the syllable-count.

C266 *sepulture*: 'burial', or possibly 'tomb', the reading of St. Y has *sepultre*, which *MED* treats as a form of the same word; but B and L agree with S on *sepulcre*. Coventry rewrites. *Sepulture* is Hoccleve's word elsewhere (*Regiment* 1610, *Jonathas* 651), and it avoids the hiatus. The two words were commonly confused in ME.

C268 Writing was removed from wax tablets by smoothing ('planing') the surface.

C269–70 'Since almost everyone is reluctant to converse with me . . .'

C271 *of your liueree*: 'one of your retinue', 'a follower or dependant of yours'. See *MED livere* n.(3) 4(e), and cf. Furn. VI 54, addressing the Knights of the Garter: 'yee been of seint Georges liueree'.

C272 *retenance*: 'retinue, band of followers': *MED retenaunce* n. (a).

C278 *repeire*: cf. C233. The word, which goes back to Latin *repatriare*, commonly implies a return home: *MED repairen* v. 1. Metre requires non-elision of *-e* before *hoom*.

C280 Kern, 'Zum Texte', p. 424, conjectures either *hem* or *men* for the second *me*; but the harder reading of the MSS must stand: the only vengeance an impatient Hoccleve could take would be upon himself.

C282 *spiryt*: The normal holograph form is *spirit*; but *Jonathas* 121 has *spiryt*, rhyming with *respyt* and *qwyt*. The form *qwyt* (here at 284) is similarly reserved for such rhymes. *Plyt* (285 here) is always so spelled, as the length of its vowel requires: Introduction, p. li. In the other two words, ⟨y⟩ spellings may suggest some lengthening of their vowels in anticipation of /pli:t/.

C287 *hertes cheertee*: cf. C81.

C289 *nat ne*: The double negative expression is emphatic, as at D523: see Kern, 'Zum Texte', p. 400. β and C read *me* for *ne*.

C291 *or*: This reading of S is challenged by the more usual *ne* in β and C (Hoccleve never uses *nor*, as in St). But metre requires that the *-e* of *stille* should elide. *Or* is unusual but not impossible in such negative expressions, e.g. D411 (where Coventry has *ne*).

C292 Selden misplaces the virgule, correctly positioned in St (supported by the points in CLY).

C293 *withynne and withoute*: 'indoors and out' (cf. C187), that is, in all circumstances.

C294 *for al þat*: 'despite all that', referring presumably to the evidence of their senses (290–2). The reading *thay* for *ay* in C and St arose from line-by-line reading, coupled with resistance to the word *ay* (cf. C350n).

C296 Hoccleve worked in the office of the Privy Seal from about 1387 until shortly before his death in the spring of 1426. On occasion he refers to his colleagues and companions (*felawes*) by name, e.g. Baillay, Hethe and Offorde in Furn. XIII 25–6.

C298 *euele*: With syncope of the second *e* and elision of the third, this word reduces to one syllable here, as at D756.

C303 Whiting S364 treats the expression as proverbial. Cf. *Regiment* 63: 'þus nat wiste I how to torne'.

C304 'But now I have made myself a promise.' The first *myself* functions as a simple first-person pronoun: Mustanoja, p. 148.

C305 *wondrynge*: See C188n.

C308 *dreeme*: The variant *deeme* has the support of S, β and C, and makes easy sense (cf. C99, 181, 192, etc.); but the harder reading *dreeme*, though found only in St, is strongly supported by its collocation with *drecche* elsewhere: see *OED dretch* v.[1] and *MED drecchen* v. and *drecchinge* ger. Thus, 'Litill rest had the king . . . For drechinge and dremyng & trobling his wittis' (*Song of Roland*, l. 80). *OED* cites Hoccleve's use of *drecche* here under sense 2, 'to be troubled in sleep'. The poet evidently compares those people who still imagine him ill to dreamers worrying and talking in their sleep.

C309–10 The Latin gloss acts as a heading: 'Here is a lamentation of a grieving man'. A. G. Rigg identified Hoccleve's source for what follows in 316–71 as the *Synonyma* of Isidore of Seville (*c.* 560–636), citing the text in *PL* 83 cols 825–68: *Speculum*, 45 (1970), 564–74. Hoccleve knew the work, however, not in its full form but in a heavily abridged version: J. A. Burrow, *Speculum*, 73 (1998), 424–28. This epitome is found, in a text very close to what Hoccleve used, under the title 'Tractatus Deflentis Hominis et Amonentis Racionis', in Bodleian Library MS Bodley 110, an early fifteenth-century English collection of religious writings. The opening of the *Tractatus* is printed from Bodley 110 in Excursus II here, up to the point at which Hoccleve ceases to render it—because, he says (372–5), the owner asked for his book back. References in the following notes are to the numbered sentences of the text in the Excursus.

C311 S has the speaker-heading *Resoun* here. BLY add *Reson* to the gloss at C309 and *Homo* to the gloss at 316. Further glosses indicate changes of speaker at C337, 340 and 342. The *Tractatus* has similar headings. Stow wrote none, but some are added in a later hand: *Reason* (C312, 337, 342) and *Thomas* (316, 340).

C316 The Latin gloss reproduces almost exactly the first two sentences of the *Tractatus*, rendered in 318–22: 'My soul is in dire straits, my heart is storm-tossed. Wherever I flee, my evils follow me, just as a shadow follows a body, and I cannot escape them'.

C323–4 Compare *Tractatus* 3: 'Non desunt michi tormenta et cruciamenta' ('Torments and tortures are not lacking for me').

C326–7 Compare *Tractatus* 4: 'Cur ego infelix natus fui in hanc vitam miseram?' ('Why was I born unhappy into this miserable life?').

C328 Hoccleve's gloss ('O death, how sweet you are to those whose life is bad') has no source in the Bodley *Tractatus*. It corresponds roughly to the passage in the unabridged *Synonyma* cited by Rigg, p. 568: 'O mors, quam dulcis es miseris! O mors, quam suavis es amare viventibus!' ('O death, how sweet you are to the miserable! O death, how delicious you are to those whose life is bitter!'), *PL* para. 19. This gloss, the only one not represented in the Bodley text, shows that Hoccleve knew the epitome in some other copy, fuller at this point.

C330 The gloss ('It is better for me to die than to live miserably') has an almost exact source in *Tractatus* 5.

C332–4 *Tractatus* 6 has: 'Plura enim ministrat dolor, et consolari non valeo' ('For sorrow supplies more, and I can get no consolation').

C335 Compare *Tractatus* 7: 'Nullus finis est dolorum meorum' ('There is no end to my sorrows').

C336 Kern, 'Zum Texte', p. 425, proposes omission of *to*, as elsewhere; but the syllable-count may be saved by counting *be a* as a single syllable: Introduction, p. xlix.

C337 The Latin gloss reproduces *Tractatus* 8–9 exactly: 'Why are you so broken in adversity? Abandon grief, drive sorrow from the heart'.

C340 Hoccleve's gloss ('How? in what way? by what method? by what counsel [or] skill?') preserves five of the eight questions asked by Homo in the unabridged *Synonyma* (*PL* col. 832, Rigg, p. 569), one more than in *Tractatus* 10, which omits *quomodo*. This word was evidently preserved in the text of the epitome used by Hoccleve.

C342 The gloss combines *Tractatus* 11 with the first part of *Tractatus* 13: 'Take up the struggles against the sorrows of the temporal world. Consider the similar fates etc.'. The plural *heuynesses*, found only in St, is supported by the Latin *tristicias* and by the reading *duresses* of S, Y and St in the following line. BLY omit *Respice similes euentus*, perhaps puzzled by the reading *silens* for *similes* as in S and C. The erroneous *silens*, presumably in the scribal archetype, is well explained by Rigg, p. 565: 'the abbreviating bar has been placed over the *e* instead of through the *l* of *siles*'.

C344–50 This stanza renders rather freely three *Tractatus* sentences: '[12] Be patient in all adversities. [13] Consider the similar fates of others: a man is more easily comforted by others' troubles. [14] Many men have suffered greater perils than you do, so that they may be purified and come to the kingdom of God.'

C345 *grettere*: The adjectival comparative ending *-ere* is a variant on more common *-er*. It occurs in rhyme also at *Learn to Die* 31 (*leuere*).

C350 Kern, 'Zum Texte', p. 426, conjectured *ay* for *euere*, to restore the syllable-count. Archetypal substitution of *euere* for *ay* can be seen three times in the holograph *Dialogue* (327, 372, 721).

C351–2 These lines neatly combine two sentences from the *Tractatus*, the first of which is cited in the gloss: '[15] Sorrow and unhappiness are common to all. [16] Tribulation has a use, and so have the pressures of this life'. The Latin supports Stow's *comon* in C352 against *comen* etc. in the rest, and also his *men* against *me*. Since Stow may have had no glosses in his exemplar, his readings are notable— evidence perhaps of inspired conjecture or of consulting a second exemplar: see Introduction, p. xxxix.

C353–4 Compare *Tractatus* 17: 'Humana temptacio reprehendit te et non interficit' ('the testing to which men are subject finds out your faults but does not kill you').

C356 The gloss ('Here God wounds those whom he is preparing for eternal salvation') corresponds to *Tractatus* 18. BLY have an additional gloss: 'Quem [Quos Y] diligo castigo', with which Rigg, p. 565, compares Apoc. 3.19 and Hebr. 12.6.

C357 Since *blisse* must have two syllables, the line is too long in all MSS. I follow Kern, 'Zum Texte', p. 462, who proposed omission of *to* before *go*. On archetypal additions of *to*, see Introduction, p. xlvii.

C358 The gloss ('Gold is melted, purged in the furnace, so that it may become purer') corresponds to *Tractatus* 19, except in reading *purgatur* for the latter's *probatur*. The image is biblical: Job 23.10, I Peter 1.7, etc. Cf. Whiting G298.

C360–2 Compare *Tractatus* 20: 'Omnia que sustines sunt ad probacionem' ('All the things you bear are to prove you').

C363 Compare *Tractatus* 21: 'Non murmures, non dicas "Quare sustineo mala?"' ('Do not complain, do not say "Why do I bear such wrongs?"').

C364 *thee takist amis*: 'misunderstand'. The word order (reversed by Coventry) avoids hiatus in *thee amis*.

C365–8 Compare *Tractatus* 22: 'Sed magis dic "Peccaui, et adhuc non sustineo tanta quanta dignus sum"' ('But rather say "I have sinned, and as yet I do not suffer as much as I deserve"'). This makes it clear that *So sore*, despite the virgule in Selden, goes with what follows: 'I must suffer as painfully for my offences as I deserve'. Cf. Furn. I 54–5.

C368–71 With *O lord, I am spilt*, Hoccleve ceases to render the *Tractatus* passage. Later in the *Tractatus*, Homo does express repentance and call for God's mercy, as Reason here advises, though in different words.

C371 *repente*: on omission of scribal *me*, see C136n.

C372–5 The *book* may have been an anthology of religious writing including the *Tractatus*, like MS Bodley 110. The story of an owner asking for it back (see D9n) serves to explain why Hoccleve stops where he does, making no further use of the Isidore epitome.

C375 *Me of his haaste vnwaar*: an absolute construction, 'I being unaware of his hurry'. See C91n.

C377 *aboue*: Hoccleve quite often uses this bookish form of cross-reference, e.g. *Jonathas* 633, 657. Elision occasionally fails, as here, before *haue*, e.g. Furn. VII 61.

said: Hoccleve's normal form is *seid*; but he uses the variant *said* once in the holographs, in the same rhyme: *Dialogue* 755.

C378 'And I consider myself very well satisfied with that.'

C379 *sythen*: Although *syn* is the regular holograph form for the conjunction, the disyllabic form is required here for the adverb, as at *Regiment* 1329.

C384 *souffrance*: Reason particularly counselled 'suffrance' or patience: C347, 349, 354.

C386 The proverbial expression 'to cast to (at) the cock', in the sense 'abandon', occurs also in Lydgate and in the Paston letters: Whiting C353, citing *MED casten* 3(c) and *cok* n(1) 5b. *MED* glosses: 'throw (sth.) at a cock or an object called "the cock"; *fig.* throw away, neglect'.

C388 The virgule after *wo* (as in Stow) is probably authorial, marking *lok* as the object of *vnpyke*. That verb consistently implies thievish activity in Middle English: *OED unpick* v. 1.

C391 *myn olde affeccioun*: that is, the former affection of others for me.

C398 A proverbial image of painful experience: Whiting B447.

C406 *tamende*: The reading of all MSS, *to amende*, gives one syllable too many. I assume elision of *to*: see D21n.

C410 *elde*: Hoccleve thanks God for his long life. Coventry's variant reflects puzzlement with the positive sense of the word here. The final *-e* fails to elide before the mid-line break.

Heading: The heading adopted here is found only in BLY (see variants). The holograph text in Durham has only Latin headings; but the evidence of the other MSS in the *Series* as a whole, where they agree, points to English headings in their archetype, as at the beginning of the *Complaint*. Exceptionally, however, they all have a Latin heading at the end of the *Dialogue*: see D826n.

Dialogue was a common genre in Medieval Latin and vernacular texts, as in the *De Consolatione Philosophiae* of Boethius and Isidore's *Synonyma*. The interlocutors vary. Hoccleve's dialogue with a friend may be compared with the *Dialogi* of Gregory the Great, where 'Gregorius', alone and miserable, is visited by his friend 'Petrus' and converses with him: *Gregoire le Grand, Dialogues*, ed. A. de Vogüé, 3 vols (Paris, 1978–80), II 10–17. In Machaut's *Voir Dit*, a melancholy narrator is visited by a friend: 'Mais, ainsi comme là pensoie | Tout seuls & merencolioie, | Je vi venir tout droit à mi | Un mien especial ami | Qui me geta de mon penser', *Le Livre du Voir-Dit*, ed. P. Paris (Paris, 1875), ll. 51–55. See A. G. Rigg on the *Dialogi* of Lawrence of Durham (*c.* 1100–1154), comparing Hoccleve: *A History of Anglo-Latin Literature 1066–1422* (Cambridge, 1992), pp. 58–61.

D1 An absolute construction, see C91n.

D2 In Machaut's *Jugement dou Roy de Navarre*, from l. 468, a solitary and melancholy narrator is similarly relieved by a visit from a friend: see C1–14n.

D3 *thow*: The Friend consistently addresses Hoccleve with the singular pronoun (the single exception is at l. 12 of the prologue to the *Jereslaus* moralisation), whereas Hoccleve consistently addresses the Friend with the more formal plural *yee*. This sustained contrast (matched by a contrast in imperative forms: D617n) evidently establishes the superior role of the Friend as counsellor. The old man in the prologue to the *Regiment* plays a similar part. He also addresses Hoccleve with the familiar singular (after one *yow* at l. 123). Hoccleve there begins with the singular form himself, but shifts to a consistent respectful plural after l. 750, once the old man has established his authority as counsellor.

D7 *By aght I woot*: 'for all I know'.

D9 *speek*: 'spoke'. This past-tense form occurs in the Durham holograph at *Jereslaus* 655 and *Learn to Die* 553; and the scribal variants there, *speke* or *spak*, correspond to those found here, reacting to what was evidently an unfamiliar form. Cf. also C150n. The past tense seems to imply that it was the Friend who lent Hoccleve the *Tractatus* book (C374), just as it is he who later supplies the moralisation to *Jereslaus* and the Latin *Jonathas*.

D15 *make it qweynte*: 'to make an issue of it', *MED queint(e* adj. 2(e). Compare *Jonathas* 642–3: 'He thoghte nat to make it qweynte and tow [tough], | And seye nay / and streyne courtesie'. Unmetrical *to* (in S and St) is to be omitted, as in C and BLY: Kern, 'Zum Texte', p. 427. Cf. D443, where all scribal copies add *to* after *thoghte*.

D17 What was first represented as a spoken outburst (C35) is treated here and hereafter as a written text: cf. D363n. See J. Simpson, 'Madness and Texts:

Hoccleve's *Series*', in *Chaucer and Fifteenth-Century Poetry*, ed. J. Boffey and J. Cowan (London, 1991), pp. 15–29.

D21 *toffende*: I assume elision of the vowel in *to*. Hoccleve writes this elision so at e.g. Goll. VIII 89 (*tapplie*) and 165 (*tescheewe*).

D22 *þat*: 'that which'.

D24 *Yee*: the form of the affirmative used in response to an open question, as also at D203, 540. On the alternative form *yis*, see D81n.

D26 Non-elision of the final *-e* in *mateere* before *ho* reflects the inverted word-order: 'refrain from that'.

D31 'I do not care that you should allude to that.'

D33 I assume that the *to* before *speke* in all MSS is an archetypal addition, as elsewhere: see Introduction, p. xlvii. Kern, 'Zum Texte', p. 427, would rather omit *a*.

D38 *forgote*: evidently a rhyming variant, like *foryite* D672, of the past participle. Hoccleve's unconstrained form was probably *foryete* (hence C80, D30), although this does not occur in the holographs.

D42 *but right now*: 'only just now'.

D44 *speke*: 'spoke'. See C150n.

D55 Omission of *to* as a scribal variant here is supported by the fact that the holographs only once show *to* after *oghten*: Kern, 'Zum Texte', p. 427. Cf. D409, 471, etc., and the variants at D157.

D58 *Syn þat*: The archetype evidently read *sithen*, a form never used in the holographs for the conjunction 'since'; but replacement by Hoccleve's regular *syn* leaves this line short of a syllable. Following Kern, 'Zum Texte', p. 427, I conjecture *syn þat*, as at D396 and 492 (cf. variants to the latter).

D61 *Wist were*: 'that it were known'.

D66 *coyn clippere*: See the digression on 'falsing of coin', which follows at D99–196, and D109n.

as wyde yblowe: 'as widely known', cf. C257.

D67–8 'Warriors against the faith' would be understood at this time as Lollard heretics, against whom Hoccleve wrote in other poems, notably Furn. II addressed to Oldcastle.

D69 *causes*: 'lawsuits'. Writers about this time commonly complain of the practice of 'maintenance', whereby lords or others lent their support to one party in a legal action regardless of the right: see J. A. Alford, *Piers Plowman: A Glossary of Legal Diction* (Woodbridge, 1988), pp. 94–5, and *MED maintenance* n. 1(a). Cf. *Regiment* 2804–6.

D70 'It would have been folly to have drawn attention to them', i.e. the crimes mentioned.

D81 An awkward line. Furnivall adds *tell* before *it*, taking *oute* as an adverb, and BLY emend similarly. But Kern, 'Zum Texte', p. 427, rightly noticed that *oute* is a verb here: *MED outen* v. 'to utter'; cf. *Jonathas* 43 and *Regiment* 1907, 2067, 3889. So: 'Am I not obliged to make it known?' Metre requires non-elision of *-e* in *oute* before the sharp syntactic break.

yis: the form of the affirmative used (as against *yee*, D24n) in response to either a negative question as here (cf. D295, 473, 535) or a negative statement (cf. D703, 754). Compare D535 with 540.

D83 *make I thynke*: 'I intend to make'. The word-order, altered without manuscript authority by Furnivall, is dictated by the requirement that both final *-e*'s should elide.

D87-8 'He would have had a lasting reputation for working such a cure on such a sick man.' Physicians were commonly criticised by writers as ineffective and expensive: C. Rawcliffe, *Medecine and Society in Later Medieval England* (Stroud, 1995), Chap. 5: 'The Physician'. The matter was of current interest as Hoccleve wrote. The parliament of 1421 received a petition requesting that physicians should be licensed, since 'many unconnyng and unapproved in the forsayd science practiseth . . .to grete harme and slaughtre of many men' (Rawcliffe, p. 120).

D90 As at C58 and 236, the archetype evidently made a pious addition (here *curteis*) to a line which may have seemed otherwise too short. But *pacient* has three syllables, as at *Learn to Die* 436.

D96 *spectacle*: 'eye-glass', as in the poem to Oldcastle (Furn. II). There, images of saints are said to prompt devotion to the saints themselves 'Right as a spectacle helpith feeble sighte, | Whan a man on the book redith or writ' (417-18).

D99-196 A digression on falsification of the coinage by washing, clipping, and counterfeiting, and on the need for judicial remedies. These were prime matters of public concern at the time of writing: see Excursus III here.

D102 *feeble moneye*: coins that lack the required weight of precious metal, the subject of D103-40.

D103 *but they gold weye*: 'unless they weigh a gold coin'. Hand-scales were commonly used for this purpose: Excursus III, pp. 123-4.

D106 *masshe*: The parliamentary petitions and statutes of the time commonly refer to *loture* 'washing' and *lavours* 'washers' of coin, along with the other offences of clipping and filing: Excursus III. *OED* cites this line and D116 as the earliest examples of the sense 'to sweat (gold or silver coin) by the application of acids' (*OED wash* v. 8, *washing* vbl. sb. 3). The purpose of 'sweating' was to extract gold from coins. The more common method was to place coins in a bag and shake them until bits of the precious metal worked off; but the term 'washing' suggests rather the use of some corrosive liquid, or perhaps a mixture of water and gravel.

D109 Coin-clippers trimmed precious metal off the edges of gold and silver coins, leaving them defective in diameter (*brede*), roundness, or both. 'Ancient and medieval coins of the same denomination varied in size and weight, were seldom perfect circles, and had plain edges. Such characteristics invited clipping', R. G. Doty, *Encyclopaedic Dictionary of Numismatics* (London, 1982), p. 57. The offence is *tonsure* in parliamentary French.

D110 This line appears to refer to the intentions of coin-clippers, or the results of their work: coins becoming continually smaller. One might expect it to begin with *So þat*, but the archetype appears to have had *Is than*, which makes no evident sense. St has *Is that*, emended to *In that* by Furnivall. The latter might be taken as a short version of *in swich wyse þat*, as at *Jereslaus* 726: 'In such a way that it would get continually smaller'. But the dictionaries record no such use of *in that*: *OED in* prep. 39, *MED in* prep. 27. For lack of a better, I allow the archetypal reading to stand, marking it as suspect with a dagger.

D111 *among*: 'preeminently among, above'. Cf. Furn VII 41, X 24, and *OED among* adv. & prep. 4b.

D113 *hool*: 'whole', a term used (Latin *integer*) to describe coins as not bent or broken. In 1498, Henry VII proclaimed that no penny 'silver and whole' should be rejected. See C. E. Challis (ed.), *A New History of the Royal Mint* (Cambridge, 1992), p. 66, and J. Craig, *The Mint* (Cambridge, 1953), p. 98. A washed or clipped coin might be, in that sense, 'whole'.

D114 *chaffare lent*: The phrase appears to refer to goods exchanged for money, as a main source of income along with wages. The unusual sense of *lent* 'supplied' may have been imposed by requirements of rhyme. If the word is taken in its normal sense, the reference would be to the pawning of valuables; but the term *chaffare* 'merchandise' tells against this.

D115 *Take*: The MSS all read *Take it*, but Kern, 'Zum Texte', p. 428, rejects *it* as unmetrical. See Mustanoja, pp. 144–5, on non-expression of the object pronoun in Middle English.

D116 'Regardless of any washing or clipping, he must consider himself satisfied.'

D117 *get*: 'gets, will get'. A contracted form of *getith*.

D118 MSS S, C and St evidently preserve the archetypal reading; β was puzzled and expands. The line evidently refers to the unlikelihood of other payment, in place of the defective coins. *It seemeth but smal* can mean 'there seems little likelihood that', with *but smal* as an adverbial phrase as in D758: 'þat sowneth but right smal to hir honour'. Addition of *right* here would supply the syllable missing in the line (it is omitted by Coventry at D758). Kern, 'Zum Texte', p. 428, would add *choys* after *othir*, comparing D126.

D122 Gold coins current at the time were the noble (6s. 8d.), the half-noble, and the quarter-noble. Quarter-nobles were commonly called 'farthings of gold' (*OED farthing* 3a, *MED ferthing* 2); and a 'halfpenny of gold' was a half noble, worth 3s. 4d. *OED* and *MED* cite the latter only from a will of 1463, understanding it as half a gold ryal; but that coin was not issued until 1465. The syllable-count requires both elision of the -*e* in *noble* and synaloepha of the -*y* in *halpeny*.

D124 'That men everywhere refuse to accept it in exchange.' The required elision of *the* is indicated, unusually, only by β. Cf. the holograph forms at D502 and 754, and Introduction, p. xxxii.

D125 'It will not pass current without his losing a great deal on it.'

D127 *been haue*: The word-order ('corrected' in C and β) saves the syllable-count by allowing elision on *haue*.

D129 *falsynge of coyn*: a general term for numismatic crime (also at 165), corresponding to 'fauxisme de monoye' in parliamentary French: see Excursus III.

D130 'Suffers great wrong in not being hanged.' The penalty of treason (cf. D153) was to be drawn and hanged: see W. R. J. Barron, *Journal of Medieval History*, 7 (1981), 187–202. Counterfeiting of coin was among the offences listed in the 1352 Statute of Treasons; and a supplementary statute of 1416 made it clear that, in addition to actual counterfeiting, 'clipping, washing and filing' of coins were also treasonable offences: see Excursus III.

D133 *Regne iustice*: 'let justice prevail'. The -*e* of *regne* does not elide before consonantal *i*-.

D134–40 As its opening words show, this stanza was added to the passage at a later date, after a new statute in May 1421 required the weighing of all gold coins: see Excursus III and Introduction, pp. lviii–lix. Hoccleve accordingly now has to distinguish between the unauthorized weighing of which he had complained in the original stanzas and the weighing required by the new statute. The unusual frequency of metrical problems in the stanza (136, 137, 140) may reflect the circumstances of its addition as a postscript.

D135 *vnhad auctoritee*: 'without having obtained authority', an absolute construction.

D136 *as now is*: The reading of S, *as þat now is*, allows regular elision of -*e* in *thanne*; but C, β and St lack *þat*, requiring non-elision at the mid-line break. For the text of the 1421 statute, see Excursus III.

D137 Even with regular substitution of *syn* for *sithen*, the line has one syllable too many. There are occasional examples of a superfluous syllable before the mid-line break (see Introduction, p. xlix); but Kern, 'Zum Texte', p. 429, regards *to* as an archetypal addition

D139 'It is now a time when we must resort to the use of weights.'

D140 Regular substitution of *syn* for *sithen* leaves the line still with one syllable too many. Kern, 'Zum Texte', p. 429, suspects scribal addition of *a* (not found in Coventry); but *it* or *þat* are arguably more suspect. Given other evidence of metrical licence in this stanza, the line is left unemended: Introduction, p. xlix.

D141–7 This stanza concerns actual counterfeiting, as distinct from washing or clipping.

D143 *copir clothe and tyn*: 'clothe copper and tin'. The word-order, normalised by β, allows elision. The production of such 'plated forgeries' is referred to in a statute of Edward II, which speaks of counterfeiters producing false pennies by covering pieces of pewter or lead with silver foil: *Statutes of the Realm*, I 219.

D150 *maintenaunce*: see D69n. The word here carries its more general meaning, 'abetting a wrong or wrongdoer', *MED maintenance* n. 2(b).

D153 *tresoun*: see D130n.

D155–7 Hoccleve refers to the legal maxim 'Consencientes et agentes pari pena punientur' ('Those who consent to a deed and those who perform it are to be punished with the same penalty'), cited in *Piers Plowman*: see J. Alford, *Piers Plowman: A Guide to the Quotations* (Binghamton, 1991), p. 86. The principle is applied to falsifiers of the coinage in *Fleta*, a law textbook of the time of Edward I: 'Qui omnes habent forte socios et fautores, vnde omnes agentes et consencientes tractari et suspendi debent' ('All these may chance to have fellows and confederates. Wherefore all those implicated, by act or assent, are liable to be drawn and hanged'): *Fleta*, vol. II, ed. and trans. H. G. Richardson and G. O. Sayles (Selden Society LXXII, London, 1955), pp. 58–9. See also *MED consenten* v. 4.

D155 *falsehede*: The holographs have only trisyllabic *falshede* or *falshode;* but they show *falsenesse* for metrical reasons besides *falsnesse*: cf. Goll. VIII 167 and Furn. II 24.

D160 *contrees*: 'parts of the country'.

D166 *and it foorth go*: 'if it becomes general'.
   many oon: two syllables only, with optional synaloepha: see Introduction, p. xlix.

D169 'Damage to the whole community is not to be underestimated.' The missing syllable would be supplied by reading *it is* with C; but this can hardly be adopted in face of the support of the other copies for non-expression of the formal subject: Mustanoja, pp. 131, 143. Kern suggests *By harm commune*, with non-elision of *-e*: 'Zum Texte', p. 429.

D170 *brode*: The adverbial form with *-e* (found in B and C) is required by both sense and metre.

D173 The Latin gloss ('the voice of the people is the voice of God') appears also against a passage in the *Regiment* where Hoccleve advises Prince Hal to win the

NOTES 93

'people's voice': 'For peples vois is Goddes voys, men seyne' (l. 2886). S. A. Gallacher, *Philological Quarterly*, 24 (1945), 12–19, traces the maxim back as far as Alcuin's letter to Charlemagne (*PL* 100 col. 438), citing also William of Malmesbury and Peter of Blois. See also H. Walther, *Proverbia Sententiaeque Latinitatis Medii Aevi* (Göttingen, 1963–67), no. 34182. On the metre, see Introduction, p. xlix.

D175 *outrers*: 'those who utter or circulate false coin'. Cited by *OED* s.v. *outer* sb.² and by *MED* s.v. *outer(e*, both following the St reading *outeris*; but *outrers* has stronger MS support (*MED outerer*, from *outren*).

D179 'However just the accusation of them may be.' See *MED enditement* 'the act of accusing or indicting a person'. The reading *enditement*, shared by S and β, is certainly authorial; but S originally wrote and then erased *entendement*, the reading of C and St: see Introduction, p. xxxviii.

D181 *notice*: 'knowledge'. The king will hear nothing of the matter; or he will be misinformed about it, as the following stanza suggests. BLY add 'Nota bene, nota'. See D. Embree, '"The King's Ignorance": A Topos for Evil Times', *Medium Aevum*, 54 (1985), 121–6, citing *Regiment* 2528–32.

D182 *Vnwasshen*: see D106n.

D184 *menes*: 'third parties'.

  lady moneye: see J. A. Yunck, *The Lineage of Lady Meed: the Development of Mediaeval Venality Satire* (Notre Dame, 1963), citing 'regina Pecunia' from Horace, *Epistulae* I vi 37, and medieval examples of the personification (pp. 16, 62–3, etc.).

D189 'What they receive will always be of good quality.' The holographs have only *receite* (once); but Chaucer has the disyllabic form, *CT* VIII 1384. For parallels to *good and fyn* referring to precious metal, see *CT* VIII 1128, 1335.

D191 *secte*: The word (which does not occur in the holographs) has a final *-e* in all the scribal copies, as in Chaucer, *CT* IV 1171; but this gives an inexact rhyme with *correct* and *infect*, neither of which can have *-e*. Perhaps Hoccleve wrote a variant form without *-e*. Kern, 'Zum Texte', p. 429, resorts to drastic emendation.

D198 Furnivall takes *Of my long tale* as dependent upon *entente* in the previous line; but the phrase makes better sense with *displese*, a verb sometimes constructed with *of*, as in Chaucer, *CT* VII 1698. See *MED displesen* v. 1, and *OED displease* v. 2c.

D200 *thende*: Elision of the definite article (cf. D502, 754) was proposed by Kern, 'Zum Texte', p. 430. See Introduction, p. xxxii.

D204 *yow*: The word, missing in S, is required by the syllable-count. Its placement in β gives one syllable too many.

D205–6 The little treatise is the second chapter of the second book of the *Horologium Sapientiae* by Heinrich Suso, written *c.* 1334: identified by B. P. Kurtz, *Modern Language Notes*, 38 (1923), 337–40. This occupies pp. 526–40 of the edition by P. Künzle, *Heinrich Seuses Horologium Sapientiae* (Freiburg, 1977). *Learn to Die*, Hoccleve's version of Suso's *ars moriendi*, follows the story of Jereslaus's wife in the *Series*.

D210 *and*: This, the reading of β and St, is challenged by *for* in Selden. S wrote the word over a deletion (perhaps deleting *and*) at the same time as adding *whanne* at the end of the line. The reading in C also shows scribal uncertainty. I adopt *and* as marginally the more difficult reading, representing an additional reason for fearing that one may die without having learned the lesson of the treatise. Suso's chief theme is the danger of being spiritually unprepared for the sudden coming of death.

D214 *lene*: a punning rhyme of the adjective with the verb *lene*. The French treatises of the time place a high value on such 'rime équivoque'.

D220 The line as it stands in all copies lacks a syllable. Furnivall supplies *ful* before *tenderly*; but I emend the latter to *tenderliche*. The adverbial ending in *-liche* can be seen in the holograph *largeliche* at D755.

D223 Suso warns that sinners should confess and repent while they still have time, mental capacity and physical strength to do so, for all three may be lacking on one's deathbed. Thus, in *Learn to Die*: 231–4, 291, 322, 423, 458 (*tyme*); 343, 347–8, 651 (*wit*); 230, 457, 479, 825 (*vigour*).

D228 The line as it stands in all copies has two syllables too many. Kern, 'Zum Texte', p. 430, emends *bigynne to* to *gynne*; and he is strongly supported by the scribal variants at D319, where all scribal copies have *bigynneth to* in place of holograph *gynneth*. Cf. D273 and the variants there.

 colde: 'grow cold'. Medieval medical theory attributed the characteristics of old age to a decline in bodily heat and the prevalence of cold humours. Suso's discussion centres on the figure of a man dying at the age of thirty (*Learn to Die* 378); but Hoccleve writes as a man of fifty-three, an age when 'ripnesse of deeth / faste vpon me haastith' (D247).

D231 *therto*: 'to that'. S has evidently misplaced the virgule. The holographs regularly write *therto* as two words.

D234 The line yields satisfactory metre and sense as it stands in SCβ, taking *mocioun* as 'prompting': *OED motion* sb. 7. However, this reading is challenged by *monicion* in St; and both *MED monicioun* n. and *OED monition* sb. cite this line as an example of the latter word: 'inspiration; urging' (*MED*), 'instruction, direction' (*OED*). With its first *n* abbeviated, *monicioun* could easily be mistaken for *mocioun*. I adopt *monicioun*, reading *thexcitynge* with *the* elided to restore the syllable-count.

D235 Hoccleve does not identify the *deuout man*, and he may be no more than a polite fiction, serving to credit *Learn to Die* not to the poet's own piety but to that of another.

D238 *fourme*: The word apparently denotes knowledge of 'the correct or appropriate way of doing something' (*MED forme* n. 8a).

D239–40 Hoccleve continued to be occupied in the writing of Latin and French as a clerk of the Privy Seal; but none of his other English compositions can be dated to the last years of his life, 1422–26. The latest datable pieces are the balades to Henry V (Goll. IX) and to Henry Somer (Furn. XVII), both of 1421: *Thomas Hoccleve*, pp. 28–31.

D244 'Wherefore I intend to stop, once this is finished.'

D245 Hoccleve takes for granted here the traditional analogy between the course of life and that of the day: J. A. Burrow, *The Ages of Man* (Oxford, 1988), pp. 56–66.

D247 β has *now* before *faste*, and S has it before *haastith*. Either reading would restore the metre, which is one syllable short in C and St (unless *-e* is unelided in *faste*). However, given the frequency of the word in the following lines, *now* must be suspect as a scribal addition (as at D326). See Introduction, p. l.

D249 Hoccleve was already complaining of failing sight before 1414 in the balade to the Duke of Bedford (Furn. XI 8–9) and, before 1415, in his balade to York (Furn. IX 55–63).

D253 The text supplied by Stow ends at D252, and the surviving part of the holograph begins here in the Durham MS. In notes and variants, holograph readings will be distinguished as H. Readings of SCBLY, recorded in the variants, will normally be commented upon only when they serve to correct writing slips in H (at D291, 373, 380, 381, 404, 426, 445, 586, 665, 667) or else may be considered as possibly preserving an authorial variant in VO: see Introduction, pp. xix–xxii. Against D253, S has 'Nota. bene. nota'.

D258–9 Compare *Regiment* 1299: 'Al þat swetnesse tourne schal to gal'. Whiting S947.

D260–2 The Latin gloss in H and all scribal copies cites a rhyming hexameter couplet of wide currency: 'Fallitur insipiens vite presentis amore | Sed noscit sapiens quanta sit plena dolore' ('The fool is deceived by love of the present life, but the wise man knows how full it is of sorrow'): H. Walther, *Proverbia Sententiaeque Latinitatis Medii Aevi* (Göttingen, 1963–67), no. 8795. In VO the opening words were evidently preceded by a heading, 'De mundi contemptu'.

D260 Syllable-count requires non-elision of *-e* in *loue* (Introduction, p. xxx). One would expect a virgule, present in S at this point.

D264 Images of Fortune's wheel commonly show a kingly figure representing prosperity and pride of life seated or enthroned at the top: see H. R. Patch, *The*

Goddess Fortuna in Mediaeval Literature (Cambridge, Mass., 1927), especially Chap. V 'Fortune's Wheel'.

D272 The scribal copies may represent a VO form of this line, perhaps 'But as soone as þat it bicome is drye'.

D276 A biblical comparison, with the tree added for rhyme: Whiting S185. In *Learn to Die* 197–9, Hoccleve renders words cited by his source Suso (ed. cit., p. 529, ll. 21–3) from Wisdom 5.8–9: 'What hath pride profited us? Or what advantage hath the boasting of riches brought us? All those things are passed away like a shadow.'

D283 *shole*: a disyllabic form employed for metrical purposes, found only here in the holographs. Hoccleve's common plural forms are *shul* (as at 285) or *shuln*.

D290 Compare the reference in *Learn to Die* to the time when 'dethes messager comth / sharp seeknesse' (533). Suso there has 'cum nuntius mortis, infirmitas gravis, adest' (ed. cit., p. 534, l. 21). The common form *messager* is replaced by *messageer* in rhyme at D293.

D291 The holograph *Dialogue* employs the paraph sign most often to mark the beginning of a new speech (295, 316, etc.); but here, as at 617 and 739, it indicates that one speaker, having finished with a subject, turns to address the other more directly: see Introduction, pp. liii–liv.

   God: so SCβ. H miswrites as *good*, anticipating the *good* that follows.

D292 *purueance*: 'provision'. Cf. *Learn to Die* 58, 258, 477. The importance of providing for death is Suso's chief theme.

D302–4 The Friend's explanation for Hoccleve's illness (repeated at 379 and 398) is contradicted by the sufferer himself (421–7). Medical authorities did regard excessive study, along with anxious thought, as among the causes of mental disorder in melancholics: R. Klibansky, E. Panofsky and F. Saxl, *Saturn and Melancholy* (London, 1964), pp. 81, 84–5, 94. Among those subject to melancholic illness, Constantinus Africanus counts 'illi qui semper sunt intenti studio': *De Melancholia*, ed. Garbers, p. 103 (Basel *Opera* I 283). But Hoccleve refers his illness to a physical cause. See Introduction, pp. lxi–lxii.

D309–13 Compare 'Numquam ubi diu fuit ignis, deficit vapor' ('Where a fire has been for any length of time, heat is never lacking'), Publilius Syrus, *Sententiae*, ed. R. A. H. Bickford-Smith (London, 1895), N13, l. 426. This work was commonly ascribed to Seneca, as in Chaucer's *Melibee*, where the same maxim is applied to the residual hostility of former enemies: 'It may nat be . . .that where greet fyr hath longe tyme endured, that ther ne dwelleth som vapour of warmnesse', *CT* VII 1185. Against l. 309, S only has the gloss 'Nota. bene. nota. Exemplum'.

D311 *plate*: probably refers to the iron fireback, often freestanding, which reflected heat from behind the fire.

D312 *seene*: an adjective, 'evident', from OE *gesene*. Like Chaucer and Gower, Hoccleve employs it in preference to the past participle *seen* where the rhyme requires final *-e*, as also at D812.

D316 *what is yow*: 'whatever is the matter with you?'

D326 Unmetrical *now* in the scribal copies evidently originated in an archetypal failure to read adverbial *sore* as disyllabic.

D327 *in existence*: 'in truth'. Cf. the Chaucerian *Romaunt of the Rose* 5549–50: misfortune makes people distinguish 'Hym that is frende in existence | From hym that is by apparence'.

D329 *me hath*: The reading *hath me* in SCβ may go back to VO. Similar small variations of word-order occur in the two holograph copies of *Learn to Die*: see Excursus I.

D333 &: The reading *or* in SCβ may go back to VO.

D344 Cicero was a prime authority on friendship. Hoccleve may or may not have known his *De Amicitia* at first hand. There Cicero speaks of stability and constancy as marks of true friendship (xviii.65): 'verae amicitiae sempiternae sunt' ('real friendships are eternal', ix.32): *De Senectute, De Amicitia, De Divinatione*, ed. and trans. W. E. Falconer (London and New York, 1923), pp. 174, 144. The discourse of Raison in the *Roman de la Rose*, 4655 ff., also draws on Cicero and portrays true friendship as unaffected by changes of fortune: 'Toujors aime qui est amis' (l. 4900).

D346–7 'It is no friendship to love well for today, or for some years either, and then give it up.'

D350 *bond*: The variant *knotte* in SCβ probably goes back to VO. Hoccleve used both words in the previous stanza.

D351–3 What is evidently a VO gloss in SCβ (not in H) cites from Proverbs 17.17: 'Omni tempore diligit qui amicus est' ('He that is a friend loveth at all times').

D359 The varied word-order in SCβ may go back to VO.
    dilate: The rhetoricians specify *dilatatio* (otherwise *amplificatio*) as one of two ways of treating subjects: 'Sunt enim artificia duo, quorum alterum est dilatandi et reliquum abreviandi materiam' ('For there are two artistic ways, one of which is dilating and the other abbreviating material'): Geoffrey of Vinsauf, *Documentum de Arte Versificandi*, II.2.1, in E. Faral, *Les Arts Poétiques du XIIe et du XIIIe Siècle* (Paris, 1924), p. 271. Cf. Goll. IX 23.

D362 *Or*: The SCβ reading *And* may go back to VO.

D363 Here as elsewhere Hoccleve elides the distinction between his persona's utterance and the literary *werk* in which it is recorded: cf. D17n, 527n.

D364 & *dul*: VO possibly read *ful dul*, as in SC.

D369 BLY add the speaker-heading *Amicus*.

D373 *at al*: This, the reading of SBLY and no doubt of VO, yields better metre and sense than H, which omits *at*. The agreement of C with H here can only be coincidental.

D376 Hoccleve's syntax is generally correct; but *þat* here, following the *þat* of 375, produces an anacoluthon.

D379 See D302–4n.

D380 *thow*: so SCβ from VO. Its unmetrical omission in H, like the writing errors at 373 and 381, suggests a weary author-copyist, here as at 373 anticipating following copy.

D381 *laborous*: I prefer this, the reading of SCLY (*MED laborous* adj., French *laboros*), to the *laborious* in H and B. The latter gives one extra syllable and evidently represents a small miswriting in H (and independently in B).

D383 *payndemayn*: a loaf or roll of fine white bread. *MED pain-demeine* n. records no other example of its use as a type of worthlessness.

D391 A common maxim, cf. Furn. III 85–6 and Whiting C470. SCβ have a Latin gloss at D386, probably from VO: 'Omnia fac cum consilio'. The source is Ecclesiasticus 32.24, cited in a gloss to *Regiment* 4933–35: 'Sine consilio nichil facias, & post factum non penitebis' ('Do thou nothing without counsel: and thou shalt not repent what thou hast done'). The version in the VO gloss occurs, for example, in the Benedictine Rule: 'Omnia fac cum consilio, et post factum non paeniteberis', *Sancti Benedicti Regula Monachorum*, ed. C. Butler (Freiburg, 1912), Chap. III, ll. 29–30. The maxim is commonly ascribed to Solomon as the supposed author of Ecclesiasticus, e.g. by Chaucer, *CT* I 3529–30, IV 1483–6, VII 1003.

D397 *it is good left*: i.e. the cause, in this case intellectual effort, is best avoided.

D398 *thoghtful studie*: cf. D302–4n. 'Much study is an affliction of the flesh', Ecclesiastes 12.12.

D399 *þat*: VO may have had *it*, as in SCβ.

D400 The paraph here marks the beginning of an elaborate simile, occupying the whole stanza. S has 'Nota. bene. nota. Exemplum'; LY have 'Exemplum'. MS B lacks ll. 400–551 by loss of leaves.

D404 *So*: The small miswriting in H, *Sa*, anticipates the following copy, as elsewhere (291, 373, 380, 426, 445).

D407–8 The gloss in SCβ identifies a biblical source: 'Nouissimus error peior [prior C] priore' ('the last error worse than the first'), Matthew 27.64.

D409 *mirour*: A 'mirror' is a salutary example to contemplate, as at D608, 646.

D413 *wisly*: 'surely', with a short vowel (OE *wislice*), as at D806.

D416 Ironical advice from the Friend: 'Carry on then, and let us see—bring your trouble back.'

D417 *heuyere*: Comparison of adverbs offers the poet a choice between *-er* and *-ere*, as the syllable-count requires: thus, *lenger* at D 441, but *lengere* at D508.

D419 *Which thee*: The SCβ variant *And þat* may derive from VO.

D420 LY (B lacks the leaf) have the speaker-heading *Thomas*.

D426 *it*: so SCβ, from VO; *is* in H. Hoccleve nowhere says more about the 'long sickness' which, he maintains, caused his breakdown. See Introduction, pp. lxi–lxii.

D435 'I do not care to make any rejoinder in this matter.'

D440 The metaphor of an author preparing his verses like a smith at an anvil goes back to Horace: 'male tornatos incudi reddere versus' ('to put badly turned verses back on the anvil'), *Ars Poetica* 441. Cf. Ovid, *Tristia* 1.7.29.

D442 *abide*: a past participle with short /i/, rhyming with *dide*. Contrast the imperative form *abyde* D306, where ⟨y⟩ indicates a long vowel, /i:/.

D445 *serche*: H has *serchee*. Doubling of final ⟨e⟩ in unstressed position occurs occasionally in ME texts (e.g *trowee* in *Sir Gawain* 813); but it is here corrected, as an inadvertent anticipation of following *see*.

D446 *fyue yeer*: H has .*v*.. C56 dates Hoccleve's recovery to five years before.

D449 L only has the speaker-heading *Amicus*.

D450 *Reed weyue*: 'to reject advice'.

D451–2 See D391n.

D456–8 All manuscripts (except B, lacking the leaf) cite Ecclesiasticus 6.6 in a gloss: 'Vnus sit tibi consiliarius inter mille' ('Let one of a thousand be thy counsellor'). LY add *Thomas* after *consiliarius*. As at D391, Ecclesiasticus ('The Wisdom of Jesus the son of Sirach') is assigned to Solomon, author of the Wisdom books. Cf. Chaucer's *Melibee*, *CT* VII 1167, where the same passage is cited and ascribed to Solomon.

D477–9 There is a similar thought in the Isidore epitome, *Tractatus*, MS Bodley 110, f. 109v: 'Nemo magis scire potest qualis fueris quam tu qui conscius es tui' ('No one can better know what you are like than you who have knowledge of yourself').

D480 *lyth*: The reading *is* in SCβ may go back to VO.

D483 Cf. Whiting A62, 'Advisement is good', and *Troilus* II 343.

D486 *it had been hard maad me to trowe*: 'it would have been hard to have made me believe'. On the omission of the auxiliary before the past participle *maad*, see C161n.

D490 ME *lappe* denotes any loosely hanging piece of clothing, by which the wearer might be caught or held. Hence, *have by the lappe* 'have in one's grasp': *MED lap(pe* n. 1(b). Cf. Hoccleve's *Complaint of the Virgin*, 'I wend, in sothfastnesse, | Have had for euere ioye be the lappe' (Egerton text, ll. 10–11, in *Regiment*, ed. Furnivall, p. xxxvii). The present line apparently expresses the Friend's general satisfaction at the way things are going; but the exact sense is unclear.

D493 *in*: The reading *by* in SCβ may go back to VO.

D495 *take of hem the lesse*: 'draw upon them [your wits] as little as possible.'

D496 One of three lines in the holograph *Dialogue* where *-e* fails to elide at the mid-line break: Introduction, p. xxx.

D502 The variants in SCβ may go back to VO: 'If I nat lightly may cacche theffect'. The H version has a better rhythm.

D508 *lengere*: trisyllabic: see D417n.

D509 *þat may nat hyndre a myte*: 'that cannot do the slightest harm'. For examples of *mite* in such expressions (also at D334), see Whiting M596–611 and *MED mite* n.(2).

D517 *now*: The reading of SCβ, *þou*, is probably an anticipation of the word in the next line, rather than a VO variant.

D522 *By*: The reading *In* of SCβ, though possibly from VO, is more likely an archetypal variant prompted by neighbouring *in*s.

D524 *wryte*: The word here refers to the physical act of writing, as against composition (*make*). Cf. *Regiment* 985–1029 on the labours of the 'writer'.

D525 *now is*: SCβ have *is now*, possibly from VO.

D527 *this book*: It becomes clear that the reference, here and at 539 and 541, is not to the work previously under discussion—the translation from Suso, yet to be undertaken—but to the *Series* itself, a work already begun (542–6). Cf. D707, 793, and nn. to D17, 363, 662.

D528 This would be September 1419: see discussion of dating, Introduction, pp. lvii–lix.

D534 *Gloucestre*: trisyllabic. Humphrey Duke of Gloucester, b. 1390, was the youngest brother of Henry V. See K. H. Vickers, *Humphrey Duke of Gloucester: A Biography* (London, 1907). He acted as regent or 'guardian and lieutenant of England' from 30 December 1419 until 2 February 1421, while Henry was in France: see Introduction, pp. lv–lviii.

is: The reading *was* in SCβ may go back to VO.

D537 *othir mo*: 'other reasons too'.

D542–3 Duke Humphrey returned to England from the French wars on three occasions: November 1415, late November or December 1419, and March or

April 1422. In the Durham holograph, but evidently not in VO, Hoccleve wrote a gloss specifying the second of these returns: 'Scilicet de secundo reditu suo de Francia' ('Concerning, that is, his second return from France'). The clarification may have been added for the benefit of the lady to whom the Durham MS is directed in its final envoy, Joan Countess of Westmorland. She was Humphrey's aunt, and so had a family interest. Seymour and others take the passage to refer to Humphrey's third return, in 1422; but see Introduction, pp. lvii–lix.

D546 'As far as any such work or activity is concerned.' VO may have had *and* for *or*, as in SCβ.

D547 *sum othir thyng*: that is, presumably, not *Learn to Die*, the work previously in question.

D549 *bownden am I deepe:* The differing word-order in SCβ may go back to VO.

D550 *God*: SCβ read *him*, possibly from VO.

D551 *balade*: 'balade stanza', such as rhyme royal: *MED balad(e* n. 2(b). A longer work in such stanzas (such as the *Series* itself) is evidently intended, rather than several short balades.

D554 *lord lige*: The unusual word-order (contrast D180), adopted to permit elision in *lige*, is 'corrected' in SCβ to the detriment of the syllable-count. The reference is to King Henry V, to whom, while he was still Prince of Wales, Hoccleve had addressed his *Regiment of Princes*.

D558 *as sad as any stoon*: 'as solid as a rock'; Whiting S767.

D561 *Vegece*: The *De Re Militari* of Vegetius (4th century AD) was widely consulted at the time, as a manual of military practice. See Carol Meale in *Book Production and Publishing in Britain, 1375–1475*, ed. J. Griffiths and D. Pearsall (Cambridge, 1989), pp. 218–19. Hoccleve recommended the book to Oldcastle as suitable reading for the heretic knight (Furn. II 196). In 1412, John Lydgate praised the future Henry V for exercising in martial games 'after the doctrine of Vygecius' (*Troy Book*, Prologue, l. 89). Humphrey himself gave a Latin Vegetius to Oxford University later in life: L. C. Y. Everest-Phillips, 'The Patronage of Humphrey, Duke of Gloucester: A Re-Evaluation', D. Phil. Thesis (York, 1983), p. 164. There is a ME translation, *Knyghthode and Bataile*, ed. R. Dyboski and Z. M. Arend (EETS, 201, 1936). On French versions, see P. Contamine, in *La Littérature Française aux XIVe et XVe Siècles*, ed. D. Poirion (Heidelberg, 1988), pp. 349–52. A copy of the French version by Jean de Vignai, now C. U. L. MS Ee. 2. 17, is inscribed 'Ceste liure est a moy Homfrey duc de Gloucestre du don Mess. Robert Roos cheualier mon cousin'.

The name *Vegece* is omitted in C, and it is added later in S (after the regular line-end stop there), B, L, and Y. Writing of S, Hammond, p. 406, suggests that 'the omission of the word is probably due to the scribe's intention of rubricking it later, as was often done with special words'. If such an omission occurred, not in S but in the scribal archetype of all five MSS, it would explain the common difficulty. C and β must then have followed the archetype in simply omitting the word,·while S and the three β descendants were able to recover it, either by conjecture or, more likely, by consulting other copies.

D564 'That no effort of mine could contribute anything.'

D566–616 Humphrey's mastery of the arts of knighthood is established by reference to his feats of arms against the French at Cherbourg, in the Cotentin peninsular, and at Rouen. These were all undertaken during the Duke's campaigning in Normandy in 1417–1419, the campaign from which he made his 'second return' to England late in 1419. For details, see Vickers, pp. 44–80.

D566 *Beyonde*: 'overseas', specifically in France, as in *Piers Plowman* B III 110.

D567 *Chirburgh*: The main military action in Humphrey's Cotentin campaign was the siege of Cherbourg, which lasted from the spring of 1418 until the town surrendered at the end of September: see Vickers, pp. 60–70. C. Allmond, *Henry V* (London, 1992), p. 120, describes the siege as 'an exploit for which he [Gloucester] rightly received much credit'. For a long early account, see the early sixteenth-century translation of Tito Livio's life of Henry V (see D576n): *The First English Life of King Henry the Fifth*, ed. C. L. Kingsford (Oxford, 1911), pp. 109–15.

D573 *Duc Henri*: The reference is to Humphrey's great-grandfather, Henry of Grosmont, the first Plantagenet Duke of Lancaster, father of John of Gaunt's wife Blanche. He died in 1361. In *Regiment* 2647–53, Hoccleve refers to the same 'good duke Henri' as a model of the just and knightly life. Henry was one of Edward III's chief captains in the French wars of that time. He also composed a French devotional treatise, *Le Livre de Seyntz Medicines*, of which Humphrey owned a copy: see W. A. Pantin, *The English Church in the Fourteenth Century* (Cambridge, 1955), p. 231n.

D576 *cloos and yle*: 'peninsular stronghold'. The Cotentin peninsular in Normandy is referred to as 'insula Constantini' in the life of Henry V written for Humphrey *c.* 1437 by Tito Livio Frulovisi: 'Magnanimus autem Princeps Humphredus Gloucestriae dux ad insulam Constantini mittitur expugnandam' ('The valiant prince, Humphrey Duke of Gloucester, is sent to conquer the isle of Constantine'): *Titi Livii Foro-Juliensis Vita Henrici Quinti Regis Angliae*, ed. T. Hearne (Oxford, 1716), p. 50. See Vickers, pp. 55–60: 'In all, it was estimated, he had taken thirty-two castles in six weeks, with very little trouble and hardly any loss of life' (p. 60).

D583 *wroot*: β substituted *wroght* for the metaphorical original: Humphrey's sword inscribed his deeds.

D584 *many a place elles*: SCβ have *many another place*, a possible VO reading.

D586 *expresse*: The curious miswriting in H, *yepresse*, must be corrected.

D587 'Lest I should chance to fall short of the gratitude due to him.'

D590 *Conueniently*: 'appropriately'. The suitability of the name is explained at 596–7.

D592 *natiuitee*: evidently a reference to Humphrey's horoscope, as Seymour suggests (n. *ad loc*), and to the influence of the planet Mars there.

D595 *into hy worthynesse*: The SCβ reading *vnto* for *into* may go back to VO; but their *prowesse* for *worthynesse* looks more like a substitution in the scribal archetype caught from *promesse* in the previous line.

D596–7 A marginal note added in the Durham MS in the seventeenth century (possibly, as Doyle suggests in his catalogue entry, by William Browne the poet, who owned the manuscript at the time) correctly interprets this etymology: 'Humfrey quasi homme feray'. At Humphrey's birth, Mars is imagined speaking through his name: 'I shall make a *man*'. The Duke himself commonly spelled his name *Homfrey*: for an example, see 561n. On the etymologising of names for purposes of praise or blame, see E. R. Curtius, *European Literature and the Latin Middle Ages*, trans. W. R. Trask (London, 1953), pp. 495–500; and E. Faral, *Les Arts Poétiques du XIIe et du XIII Siècle* (Paris, 1924), pp. 65–7. Cf. *Jonathas* 634–6, where the wicked Fellicula is said to take her name from *fel* 'gall'.

D601 *Duely*: The word has three syllables.

D602 'Has enough with which to promote his renown.'

D610–16 After the surrender of Cherbourg, Humphrey in November 1418 joined his brother Henry, who was already besieging Rouen. The town surrendered in January 1419. See Vickers, pp. 70–4. Hoccleve's praise of the Duke for taking up a position dangerously near the walls of Rouen is matched in contemporary sources. John Page, who himself fought in the siege, writes: 'At the Port Synt Hyllarye | Fulle manfully loggyd he. | In caste of stone, in schot of quarelle, | He dradde hym for noo perelle, | But wanne worschyppe with his werre, | And lay hys enmys fulle nerre | Thanne any man that there was | Be xl. rode and more in spas', *The Siege of Rouen*, ed. J. Gairdner in *The Historical Collections of a Citizen of London in the Fifteenth Century* (Camden Society, London, 1876), p. 11. See also *The Brut*, ed. F. W. D. Brie (EETS, 131, 136, 1906–8), p. 397.

D611 *whethir*: The conjunction introduces a question presenting alternatives, here rhetorical as at *CT* III 2069.

D617 *shoue at the cart*: 'lend a hand'; Whiting C61. Hoccleve sometimes, as here, employs the more familiar singular imperative form when addressing the Friend (cf. D429, 441, 658, 775); but he uses more often the polite plural form, as at 623 here. The Friend always uses singular forms to him (as at 673). Cf. D3n.

D620 The Friend politely disclaims his own indispensibility. *Ascaunce* is obscure. The context suggests some sense such as 'indeed', proposed by Seymour in his note; but the dictionaries lend no support. Pryor's glossary and Hammond's note identify the word as modern *askance*, used by Shakespeare as a verb, 'turn away'; but this word is not recorded until the sixteenth century, and Shakespeare's use is highly idiosyncratic. There is the well-attested ME word, *MED ascaunce* adv. and conj., meaning 'as if' or 'as if to say'; but the senses offered by *MED* for the present use do not fit the context: '2(b) with affectation, factitiously, insincerely; deceptively'.

D621–2 *no cheuissance | Can I*: 'I do not know how to proceed': *MED chevisaunce* n. 2, 'a provision or arrangement for accomplishing something'.

D630 *on heed*: 'impetuously, headlong': *MED hed* n.(1) 3(c).

D631 *þat*: 'that which, what', object of *haue* in 633 and subject of *needith* there. The difficult syntax prompted addition of *to* after *þat* in β and also in S. See Introduction, pp. xxv and xxxvii.

D638–9 The Latin gloss in H and all scribal copies cites ll. 43–4 from Geoffrey of Vinsauf's *Poetria Nova*, ed. Faral, *Les Arts Poétiques*, p. 198: 'If anyone sets out to build a house, his rash hand does not rush into action'. Chaucer imitated the same passage in *Troilus* I 1065–9, applying it to the scheming of Pandarus. Like Vinsauf, Hoccleve speaks of planning a poem. His version shows no verbal similarities to Chaucer's, and he evidently knew at least the following lines up to *Poetria Nova* l. 59: see nn. to D640–2, 645–7, 653.

D640–2 The Vinsauf gloss ends with *etc.* in H, and the present lines correspond in sense to the following lines (44–8) in the *Poetria Nova*, where Vinsauf speaks of how a house-builder plans his designs mentally in advance. The *mental ye* may be identified with the third eye of prudence (cf. 653), looking towards the future, as in *Troilus* V 744–49.

D645–7 Geoffrey of Vinsauf uses the same image of a mirror as he turns from the house-builder to warn poets against over-hasty beginning: 'Ipsa poesis | Spectet in hoc speculo quae lex sit danda poetis. | Non manus ad calamum praeceps, non lingua sit ardens | Ad verbum' ('Poetry itself may see in this mirror what law should govern poets. The hand should not be too quick to the pen, nor the tongue too eager for utterance', ll. 48–51).

D653 *leue*: Final -*e* elides before the initial /h/ of *Who*, as observed by Kern, 'Zum Texte', p. 413.

   prudence: Vinsauf also treats artistic foresight as a species of prudence: 'Opus totum prudens in pectoris arcem | Contrahe' ('Prudently assemble the whole work into the citadel of your breast', ll. 58–9).

D659 *tyme*: SCβ have *while*, a possible VO reading.

D660 S with Cβ reads: 'And aftirwarde / þus he tolde his entente'. Since Hoccleve's *aftirward* has no final -*e*, this is a possible VO version of the line. The addition of *þat* above the line in H following *aftir* suggests rewriting there.

D661 *sauf bettre auys*: 'subject to any better opinion.'

D662 *Lente*: The present conversation was earlier represented as taking place immediately after the conclusion of Hoccleve's complaining, which itself took place on the morning after a bad night at the end of November (*Complaint* 17). The present reference to Lent therefore introduces an inconsistency into the narrative chronology. The season is obviously appropriate to the penitential theme in what follows; but, since elsewhere Hoccleve speaks as if already engaged on writing that text in which his conversation with the Friend is recorded (nn. to D17, 363, 527), it may be that Lent here also represents the time of writing. In 1420, Lent extended from 21 February to 7 April.

D663 *man*: SCβ have *wight*, a likely VO reading.

repente: Contrition, confession (665) and satisfaction (666) are the three parts of the sacrament of penance.

D665 *thee*: H has *the*; but Hoccleve consistently distinguishes the pronoun from the article.

D667 *wyte*: 'blame'. Hoccleve wrote *wyt* in H; but he never spells 'wit', with its short vowel, so. The verb for 'blame' is elsewhere *wyte* (*Learn to Die* 380), and the corresponding noun, OE *wite* with /i:/, should be spelled the same, with -*y*- and -*e*. The offence against women, with which the rest of the *Dialogue* deals, is later identified as Hoccleve's *Letter of Cupid*: cf. 754 and n. See generally J. Mann, *Apologies to Women* (Inaugural Lecture, Cambridge, 1991), discussing *Dialogue* on pp. 20–22.

D669 *quarter sak*: a large sack, probably one capable of holding eight bushels of grain: *MED quarter(e* n. 5(c).

D670 *Which*: The variant *That* in SCβ, like the reverse variant at 672, may go back to VO.

D679 The punctuation mark at the end of this stanza in H, like a large capital S slightly tilted forward, indicates that the sentence remains to be completed in the next stanza. So also at D770. See Introduction, p. lv.

D680 *Bewar*: The variant *Be wys* in SCβ may go back to VO. The form *bewar* varies with *be waar* (cf. 668 above) in the holographs.

D683 Proverbial: Whiting F194.

D691 *make partie*: 'do battle, take them on': *MED partie* n. 6(a) or (b), and *Regiment* 2793.

D694–7 So the Wife of Bath in her Prologue: 'I hate hym that my vices telleth me, | And so doo mo, God woot, of us than I', *CT* III 662–3; also her Tale, III 937–44.

D694 *auctrice*: *MED* defines the word 'a woman whose opinion is accepted as authoritative', recording it only here. This unusual feminine form of *auctor* puzzled the scribes of C and β.

D699 *hem haast*: The reading *hast hem* in SCβ may go back to VO.

D706 *to haue*: Since *ladyes* can have either two or three syllables (Introduction, p. xxx), the reading *for to haue* in SCβ may go back to VO.

D707 *shewen hem*: The reading *hem shewe* in SCβ may go back to VO. On the part played by writings in more or less flirtateous conversation between men and women, see J. Stevens, *Music and Poetry in the Early Tudor Court* (2nd edn, Cambridge, 1979).

D708–9 'Good lordship' referred specifically at this time to the patronage extended by persons of influence to their clients (cf. Furn. XII 10, Goll. I 42). One function of a good lord was to act as *mene* or intermediary in the client's interest. Such third-party advocacy is commonly referred to in both secular and religious contexts, e.g. Furn. XVI 22–24, X 44, 83.

D713 A gesture of contrition: cf. Gower's *Confessio Amantis* I 661–63, 'With *mea culpa*, which he seith, | Upon his brest fullofte he leith | His hond'.

D718 *take on thee*: 'accept, submit to'. The ensuing lines on women's power in dominating men recall the Wife of Bath's assertion of *maistrie* (cf. D732).

D722 *with*: The reading in SCβ represents a possible *thurgh* in VO.

D724–6 The gloss in H and VO cites God's words to the serpent from Genesis 3.15 in their Vulgate form (with *ipsa* 'she', where AV has 'it'): 'she shall crush thy head'. The rest of God's words derive from Genesis 3.13–14. The Devil, having overcome Eve in the form of a serpent, will himself be overcome through her descendent Mary.

D727 The SCβ variants *O* for *now* and *on* for *of* may go back to VO. The argument is facetious: if woman could overcome the Devil, she will have no difficulty overcoming a man.

D732 H has a long gap between *axith* and *haue*, filled with a horizontal line. SCβ have unmetrical *to* before *haue*; but the length of the gap in H implies a longer word deleted.

D733–4 The gloss in H and VO cites Genesis 3.16: 'thou shalt be under thy husband's power, and he shall have dominion over thee.'

D736 'Let him give up and submit': Whiting A251 'To hang up one's ax'. *Regiment* 5103–194 offer unserious arguments for the proposition that men should seek peace with their wives by submitting to female sovereignty.

D741 *haue hokir*: 'feel scorn'. The SCβ reading *hoker haue* may go back to VO.

D742 *pleye a soleyn*: 'act the malcontent': *MED solein(e* adj. 4(d).

D745 'Though it [women's goodwill] is hard to get . . .'. Applied to women themselves, *dangerous* means 'standoffish, difficult to please'.

D746 *hard*: Here as at 750 the word refers, not to difficulty, but to painful consequences.

D749 *Thomas han been*: The word-order of SCβ may go back to VO.

D751 'In the name of him who died [Christ], what have I done wrong?'

D754 Hoccleve had made his version (Goll. VIII) of the *Epistre au Dieu d'Amours* by Christine de Pizan some twenty years earlier, in 1402. The two poems are edited together by T. S. Fenster and M. C. Erler, *Poems of Cupid, God of Love* (Leiden, 1990). The *Letter of Cupid* was printed in sixteenth-century 'Chaucers'; and Speght's 1598 edition notes that the poem 'gat him such hatred among the gentlewomen of the Court, that he was inforced to recant in that booke of his, called *Planctus proprius*' (Arguments, c6a). Speght probably derived this information from John Stow, in whose hand a note 'Epistle of Cupid' stands against the present line in the Durham MS. It is unlikely that Stow had any other authority than the *Dialogue* itself. If gentlewomen did in fact object to Hoccleve's poem, it is hard to see why. Like its French original, the *Letter* takes the form of a communication from the God of Love rehearsing complaints received by him from ladies who have suffered from the doubleness and misogyny of men. Hoccleve's Cupid follows Christine's in quoting instances of men's calumnies against women (*Letter* 99–112, 127–33, 197–217, etc.), but only as examples of wicked talk. J. V. Fleming concludes that the *Letter* faithfully preserves the spirit of Christine's 'anti-anti-feminism', *Medium Aevum*, 40 (1971), 21–40, p. 24; and Jill Mann sees Hoccleve as 'trying to create a controversial atmosphere' out of nothing, in somewhat mechanical imitation of Chaucer's apologies to women: *Apologies to Women* (Inaugural Lecture, Cambridge, 1991), p. 20. However, D. Bornstein finds evidence of actual antifeminism in Hoccleve's version: 'Hoccleve managed to laugh at women while ostensibly defending them': *English Language Notes*, 19 (1981–2), 7–14, p. 14. Such apologies, for real or imagined offences, were fashionable at the time, as Mann shows.

D755 *largeliche*: 'intemperately, without proper restraint'; cf. 'of tonge large', *Troilus* V 804.

D756 *swart wrooth*: The reading *blak wrooth* in SCβ may go back to VO.

D760–3 Since the misogynist passages in his *Letter* all represent slanders said to be uttered by wicked men (*folkes tales*), Hoccleve bases his defence on the distinction between those utterances of an 'author' which he 'affirms' in his own person and those which he only 'reports'. The corresponding Latin terms, *auctor, affirmare* and *reportare*, were commonly used by medieval writers and exegetes to point the same distinction: A. J. Minnis, *Medieval Theory of Authorship* (London, 1984), pp. 100–2, 193–200. As Hoccleve may have known, similar arguments were used by writers who defended Jean de Meun against those, including Christine, who accused him of antifeminism, in the course of 'la querelle de la Rose'. Cf. also Alain Chartier's 'Excusacion' for having offended women by his *Belle Dame sans Mercy*, ed. J. C. Laidlaw, *The Poetical Works of Alain Chartier* (Cambridge, 1974), ll. 193–216.

D760 *therof was I*: The different word-order may go back to VO.

D764 *reherce*: 'report'. Chaucer uses the term in similar contexts, *CT* I 732, 3170, 3173. See Minnis, *Medieval Theory of Authorship*, pp. 198–9.

D770 On the punctuation at the end of this stanza in H, see D679n.

D771 All scribal copies write 'Nota. bene. nota' against this line, probably from VO.

D772 *conpleynyngly* : 'by way of complaint'. In both the *Epistre* and the *Letter*, affronted ladies 'conpleynen hem' (*Letter* 190) about the slanders of men. Their accusatory mode is endorsed by Cupid, by Christine, and here by Hoccleve.

D775 *What stikith by*: The expression is obscure. *MED stiken* v. cites the line as its sole example of sense 6(f), 'what endures, what remains'; but this does not well fit the context. Hammond glosses *stikith by* 'is close at hand', taking *by* in the sense 'nearby' (*MED bi* adv. 1(a)). *Stikith* could then be understood as referring to a hostile thrust (*MED stiken* 1): Hoccleve may be asking what, in his book, came anywhere close to injuring the reputation of women—expecting the answer 'nothing'.

D778 Proverbial: Whiting W204.

D781 *neuere it yit I say*: 'I have never seen it to this day.' The different word-order in SCβ may go back to VO.

D789 *Thy kut to keepe*: 'to look after yourself' (?). Whiting C656 cites two instances from the *Tale of Beryn*, ll. 1309, 1805, which also concern survival in difficult circumstances. *MED cut* n.(2) 2(b) gives a different interpretation.

D804 *portreye*: 'adorn, embellish', i.e. with rhetorical art.

D806 This line, marked with a paraph, begins an address to ladies, in three stanzas like a balade. Hoccleve's poem to Oldcastle (Furn. II) similarly ends with a three-stanza address to the knight.

D808 *the*: The variant *his* in SCβ may go back to VO.

D810 *byte me the crowe*: 'may the crow bite me', i.e. 'may the carrion crow feed on my corpse' (*MED croue* n. 3): Whiting C573.

D812 *hath it & shal be seene*: The form *be* can represent both the infinitive and, as at D266, the past participle, and it has both functions here: 'it has been and will be evident'. On *seene*, see D312n.

D819 *me putte atte werre*: 'get the better of me'. *Werre* 'worse' rhymes with *werre* 'war', an example of 'rime équivoque' in the French manner.

D820 *Romayn Deedis*: The *Gesta Romanorum*, a popular Latin compilation of stories made towards the end of the thirteenth century, is Hoccleve's source for the story of the virtuous Roman empress, Jereslaus's wife, which immediately follows in the *Series*: see J. Mitchell, *Thomas Hoccleve: A Study in Early Fifteenth-Century English Poetic* (Urbana, Ill., 1968), pp. 44–7, 86–91.

D824 Mention of France prompts incongruous thoughts of knights spurring their prancing steeds into battle. The collocation of *prike* and *praunce* is common: *MED priken* v. 4b.

D825–6 The variants in SCβ evidently represent an alternative VO version of this couplet: 'Wole I translate / and þat my gilt, I hope, | Shal pourge as cleene / as keuerchiefs dooth sope'. The version in H avoids placing the object *gilt* before the verb *pourge* and may be regarded as a revision to avoid that awkwardness.

D826 The *Dialogue* has exactly twice as many lines as the *Complaint*, which has 413 (counting the Prologue as part of the *Complaint*)—appropriately enough, if one sees the latter as a monologue. In H, the line is followed by the heading 'Fabula de quadam Imperatrice Romana'. SCβ have 'Explicit dialogus & incipit quedam fabula de quadam bona & nobili Imperatrice Romana' (Y omits 'bona'). C and BLY follow this with 'capitulo tercio', identifying *Jereslaus' Wife* as the third 'chapter' of the whole work.

EXCURSUS I: THE TWO
HOLOGRAPHS OF *LEARN TO DIE*

Learn to Die, alone among Hoccleve's writings, survives in two holograph copies: in the Durham copy of the *Series*, and as a separate item in Huntington HM 744, a collection of shorter pieces. The text of the latter breaks off at line 672 because the manuscript has lost its final leaves. John M. Bowers has published a valuable comparative study of the two texts, but the matter merits further consideration here.[1] I have argued in the Introduction that the scribal copies of the *Complaint* and *Dialogue* descend, not from the Durham holograph, but from a lost 'Variant Original'. It is therefore a matter of some interest to notice the extent and character of substantive variation between the two existing authorial copies of *Learn to Die*, even though one cannot assume that Hoccleve varied texts of the *Complaint-Dialogue* in just the same way or to just the same extent. The two *Learn to Die* copies also provide evidence for the study of the poet's orthography, showing how far he was consistent in writing out what are most often substantively the same lines.[2]

Substantive Variation

Not counting five slips of the pen listed below (n.18), I find 69 substantive variants between Durham and Huntington: 15 differences in word-order, 31 substitutions of one word for another, and 23 rather more extensively revised lines. Bowers may give a misleading impression of the extent of such substantive variation. He remarks, for instance, that Hoccleve 'routinely allowed substitutions of an almost indifferent nature' and that he 'engaged in all manner of minute, local, inconsequential, even

[1] J. M. Bowers, 'Hoccleve's Two Copies of *Lerne to Dye*: Implications for Textual Critics', *Papers of the Bibliographical Society of America*, 83 (1989), 437–72.
[2] Gollancz did not include the Huntington *Learn to Die* in his edition of that manuscript, because Furnivall had already printed the Durham text. I cite from photocopy supplied by the Huntington Library. I have also compared the Furnivall text of Durham, in the revised EETS edition, with the manuscript itself. This shows nine erroneous editorial readings, where Durham in fact agrees with Huntington. The correct readings are: 63 wey, 84 thee, 108 ful, 148 conplaynte, 160 Shee, 185 bittir, 296 yee, 642 conpleyne, 661 manace. At 660, Durham has *pows*, not *powr* as reported in the EETS footnote. But at 481 it omits the *i* in *satisfaccioun*.

inadvertent alterations'.[3] Yet sixty-nine variants in ninety-six stanzas of seven lines each is no very great number, and many of them are indeed minute and inconsequential. Since, however, this is a very rare opportunity to observe authorial variation in a medieval English text, I shall present all the evidence here.[4] I give the Durham readings first, followed by that of Huntington.

Differences in Word-Order. 56 is therof] therof is; 138 put been] be put; 193 am weery] weery am; 279 Leet y] I leet; 318 thus had it] it had thus; 379 y haue] haue I; 441 me now] now me; 458 tyme han eek] han eek tyme; 472 heere aftir y] I heer aftir; 484 it is] is it; 506 y am] am I; 513 me leuen] leuen me; 597 it shal] shal it; 651 now so] so now; 667 of al] al of. It is not easy to see any motivation for many of these changes, though Huntington has a better rhythm at 193, and Durham at 138. The syllable-count is preserved in every case, most interestingly at line 597: þat nat oonly dye it shal nat thee gaste] That oonly die shal it nat the gaste. It seems likely that the first *nat* was mistakenly omitted in a common master copy. In Durham, Hoccleve first wrote the line without the word and then supplied it above the line. In Huntington, on the other hand, he repaired the metre but not the sense, by a change in word-order which prevents elision on *die* and so supplies the missing syllable.[5]

Single-word Substitutions. 15 so] to; 21 lerne] leere; 69 tho] the; 74 ful] right; 85 now] inward; 101 eternel] eterne; 123 A] O; 139 this] the; 147 this] the; 205 preef] way; 208 by] with; 216 Continuelly] Anoon rightes; 231 dayes] yeeres; 253 the] þat; 272 arn] be; 280 beten] scourgid; 297 youthe] dayes; 310 right] ful; 335 þat] which; 336 it] this; 350 cape] gape; 371 al] now; 376 me] him; 377 alle] ny; 399 synfully] folyly; 451 ful] right; 460 Tresors] Tresor; 520 profyten] auaille; 528 which] þat; 588 men] folk; 672 vpon] on. Of these thirty-one variants, some are trivial and possibly inadvertent. All, it may be noted, preserve the syllable-count.[6] Eight show one copy closer than the other to the poem's

---

[3] 'Two Copies', 443, 447. See also D. Pearsall, 'Theory and Practice in Middle English Editing', *Text*, 7 (1994), 107–26, p. 118: the two holographs 'vary considerably not only in spelling but in substantive readings. The variants are significant but directionless'.

[4] There is considerable variation in the marginal Latin speaker-headings and glosses from the Latin source. Durham has only three speaker-headings, at lines 15, 29, and 37, to which Huntington adds six more (323, 337, 467, 477, 515, 553). However, Huntington omits twelve of Durham's twenty-one Latin glosses, those at lines 34, 199, 218, 344, 365, 507, 512, 554, 596, 616, 622, and 631.

[5] Durham gives the Latin original in a gloss: '..vt non solum mori non timeas..': see Suso's *Horologium Sapientiae*, ed. P. Künzle (Freiburg, 1977), p. 535, l. 21.

[6] At line 85 'Beholde now' and 'Beholde inward' have the same syllabic value, as do 'Awayte vpon' and 'Awayten on' at 672.

Latin source, Suso's *Horologium Sapientiae*. In one of these, Huntington is the closer: it has *yeeres* for Durham's *dayes* at 231, where Suso has *annos*.[7] In the other seven, Durham is closer: at lines 85 (Suso *nunc*, 528.3), 205 (Suso *argumentum*, 529.26), 216 (Suso *continuo*, 530.5), 297 (Suso *iuventutis*, 531.3), 377 (Suso *omnes*, 532.11), 460 (Suso *thesauros*, 533.23), and 520 (Suso *proficiunt*, 534.17–18).

More Extensively Revised Lines. Of the twenty-three variants which remain, thirteen represent small readjustments in one or other copy: 13 Sotil matires right profownde] Sotile materes profounde; 150 he hath] hath vnto; 163 many anothir eek] many oon also; 275 telle] telle or; 301 whyle it tyme is] whil tyme is your; 304 wrecchidnesses in whiche] wrecchidnesse in which þat; 308 be told vnto] to be told to; 322 grantid] lent to; 332 to thee] seye and; 431 maneere] manere of; 527 ne haan tho wrecches noon] han tho wrecches right noon; 583 lyke] list to; 622 shal go to] gooth vnto. In all these, the syllable-count is correct.[8] At line 13, Durham is closer to Suso's Latin (*profundissimas*, 526.21); also at 322 (Suso *concessum*, 531.11); but Huntington is closer at 304, with its singular form (*miseriam*, 531.5).

The remaining ten lines, where more substantial variation is in question, must be set out in full: 117 Thy comynge vnto me was vncerteyn] Thyn hour was vnto me ful vncerteyn; 212 Twynneth the eir which þat continuelly] Twynneth the eir which foorthwith redily; 220 Which the wynd vp reisith for his lightnesse] With the wynd blowe away for his lightnesse; 393 O now this hour gretter ioie & gladnesse] O now this day more ioie and gladnesse; 483 þat thee mighten the blisse of heuene reue] That heuenes blisse mighten thee byreue; 524 And eres han also and may nat heere] Eres also and may nat with hem heere; 570 Of the world vertu gooth so faste abak] Of the world vertu is so dryue abak; 621 The rightwys man or slee him sodeynly] The good lyuere or slee him sodeynly; 642 Hensfoorth conpleyne weepe & crye & grede] Hensfoorth weepe and conpleyne & crie & grede; 655 And my look ful dym & heuy as leed] And dim my look and as heuy as leed. The syllable-count is correct in every case.[9] Three variants show Durham

---

[7] Ed. Künzle, 530.13 (citing by page and line).

[8] At line 13 Huntington saves it by an unusual plural ending *-e* on a disyllabic adjective. At 150 Durham employs the occasional licence by which *-e* fails to elide before the mid-line break: 'And in this wyse / he hath him answerd'. Huntington avoids this by adding an extra syllable later in the line: 'And in this wyse / hath vnto him answerd'. The variant at 163 shows synaloepha of *-y* before *anothir* but not before *oon*: compare, for example, *Dialogue* 336 and 557. At 301 *whil* in non-eliding position matches elided *whyle*.

[9] At line 393 Huntington's *more* has no elision before consonantal *i* in *ioie*.

closer to Suso's Latin than Huntington: at lines 212 (Suso *continuo*, 530.4), 220 (Suso *tollitur*, 530.7), and 393 (Suso *hora*, 532.23). Huntington's 'foorthwith redily' for Durham's 'continuelly' at 212 is matched by its 'Anoon rightes' for Durham's 'Continuelly' later in the same stanza (line 216, noted above). The simile of the arrow in this stanza, like the surrounding similes, is derived *via* Suso from the Wisdom of Solomon.[10] The Huntington readings might be understood as revisions prompted by uneasiness at the idea of a continual ceasing to be, as at Durham 216, which follows the Latin. The Huntington version, 'Anoon rightes I styntid for to be', expresses the rather easier idea that we begin to die from the moment of our birth.

Variation in Accidentals

The only orthographic variations between the Durham and Huntington copies which can safely be ascribed to general changes in Hoccleve's spelling practice concern the two letters *y* and *i*. As will be noticed below, his usage in Durham as a whole increasingly prefers *y* to *I* for the first person singular pronoun, where that occurs in the body of the line, not at the beginning or end. Accordingly, in the 672 lines of *Learn to Die* where Huntington is available for comparison, we find that it never writes anything but *I* in that position, whereas Durham has only nine cases of mid-line *I* as against 118 of *y*. In the spelling of other words, too, Durham shows some preference for *y* over *i*.[11]

There remain about one hundred and forty other small differences in spelling. One quite common type involves variation between single and double vowel writings: *a/aa* (11x), *e/ee* (21x), and *o/oo* (4x). Both copies show both types, which seem to have been in free variation, though *aa* predominates in Huntington.[12] There are also some twenty variations between *i* and *e* in the verb inflexions *-est/-ist*, *-eth/-ith*, and *-ed/-id*, again with no marked preference in either manuscript. Thus, Durham 64 has *despended* for Huntington's *despendid* and *haddest* for *haddist* at 613; but it has *entendid* for Huntington's *entended* at 409 and

---

[10] Suso 530.3–5: 'Aut tamquam sagitta emissa in locum destinatum; divisus aer continuo in se reclusus est, ut ignoretur transitus illius. Sic et ego natus continuo desini esse, et virtutis quidem signum nullum valui ostendere'. From Wisdom 5.12–13.

[11] Huntington has *y* for Durham's *i* in: enuirond 99, certainly 159, might 208, obeissance 334, preid 420, sodein 555, desir 584. It has *i* for Durham's *y* in: hye 15, 95, 391, 534; dye 23, 37, 93, 131, 145, 392, 546, 597, 622; bysyly 88; crye 96, 124, 642; lye 151, 537; sayllynge 201; brydil 237; whyle 301, 541; synfully 361; seyd 395; whyles 457, 611; purueyour 502; despysed 560; leye 602; dym 655.

[12] Huntington has *a* for Durham's *aa* in *haan* 527, 531; but it has *aa* for *a* in *han* 478, 545, 548, 566, as well as in *art* 40, *artes* 42, and *part* 433, 521, 602.

mightist for *mightest* at 551. The reverse concordance to the Hoccleve holographs shows considerable variation generally in these endings where they occur after stems of verbs ending in certain consonants (including -*d* and -*t*). After some other stem endings, however, there is not variation. Thus, stems in -*m* always have -*est*, -*eth*, or -*ed*, whereas stems in -*k* always have -*ist*, -*ith*, or -*id*.

More significant, given the poet's concern with the syllable-count, are the thirty-two variations affecting final -*e* (including those represented by bars through *ll* and flourishes on *r*). These mostly occur in words which, as the concordance confirms, Hoccleve generally writes sometimes with and sometimes without -*e*: *heer* 472; *hir* 172, 665; *ther* 10, 40, 135, 310, 507, 558; *wher* 214, 388; *whil* 301; *your* 295; *second* 24; *many* 401; *than/thanne* 397; *had/hadde* 92, 492; *nad/nadde* 104. In two other cases, -*e* is an optional plural ending present in one copy only: *sotile* 13 (Huntington) and *whiche* 304 (Durham). At line 580, Durham has what may be regarded as a writing error: past participial *hold* as against the regular Hocclevian *holde* in Huntington. Ten other lines show variation in gerunds and present participles between -*ynge* and -*yng*.[13] It might be thought that these variants would disturb the syllabic structure of the line; but variant -*e*'s are silenced by elision in all but three cases. At line 13, the unelided plural -*e* on *sotile* in Huntington compensates for the absence in that copy of Durham's *right*. At 492, Durham's *hadde* as against Huntington's *had* reflects variant pronunciations of the word *purgatorie* earlier in the line, either with or without its third syllable.[14] In only one line does Hoccleve write (or rather, indicate with a flourish) a hypermetrical -*e*: in *where*, Durham 214. A similar care for syllables marks the four variations between the inflexional forms -*e* and -*en* in verbs. Two of these (*weenen* at 525 and the first *comen* at 134) occur in non-eliding position; and the other two have compensating syllables elsewhere in the line: 203 Whos kerf nat fownden is whan past is shee] Whos kerf nat fownde is whan passid is shee; 672 Awayte vpon my soule miserable] Awayten on my soule miserable.[15]

There further remain some fifty miscellaneous variations between the spelling forms of the two copies. These include such things as variant forms of prefixes (*con-/com-* 100) and suffixes (-*on/-oun* 131, 366, 447, 481, 582, 584). Durham has -*an*- where Huntington shows -*aun*- in

---

[13] Durham has -*ynge* as against Huntington's -*yng* (the latter with an otiose final hook) at 20, 35 (hauynge), 55, 129, 169, 241, 256, 616, 638, all in eliding positions. See Jefferson, 'The Hoccleve Holographs', 104. Jefferson notes most of the other variants cited here.

[14] The concordance shows the poet elsewhere preferring *purgat'rie*.

[15] Variation between *be* and *been* (354, 365, 629) has no metrical consequences.

words such as *change* (137, 229, 280, 329, 331, 333, 334, 494, 643), *-on-* in words such as *stonde* where Huntington has *-an-* (287, 529, 657), and *shul* where Huntington has *shuln* (461, 531). There is variation between initial *c-* and *k-* (208, 246, 412, 663) and between *at the* and *atte* (460, 486, 615). These slight differences carry no metrical significance; but it may be noted that the poet sometimes takes elision of *the* for granted and sometimes indicates it: compare *thaftirclap* with *the aftirclap* at 243, and *the iniquitee* with *thiniquitee* at 569.

Relationship between the Two Copies

Hoccleve made both the Huntington and the Durham copies in the period between 1422 and his death in 1426.[16] There is one piece of evidence suggesting that Durham was made later than Huntington. This concerns the poet's way of writing the first person singular pronoun. He at all times quite consistently wrote *I* for this pronoun at the beginning of a verse line and *y* at the line end. Where it occurs within the body of the line, however, his practice varied rather remarkably. In that mid-line position he always writes *I*, never *y*, in Huntington; but in Durham a change can be seen. In the first holograph text there, the latter part of the *Dialogue*, mid-line *I* still prevails, with only four examples of *y* against 123 of *I*; but the ratio shifts in the rest of the *Series*, as follows: mid-line *y* 72, mid-line *I* 102 in *Jereslaus*; mid-line *y* 159, mid-line *I* 12 in the whole *Learn to Die*; 85 mid-line *y*, 25 mid-line *I* in *Jonathas*. The simplest explanation of these figures is that Huntington represents Hoccleve's older practice, which he is still largely following in the Durham *Dialogue*, but which he moves away from in the later texts there, coming, for whatever reason, to prefer *y* to *I*.[17]

One might suppose that the question of priority between the two copying jobs could be settled by study of the variants themselves, but this is hardly the case. In many of the variants the direction of change is quite indeterminable. Furthermore, what do appear to be later readings can be found in both copies. Some of the evidence supports the priority of Durham, notably in those places where one copy is closer to the Latin source than the other. Out of the fourteen such places noted above, Durham is closer to Suso in twelve and so may be held to have generally the earlier, more literal renderings. However, this evidence does not

---

[16] See my *Thomas Hoccleve*, p. 30.

[17] My figures are derived from the entries under *I* and *y* in the concordance. See Bowers, 'Two Copies', 455. In other contexts Hoccleve commonly represents long /i/ (as in the pronoun) by the letter *y* (*fyr*, *wyf*, etc.).

necessarily conflict with the more powerful orthographic evidence in favour of Huntington as the earlier copy; for under certain circumstances 'earlier' readings can appear in a later copy. It is, after all, highly unlikely that Hoccleve copied *Learn to Die* into the Durham *Series* from the text of that poem as a separate item in Huntington.[18] The more likely supposition is that both copies were taken at different times from the poet's working copy or foul papers.[19] If that is the case, two kinds of change are to be reckoned with: changes in the working copy itself, and changes made in the act of transcribing from that copy but not registered in it. These may be imagined as, respectively, horizontal and vertical variations. Hence it is possible, on this hypothesis, that in writing an earlier, Huntington copy Hoccleve made changes introducing 'later' readings without entering them on the working copy, from which, accordingly, 'earlier' readings could have been allowed to stand unchanged on a later occasion in Durham. This argument is, of course, reversible, so far as the priority of copying jobs is concerned; but reversal would require a more elaborate explanation of the orthographic evidence.[20]

Regardless of which copy one chooses to regard as the earlier, the existence of a second holograph of *Learn to Die* (alone among the *Series* pieces) makes it possible to throw a little more light upon the 'Variant Original' from which the scribal copies of *Learn to Die* and the rest of the *Series* descend. For, if one introduces the ancestral readings of these scribal copies into the comparison, it is evident that they agree now with Huntington and now with Durham, though more often with the latter.[21] This state of affairs is most easily explained by supposing that VO represents the evolution of the text at a stage somewhere between those represented by Hoccleve's two fair copies of *Learn to Die*. It follows

[18] Nor is the Durham copy, prepared for presentation to the Countess of Westmorland, a likely exemplar for the Huntington *Learn to Die*. Each copy contains transcriptional slips not found in the other. In Durham Hoccleve writes *thogh* for *thow* (607); Huntington omits *no* (155) and *nat* (597), and writes *of* for *to* (628) and *freendes* for *feendes* (671).

[19] Bowers speaks of the 'likelihood that both copies radiated independently from a single lost exemplar, which itself may have undergone one or more stages of retouching between the occasions on which the poet executed these two transcriptions', 'Two Copies', 457–8.

[20] Scholarly opinion is divided. On the strength only of the Huntington readings recorded by Furnivall in the EETS edition, Kern took that copy to represent a later, revised version: 'Zum Texte', 443. So also Pryor, p. 123. Bowers sees Durham as the later: 'Two Copies', 457, and 'Hoccleve's Huntington Holographs', 38–42.

[21] The best representative of the scribal copies, MS Selden, has readings at 67 of the 69 places where substantive variation is in question (it lacks lines 1–21 by loss of leaf). Of these, 42 agree with Durham, 25 with Huntington.

that, if Durham is indeed later than Huntington, it must also be later than VO. However, comparison of the readings of Durham with those attributable to VO throughout the *Series* yields (as in the holograph *Dialogue*, above pp. xxi–xxii) quite uncertain results. The variants are rarely substantial enough to allow significant comparison with the Latin sources;[22] the frequent differences in word-order yield rhythms which may be preferred sometimes in Durham and sometimes in VO; nor would it be easy to agree which version has the greater number of improved readings overall. Perhaps a fuller study of the whole matter would succeed in clarifying what appears to have been a complex process of largely trivial tinkering, both in Hoccleve's working material and also in the process of making fair copies from it.

Conclusion

The main aim of this excursus has been to study textual variation in the one Hoccleve poem which survives in two copies made by the author himself. I find sixty-nine substantive variants, together with some 140 orthographic variants (not counting *i/y*), in 672 lines of verse. Much trivial and tiresome detail has been given, because it seems to me important to show how even the 'substantive' variants rarely involve more than slight rewordings, or reorderings of words. Only ten of the 672 lines undergo anything approaching extensive revision. It has become customary to stress the instability or 'mouvance' of medieval vernacular texts.[23] In this particular case, however, one may be struck rather by the overall stability of the text, given the opportunities for both horizontal and vertical variation that the poet evidently enjoyed. Readings peculiar to Durham or to Huntington can sometimes be seen to strengthen or sharpen meaning; but more commonly, where inadvertence is not in question, Hoccleve's eye seems to have been caught by tiny infelicities in expression. Particularly striking is his meticulous and consistent preservation of the syllable-count in all the variants: I find only one case (*where* at Durham 214) where variation brings a breach of the poet's rules.

---

[22] Durham keeps closer to Suso than VO in *Learn to Die* on ten occasions as against three; but the opposite is the case in the two *Gesta* stories (*Jereslaus* VO 4 to Durham 0, *Jonathas* VO 3 to Durham 1).

[23] The term 'mouvance' was coined by Paul Zumthor: see his *Essai de Poétique Médiévale* (Paris, 1972), p. 507. His discussion on pp. 70–3 speaks of 'une mobilité essentielle du texte médiéval'; but he makes exceptions for certain fourteenth- and fifteenth-century poets, naming Guillaume de Machaut and Charles d'Orléans, 'dans l'entourage desquels perce un certain souci de contrôler et de fixer le texte' (p. 72).

EXCURSUS II: *TRACTATUS DEFLENTIS HOMINIS ET AMONENTIS RACIONIS*

The following is a text of the epitome of the *Synonyma* of Isidore of Seville as found on ff. 106v-111r in Bodleian Library MS Bodley 110, up to the point where the rendering by Hoccleve (*Complaint* 316–71) breaks off. I supply modern punctuation, and number the sentences for convenience of reference in the notes. See further the note to *Complaint* 309–10, and J. A. Burrow, 'Hoccleve's *Complaint* and Isidore of Seville Again', *Speculum*, 73 (1998), 424–8.

[f. 106v] Hic introducuntur persone duorum, deflentis Hominis et amonentis Racionis.

[1] O Homo: Anima mea in angustijs est, et cor meum in doloribus fluctuat. [2] Vbicumque fugero, mala mea sequntur me, sicut vmbra prosequitur corpus, non possum fugere ea. [3] Non desunt michi tormenta et cruciamenta. [4] Cur ego infelix natus fui in hanc vitam miseram? [5] Melius est mihi mori quam infeliciter viuere. [6] Plura enim ministrat dolor, et consolari non valeo. [7] Nullus finis est dolorum meorum. [8] Racio: Quare tantum frangeris in aduersis? [9] Omitte tristiciam, repelle dolorem a corde. [10] Homo: Qualiter? qua racione? quo consilio? quo ingenio? [11] Racio: Luctamen sume contra temporales tristicias. [12] Esto paciens in cunctis aduersitatibus. [13] Respice similes euentus aliorum: facilius consolatur homo alienis malis. [14] Multi homines [f. 107r] maiora pericula sustinuerunt quam tu, vt purgati peruenirent ad regnum Dei. [15] Dolor et tristicia sunt communia omnibus. [16] Vtilis est tribulacio et vtiles sunt pressure huius vite. [17] Humana temptacio reprehendit te et non interficit. [18] Semper hic Deus vulnerat eos quos preparat ad eternam salutem. [19] Aurum decoquitur et probatur in fornace, vt purius fiat. [20] Omnia que sustines sunt ad probacionem. [21] Non murmures, non dicas 'Quare sustineo mala?' [22] Sed magis dic 'Peccaui, et adhuc non sustineo tanta quanta dignus sum'.

EXCURSUS III: FALSING OF COIN, *DIALOGUE* 99-196

Hoccleve's digression on 'falsynge of coyn' (*Dial.* 129, 165) is prompted by a passing reference to coin-clipping earlier in the *Dialogue* (l. 66). The first part of the digression concerns 'feeble moneye' (102), that is, coin which falls short of its prescribed size and weight. The two criminal processes to which he here refers are clipping (109, 116) and washing (106, 116). Clipping reduces the coin 'in brede and in rowndnesse' (109), leaving it 'narw and smal' (123); washing reduces its thickness (107), leaving it thin (123). Hoccleve is concerned, not with the processes themselves (on which see the notes to ll. 106 and 109), but with the consequences for users. The poor have no choice but to accept underweight gold coins, provided they are undamaged ('hool', 113); yet when they attempt to spend or exchange these, other people insist on weighing them, and either refuse them outright or accept them at much less than their face value (104-5, 124-5). There follows a stanza (134-40) which Hoccleve added some time after writing the rest of the passage, in which he acknowledges that the weighing of gold coins has now been authorised, and indeed required, by a statute (May 1421). The original digression then resumes with a stanza concerned with the counterfeiting and 'plating' of coins, crimes even worse than clipping or washing (141-7). The rest of the passage complains that falsers of coin are aided and abetted by powerful folk, and calls for all those involved to be punished as traitors (152-4, cf. 130).

Numismatic crime was no new thing in England, as the poet remarks ('nat begonne of neewe', 165); but in the later years of Henry V such offences were quite exceptionally prevalent. One modern scholar speaks of 'an epidemic of counterfeiting coin which swept the country from 1415 onwards'.[1] The same writer notes that after 1417 counterfeiting took over from Lollardy as the treasonable offence most preoccupying the authorities.[2] In the *Dialogue*, Hoccleve speaks as one who has

---

[1] Edward Powell, in *Henry V: The Practice of Kingship*, ed. G. L. Harriss, 2nd edn (Stroud, 1993), p. 73. For help with this Excursus I am indebted to Dr Challis, Mr Mayhew, and Professor Tuck.

[2] Edward Powell, *Kingship, Law, and Society: Criminal Justice in the Reign of Henry V* (Oxford, 1989), pp. 252-3. Hoccleve's writings reflect a similar shift of interest: the last

himself suffered from light coin (127–8), and he must also have heard the matter discussed in official London circles: Henry Somer, a fellow member of his dining club to whom he addressed a balade in the spring of 1421, was warden of the exchange and mint in the Tower of London.[3] The 'epidemic of counterfeiting' at this time had a general cause: a Europe-wide shortage of gold and silver in the early fifteenth century, a 'bullion famine' which led to a rise in the price of precious metals, and also to a fall in the output of mints and a consequent shortage of coin.[4] In England, these developments were exacerbated by the financial effects of Henry V's wars.

The documents of the time provide much evidence of official concern about, and reaction to, the epidemic. Prosecutions for coinage offences were frequent. 'Between 1418 and the end of the reign there was a spate of counterfeiting cases'.[5] Thus in June 1419 John Peyntour was indicted for having 'feloniously and traitorously by divers instruments sweated and clipped genuine English money of the said king [Henry V], to wit nobles of choice gold called "Edwardes", and other nobles, half nobles and "fertlynges" of good gold and true weight, and also [silver] groats, pence, halfpence, and other pence called "penyes of topens" to the sum of 40l., and of having coined and manufactured bad and counterfeit money, to wit gilt nobles, half nobles and farthings, groats, half-groats, pence and halfpence of false and bad metal but seeming to be good money, to the sum of 100l.'[6] Parliament was also much concerned with the matter. Already in November 1414, parliament agreed that the king should take measures 'pur ouster les damages, meschiefs, & deceites, qe se habundent dedeinz le Roialme parmy les lavours, tonsours, &

poem in which he addresses the question of Lollardy (Furnivall nos V and VI) probably dates from 1416.

[3] *Calendar of Patent Rolls 1408–1413*, p. 353: November 29, 1411, 'Grant for life to Henry Somer of the office of keeper of the exchange and mint in the Tower of London and the keeping of the coinages of gold and silver within the realm'. The appointment was confirmed by Henry V, and by Henry VI in December 1422 (*CPR 1422–1429*, p. 72). On the date of the Somer balade, see my *Thomas Hoccleve*, pp. 28–9.

[4] See generally J. Day, 'The Great Bullion Famine of the Fifteenth Century', *Past and Present*, 79 (1978), 3–54; also Powell, *Kingship, Law, and Society*, pp. 258–61. The output of gold and silver coins from English mints 'declined by about two-thirds between 1417 and 1419', J. H. A. Munro, *Wool, Cloth, and Gold: The Struggle for Bullion in Anglo-Burgundian Trade, 1340–1478* (Brussels and Toronto, 1972), p. 72.

[5] Powell, *Kingship, Law, and Society*, p. 260. Powell dates the 'height of the crisis' to 1419. He notes 114 indictments in king's bench for counterfeiting between 1418 and 1421, compared with 54 between 1414 and 1417.

[6] *Calendar of Patent Rolls 1429–36*, pp. 592–3.

contrefaitours [washers, clippers, and counterfeiters]'.[7] In the parliament of spring 1416, the Commons petitioned that the reference to counterfeiting in Edward III's Statute of Treasons (1352) should be understood to include in its scope 'le tonsure, loture, fylinge, & autre fauxisne de vostre Moneye [clipping, washing, filing, and other falsing of your money]'.[8] This request to the king was met in a statute of the same parliament: 'qe tieux tonsure, loture, & filer soient adjuggez pur traison; et qe ceux qi tondent, lavent, & filent la moneie de la terre soient adjuggez traitours a Roi & a le roialme & encourgent la peine du traison'.[9]

The statute to which Hoccleve himself refers (*Dial.* 136–40) was issued at the parliament of 2 May 1421. It ordained that, from Christmas Eve 1421, no one should accept any English gold coin in payment unless it was of correct weight. In the meantime, all the many defective gold coins must be sent to the mint to be recoined with the correct weight and alloy; and during this period the king waived the tax due to him on all minting (his 'seignorage'), though people would still have to pay the mint's own charge. The text of the statute is as follows:[10] 'Item, pur ouster periles & deceites queux longement ont contenus dedeinz le Roialme parmy les lavours, tonsours, & contrefaitours de la moneie D'engleterre, a tres graundes meschiefs & damages a toutz gentz de mesme le Roialme; le Roi, par advis & assent de toutz les Seigneurs & Communes assembles en cest parlement, ad ordeinez & estables qe, de la veille del feste de Nouel prochein a venir enavant, nulle liege du Roy receivera ascune moneie d'or Engleis en paiment sinon par les pois du Roy sur ceo ordeines. Et pur tant qe graunde partie del or de present currant en paiement n'est mye de droiturell pois ne de bon allaie, y faute ceo remettre a le cune, au fyne q'il poet estre novelment cunez de joust pois & bone alleie; & ce serra estre a graunde perde & costages des subditz du Roy, s'il ne luy plest eux relever en ceo cas; si ad le Roi de sa grace especiale remis & pardonez a toutz ses liges, qi parentre cy & le dit

---

[7] *Rotuli Parliamentorum*, IV 35 (c. 12).

[8] *Rotuli Parliamentorum*, IV 82 (c. 40). Two other petitions at this parliament may be noted. One (c. 41) complains that too many of those held in custody 'pur la controfaiture, tonsure, loture, & autre fauxisme de vostre Monoye' are managing to escape their keepers; the other (c. 42) asks that Justices of Assises and Justices of Peace should be given more powers in the matter, since 'le contrefaiture, tonsure, & loture, & autre fauxisme de vostre Moneye est le pluis usee & pluis habounde de jour en jour qe ne soleit'.

[9] *Statutes of the Realm*, II 195: 4 Henry V c. 6. On this supplementary treason statute of 1416, see J. G. Bellamy, *The Law of Treason in England in the Later Middle Ages* (Cambridge, 1970), p. 130.

[10] *Statutes of the Realm*, II 208–9: 9 Henry V st. 1 c. 11. *Rotuli Parliamentorum*, IV 130 (c. 7), has the same text in the form of a petition.

fest de Nouelle ferront cuner de novel a le cunage du Roy dedeinz le
Toure de Loundres lour monoie d'or qe ne soit de joust pois ne de bone
allaie, c'est assavoir tout ceo qe a luy appartient pur celle novelle cunage
de tiel ore, come desuis; Salvez a le Mestre del Mynte & as autres
Officeres d'icelle ceo qe a eux appartient resonablement'.

This recoinage statute was a major public event in its time. A writer
of the *Brut*, after recording the return of Henry and Katherine from
France and the coronation of the queen in February 1421, notes it: 'Also
þe same yeer, Anon after Ester, þe King held a parlement at
Westmynster, at which it was ordeyned þat þe gold in Englissh
coygne shuld be weyed, & none receyved but by weght'.[11] Similarly
another fifteenth-century chronicle: 'And in thys Parlymentt was
ordaynyde, by cause that golde was gretely a payryde by clyppyng
and waschynge, that no man shulde aftyr Crystysmas nexte aftyr put
forthe no enpayryd golde in no paymente uppon payne of furfeture
there of; where fore every man for the moste party ordaynyd hym
balans.'[12] So it is not surprising that Hoccleve felt called upon to add his
stanza as a postscript, in which he distinguishes between the
unauthorised weighing that he had complained of in the original passage
(written before May 1421) and the weighing now required by statute:
'Now tyme it is vnto weightes vs drawe | Syn þat the parlement hath
maad it a lawe' (139–40). In the period up to Christmas Eve 1421,
people had to resort to weights in order to determine which gold coins
should be recoined. The processes of weighing, exchanging and minting
during this period evidently gave rise to a number of difficulties, which
were addressed in no less than eight statutes in the parliament of 1
December 1421. One of these concerns the supply of just weights: the
king is to order 'bones & joustz pois del noble, demy noble & ferling
d'or, ovesqe les rates a ceo necessaries', to be supplied to every city,
borough and town, so that honest citizens will not be deceived by 'faues
Controvours & ceux qi usent fauxes pois en deceit de le poeple'.[13]
Weights were also necessary, of course, for the time after Christmas
1421, when 'no subject of the king shall receive any English gold money

---

[11] *The Brut*, ed. F. W. D. Brie (EETS, 131, 136, 1906, 1908), p. 492.
[12] *Gregory's Chronicle*, ed. J. Gairdner in *The Historical Collections of a Citizen of London in the Fifteenth Century* (Camden Society, London, 1876), p. 142.
[13] *Statutes of the Realm*, II 210: 9 Henry V st. 2 c. 7. See Sir John Craig, *The Mint: A History of the London Mint from A. D. 287 to 1948* (Cambridge, 1953), pp. 85–6. The December statutes respond to a series of petitions submitted at the same parliament: *Rotuli Parliamentorum*, IV 154–5 (cc. 15–22).

in payment save by the king's weight ordained for it'. This is the period, in the last year of Henry's reign, described by an author of the *Brut*: 'And in þat tyme þe gold of þe realme went by weght; And euery man had a payr ballaunce And weghttes in hys sleve for þe gold'.[14]

[14] *Brut*, p. 448. Vermeer's picture 'Woman Holding a Balance' shows the kind of hand-scales in question.

GLOSSARY

The glossary is selective, mainly registering divergences from Modern English; but forms representing Hoccleve's usage are included even where they would now present no difficulty. Line references prefixed by the letters C and D refer to the *Complaint* and *Dialogue*, respectively. The Selden text of the non-holograph section is not included in the glossary. All references to the edited text of that section (the whole *Complaint* and the *Dialogue* up to l. 252) are distinguished by an asterisk, thus: C153*, D202*, but D382. Also asterisked are three cases of editorial emendation in the holograph *Dialogue*. Authority for the forms so marked lies, in almost all cases, with the corpus of Hoccleve holographs, as explained in the Introduction, pp. xl–xlvi. Up to three examples are normally cited from both the non-holograph and the holograph sections. The note (*in rhyme*) indicates that a form is one used by Hoccleve only, or almost only, in that position.

Vocalic *y* is treated as *i*, but consonantal *y* has its usual place after *x*; consonantal *i* is treated as *j*; *u* and *v* are separated according to function.

abasshe *pr. pl. hem* ~ are ashamed D108*.
abaten *v.* fall C74*; lose strength D355; **abated** *pa. t.* C25*.
abyde *v.* wait D224*; *imp. sg.* D306; **abood** *pa. t. sg.* D571; **abide** *pp.* D442.
abieth *pr. 3 sg.* pays for D497.
abood *n.* pause C129*.
aboute *adv.* ~ *brynge* perform D299.
aboute *prep.* about D302; near C83*.
aboue *adv.* above C377*.
abregge *v.* fall short of D587.
accord *n. of swich* ~ in such agreement C59*.
accordith *pr. 3 sg.* agrees D351, 448.
adayes *adv.* daily C186*; ~ *now* nowadays D250*.
Adam Adam D722.
adoun *adv.* down C13*, D195*, D736.
affeccioun *n.* friendly relationships C391*; good graces D676.
affermed *pa. t.* ~ *on* affirmed of D763.
affrighte *pa. t.* alarmed C46*.
agayn *see* **ageyn** *adv.*
agast *adj.* afraid D474.
ageyn *adv.* again C93*, 182*, 231*, D678; back C64*, 180*, 374*; **agayn** (*in rhyme*) C233*, D380.
ageyn *prep.* against C342*, D68*, D766; in preparation for D293.
aght *n.* anything D7*, 202*, D395, 470, 794.
aght *adv.* at all D201*.
agilt *pp.* done wrong C366*, D751.

agoon *ppl. adj.* gone by, past C171*, D161*. *adv.* ago D8*, 42*.
ay *adv.* always C131*, 134*, 196*, D327, 341, 349.
aylastynge *ppl. adj.* everlasting C350*.
al *conj.* although C254*.
alday *adv.* always C170*.
algate *adv.* nevertheless C246*, D361; at all times D189*.
allegge *v.* adduce D588.
Alle Halwemesse *n. phr.* All Saints' Day (Nov. 1) C55*.
also *conj.* as D491, 798.
alway *adv.* always C216*, D110*, 176*; **alwey** (*in rhyme*) D591.
amendement *n.* reformation D91*.
amendid *pp.* improved C161*; made amends for D700; ~ *me* reformed D69*.
amis *adj.* wrong D82*. *adv.* wrongly C94*, 138*, 139*, D471.
among *adv.* from time to time C281*, D792.
among *prep.* preeminently among, above D111*.
and *conj.* if C241*, D166*, D766.
angwisshous *adj.* anguished C316*.
annexid *pp.* joined D335.
annoyed *pp.* damaged, injured D112*.
anoon *adv.* at once C169*, D10*, 17*, D504.
anothir *adj.* another D478; *al* ~ quite different D252*.
apaid *pp.* satisfied, pleased C378*, D756.

apalle v. cloud over C74*.
appeire v. harm C277*; appeirith pr. 3 sg. deteriorates D249*.
applied pp. directed D242*.
apt adj. fit C124*.
aqweynte v. acquaint; neewe to ~ newly acquainted D320; pp. D321.
areest n. stopping C129*.
arn pr. 3 pl. are C352*.
as conj. as if C77*, 144*.
ascaunce adv. D620 (see note).
assay n. test C217*; putte in ~ put to the test D710; at assayes when put to the test D278.
assaye v. put to the test C210*.
asslakith pr. 3 sg. slackens D507.
atte prep. + def. art. at the D819.
auctoritee n. authority D135*; pl. D360.
auctour n. author, originator D760.
auctrice n. female authority D694.
audience n. hearing D44*.
auaille v. ~ to assist, advance D530.
auante v. me ~ boast, claim D752.
auauntage n. advantage D607.
auenture n. fortune C273*.
auys n. opinion D510, 661; consideration D633, 650.
auisament n. consideration D483, 639.
auyse v. ~ me consider D628; pr. 2 sg. subj. thee ~ D684; auysed pp. ~ of informed about D40*; ~ be wel have well considered D648.
away adv. away C400*, D310; al ~ altogether C345*; al aweye (in rhyme) C80*.
awe n. reverential fear, awe C399*.
awry adv. askance C76*.
axe v. ask D816; axith pr. 3 sg. D91*, 138*, 732; axynge pr. p. D716; axid pp. C295*.

baar see bere.
balade n. balade stanza D551.
balaunce n. weighing-scales D601.
bataillous adj. warlike D592.
Bathe Bath D694.
be(en) v. be C203*, 222*, D265, 282; pr. pl. C96*, 200*, 213*, D19*, D277, 282, 312; be pr. sg. subj. C246*, D244*, D267, 305, 307; be(en) pp. C4*, 59*, 152*, D266, 356, 440.
beer see bere.
befalle v. occur D395.
beforn adv. before, previously D408.

beforn prep. before D483, 568, 579.
begonne pp. begun D165*.
begoon pp. wel ~ happily placed C11*.
behight pp. promised C111*.
benedicitee exclam. bless me D316.
benefice n. beneficial action D92*; pl. C412*.
bere pr. pl. bear C347*; imp. sg. C361*; beer (in rhyme) pa. t. 1 sg. carried C122*; baar pa. t. 3 sg. ~ him conducted himself D616; born pp. borne C178*.
besom n. broom D286.
beste adj. wk. best. as n. C175*, D300; for my ~ in my best interests C394*.
bet adv. compar. better D40*, 98*, 128*, D352.
bete v. beat C186*; pp. hammered out D440.
bethoghte pa. t. ~ me reflected C274*.
betid pp. harde ~ severely afflicted C215*.
betwixt prep. between C249*.
bewar imp. beware D680.
beyonde adv. overseas D566.
by prep. concerning C85*.
bicomen pp. become D272.
byheeste n. promise D598.
bireft pp. taken away from D285; byreft D396.
biried pp. buried C230*.
byseeche pr. 1 sg. beg D657.
bisy adj. busy D302, 788.
bisye v. me ~ busy myself D506; imp. sg. ~ thee busy yourself D384.
bisynesse n. activity D381, 546.
bistad pp. wo ~ distressed C146*.
bit pr. 3 sg. bids D391, 452, 457.
bytake pr. 1 sg. commit D789.
bywreye v. reveal D599.
blak adj. as n. black (ink) D670.
blyue adv. quickly D257; soon D542; as ~ D204*.
blowe pp. blown, spread C257*; yblowe D66*.
bolned pa. t. swelled C30*.
bond n. bond, link D350; binding obligation D340.
bontees n. pl. good graces D814.
boon n. bone C398*.
boote n. remedy, cure C49*.
born see bere.
bowe pr. 2 sg. subj. bow, submit D715.
bownden pp. duty bound D549.
braynseek adj. mentally ill C129*.

brast *pa. t. 1 sg.* burst C35*.

brede *n.* breadth, diameter D109*.

breest *n.* breast D713.

breewith *pr. 3 sg.* brews, brings about D72*.

breke *v.* break D654, 725, 728; ybroken *pp.* D726.

brent *pp.* burnt D500.

brode *adv.* broad D170*.

brondes *n. pl.* pieces of burnt wood D685.

brotil *adj.* brittle, uncertain D278.

broun *adj.* brown C2*.

bukkissh *adj.* disturbed C123*.

but *adv.* only, save C219*, 254*, D91*, D374, 758, 761. *conj.* unless C369*, D103*, 209*, D394, 637, 810; without it happening that D125*; ~ *if* unless D82*, 193*; without it happening that C264*.

buxum *adj.* yielding, submissive D687.

cacche *v.* catch, achieve D502; caght *pp.* acquired C375*; suffered D375; kaght contracted D398.

calle *v.* invite C75*.

cam *pa. t. 1 sg.* came C34*, D7*; *pa. t. 3 sg.* C20*, 55*, 91*, D575, 610, 808.

can *pr. 1 sg.* know D622; can say C224*, D407; *pr. 3 sg.* knows C241*, D565.

cancre *pr. 3 sg. subj.* corrode D325.

cas *n.* case C170*, D78*, 127*, D462, 742, 761.

caste *pr. 1 sg.* throw; ~ *to the cok* abandon C386*; *pa. t.* threw C42*, 76*; considered C135*; cast *pp.* planned D641.

catel *n.* movable property D281.

causes *n. pl.* lawsuits D69*.

certeyn *adj. as n. in* ~ certainly D438.

certein *adv.* certainly D203*, D621.

certes *adv.* certainly D328, 643.

cesse *v.* stop D244*.

chaffare *n.* merchandise D114*.

charged *pp.* commanded D137*.

chaunce *n.* fortune D291; chance (*in rhyme*) C273*.

cheere *n.* face, expression C74*, 149*, 158*, D817.

cheertee *n.* affection C81*, 287*, D777.

cheese *v.* choose D74*, 126*; *imp. sg.* D680.

cheste *n.* chest D301.

cheuissance *n.* way to proceed D621.

Chirburgh Cherbourg D567, 575, 611.

clappe *pr. pl.* chatter D489.

cleene *adv.* clean, completely D310, 676, 826.

clenner *adj. compar.* purer C359*.

clippe *v.* clip D109*.

clippynge *vbl. n.* clipping (of coins) D116*.

cloos *n.* stronghold D576.

cloos *adj.* secret, private C32*, 145*, D28*.

clothe *pr. pl.* clothe, enclose D143*.

cofre *n.* strong-box D115*.

cok *n.* cock C386*.

colde *v.* grow cold D228*.

commune *n.* community D172*.

commune *v.* hold a conversation C218*, 269*.

commune *adj.* common C352*, D169*, D599.

communynge *n.* conversation C217*, D470.

conceit *n.* power of comprehension, understanding C253*, D250*, D364, 445, 461; idea D383, 423, 591; *pl.* C168*.

concludith *pr. 3 sg.* reaches a conclusion D779.

condicions *n. pl.* dispositions D769.

confesse *v.* declare D94*; *imp. sg. thee* ~ make confession D665.

conforte *v. me* ~ take comfort C392*.

conpaignie *n.* company C76*.

conpleynyngly *adv.* by way of complaint D772.

conseil *n.* a secret C44*; advice D391, 452, 622.

conseille *v.* give advice D464; consaille (*in rhyme*) D462; *pr. pl.* D50*.

Constantyn Cotentin D576.

contenance *n.* expression C149*, 166*, 214*; *straunge* ~ distant regard C70*.

contrarie *v.* run counter to D767.

contrees *n. pl.* parts of the country D160*.

conueniently *adv.* appropriately D590.

copir *n.* copper D143*.

correccioun *n. do* ~ *of* make amends for D674.

correct *pp.* corrected D193*.

coupable *adj.* culpable, guilty D688.

couenable *adj.* fitting D635.

couenant *n.* agreement D535.

couetyse *n.* covetousness D146*.

craft *n.* skill D682.

Cryst Christ C223*.

crowe *n.* carrion crow D810.
Cupyde Cupid D754.
curteys *adj.* courteous, gracious C236*.
curteisly *adv.* graciously D80*.

daliance *n.* friendly conversation C69*, D706.
dangerous *adj.* hard to get D745.
dar *pr. 1 sg.* dare D100*, 187*, D752.
debat *n.* conflict C247*.
deed *adj.* dead C81*.
deede *n.* deed, action C224*, D299, 574; **Deedis** *pl.* D820.
deel *n.* deal D128*; *nat a* ~ not a bit D263.
deeme *v.* judge, consider, suppose C181*, 192*, 289*, D471; *pr. 1 sg.* C394*; **deemeth** *pr. 3 sg.* C208*; **deeme(n)** *pr. pl.* C99*, 207*, 223*, D421, 809; **deeme** *pr. subj.* C264*, D305; **deemeth** *imp. pl.* D429; **deemed** *pa. t.* C141*.
deemynge *vbl. n.* speculation, supposition D432, 540.
deere *adv.* dearly D497.
deffaute *n.* fault C288*; lack D643.
deffectif *adj.* defective D188*.
degree *n.* rank D704.
deyntee *n.* delight D695.
delen *v.* deal C66*.
delyt *n.* pleasure C28*.
depeynted *pp.* depicted, inscribed D670.
dere *v.* harm C348*, D711.
derk *adj.* dark D364.
desdeyn *n.* disdain C66*, D411, 741.
desdeynest *pr. 2 sg.* disdain D453.
despeire *pr. 1 sg. me* ~ fall into despair C275*.
despente *pa. t.* employed; *mis* ~ wasted C401*.
desport *n.* entertainment D705.
dette *n.* debt D532.
dyde *pa. t.* died D751.
died *pp.* dyed C6*.
dilate *v.* amplify D359.
dirk *adj.* dark C292*; **dirke** *wk.* C25*.
discreet *adj.* rational, sensible C245*, 251*.
disese *n.* distress, illness C344*, 360*, 388*, D422.
displesance *n. take in* ~ be displeased at D370.
displesith *pr. 3 sg.* displeases D786; **displese** *pr. 3 sg. subj.* may it displease D198*.

disposicioun *n.* physical condition D377, 519.
disseuerance *n.* parting, breach C248*.
dyuerse *adj. pl.* various D160*.
dominacioun *n.* domination D734.
doom *n.* judgement C201*, 244*, 393*, D483.
doon *v.* do C341*, D712; **doost** *pr. 2 sg.* D679; **dooth** *pr. 3 sg.* D276, 280, 780; **doon** *pr. pl.* D141*; **do** *imp. sg.* ~ *foorth* carry on D416, 523; **dide** *pa. t.* D14*, 98*, D389, 418, 444; **doon** *pp.* C179*, D18*, 88*, D258, 486, 752.
dote *pr. 1 sg.* am weak-minded D36*.
doute *n.* doubt, uncertainty C294*.
doute *imp. sg.* doubt D373.
doutelees *adv.* doubtless, certainly C219*, D581, 757.
drawe *v.* draw; *vs* ~ *vnto* resort to D139*; ~ *along* draw out, discuss at length D359.
drecche *v.* be troubled in sleep C308*.
dreede *n.* fear D401; **drede** (*in rhyme*) *no* ~ no doubt D390.
dreede *v.* fear C115*; *pr. 1 sg.* D176*, 190*, D296, 474; **dredde** *pa. t.* feared to D799.
dresse *v. refl.* address oneself C119*, D492.
dronkenesse *n.* drunkenness C225*.
droupynge *ppl. adj.* downcast C146*.
duely *adv.* justly D601.
dullith *pr. 3 sg.* grows dull D507.
duresses *n. pl.* hardships C343*.
dwelle *v.* linger D358.

edifie *v.* build D638; contribute D564.
eek *adv.* also C73*, 127*, 141*, D382, 423, 771.
eelde *v.* grow old C33*.
eer *adv.* previously D365, 418, 451.
eerthely *adj.* earthly D274.
Eeues *n. gen.* Eve's D722.
effectuelly *adv.* earnestly C312*.
eft *adv.* again D394, 401.
egal *adj.* equal D156*.
elde *n.* advanced age C410*.
eleccioun *n.* choice; *in thyn* ~ for you to choose D677.
elles *adv.* else D192*, 202*, D362; otherwise C231*, D25*, D642, 778; elsewhere D584.
empryse *n.* undertaking D514.

enablith *pr. 3 sg.* ~ *to* qualifies for C350*.
encombrous *adj.* burdensome C318*.
encorage *v.* hearten D604.
encrece *v.* increase D563.
encrees *n.* increase D580.
enditement *n.* indictment, accusation D179*.
enformed *pp.* informed D183*.
enhaunce *v.* promote D602.
ensaumple *v.* set an example D604.
ensurid *pp.* promised C304*.
entencioun *n.* intention D45*.
entente *n.* intention C404*, D22*, D295; meaning D197*; *his* ~ what he had in mind D660.
enticement *n.* tempting D725.
ere *n.* ear C91*, 134*, D585.
ernest *n.* a serious matter D256.
errour *n.* error C164*, D407, 460; wrong-doing D193*.
erst *adv.* at first D378.
eschapid *pp.* escaped D400.
eschue *v.* escape C322*; **eschuen** *pr. pl.* refuse D124*; **eschue** *imp. sg.* avoid D397.
ese *n.* comfort D743.
esid *pp.* eased, relieved C313*.
esily *adv.* calmly C178*.
euele *adv.* badly C298*; ~ *apaid* ill-pleased D756.
euene *adv.* exactly D389.
euerydeel *adv.* in every detail C299*.
excitacioun *n.* urging D437.
existence *n. in* ~ in truth D327.
expresse *v.* describe D586*.

fadir *n. gen. sg.* father's D759; **fadres** *pl.* forefathers D748.
fay *n.* faith D782.
faille *n.* fail; *sanz* ~ without fail D461; *it is no* ~ certainly D529.
fayn *adv.* gladly C160*, 175*, D308, 547.
fal *n.* fall C115*, D158*, D375.
falle *v.* occur C99*, D287; **fil** fell *pa. t. sg.* D388; **yfalle** *pp.* D393.
fals *adj.* false D68*, 146*, 187*; **false** *wk.* D108*, 191*; *pl.* D174*.
falshede *n.* falsehood, deceit D119*, 196*; **falsehede** D155*.
falsynge *n.* falsification D129*, 165*.
fame *n.* repute D599.
fare *n.* business, fuss C337*.
farest *pr. 2 sg. so* ~ *thow* so it is with you

D404; **fare** *imp. sg.* ~ *weel* farewell D797.
farwel *interj.* farewell C267*, 270*, 386*, D273.
faste *adv.* vigorously C187*, D12*; rapidly D247*.
fauour *n.* favourable regard C23*.
fed *pp.* fed, satisfied C315*.
feend *n.* fiend D727.
feere *n.* partner D739.
feynte *v.* grow weak D319.
felawes *n. pl.* companions, colleagues C296*.
felle *adj. pl.* shrewd D681.
fer *adj.* far off D119*. *adv.* far C233*, D245*, D304, 529, 814; **ferre** *compar.* further C198*.
fere *n.* fear C90*, 151*, D586, 611, 823.
ferfoorth *adv.* far; *so* ~ to such an extent C228*, D36*.
fern *adv. in n. phr. of* ~ *agoon* from long ago D8*.
ferre *see* **fer**.
fil *see* **falle**.
fyn *adj.* pure D189*; **fyner** *compar.* C359*.
fyr *n.* fire D309, 312, 683; **fyre** *dat. on* ~ alight C62*.
flitte *v.* shift D340.
flour *n.* flower D268.
fo *n.* foe C333*, D75*, D809.
fold *n. by many* ~ many times over C331*, D352, 522.
foltissh *adj.* foolish C243*, D147*.
folwe(n) *v.* follow D453, 553, 720; **folwith** *pr. 3 sg.* D574; **folwen** *pr. pl.* C320*.
fond *pa. t. 1 sg.* found C195*.
fonde *v.* try D236*.
foorth *adv.* forward D630; henceforth C167*; *hens* ~ henceforth C387*; *do* ~ carry on D416, 523; ~ *go* circulate D23*, become general D166*.
foote *n. dat.* foot C6*, 13*, 48*.
for *conj.* because; ~ *þat* D770.
for *prep.* despite C294*, D395, 685; so far as concerns D546.
forbeede *pr. 3 sg. subj.* forbid C223*.
forborn *pp.* refrained from D410.
force *n. no* ~ it does not matter C336*, D530.
foreward *n.* pledge D337.
forgat *pa. t. 3. sg.* forgot C39*; **foryete** *pp.* forgotten C80*, D30*; **foryite** (*in rhyme*) D672; **forgote** (*in rhyme*) D38*.

forgoon v. forgo, lose C12*; forgo D283.
forsake ppl. adj. forsaken, deserted C67*.
forsighte n. foresight D643.
forthy adv. therefore D428.
forwhy adv. wherefore C144*, D729.
foryete, foryite, see forgat.
foryeue v. forgive D710; pp. D672.
fourme n. method D238*; fashion D805.
fourneys n. furnace C358*.
fownde(n) pp. found C222*, 383*.
France France D543, 823.
freeltee n. frailty D71*.
freendly adj. friendly C338*, D412.
freendlyhede n. friendliness D387.
freyned pp. asked C295*.
fro prep. from C79*, 183*, 229*, D256, 340, 343.
froward adj. perverse D386.
ful adv. very C24*, 46*, 176*, D270, 285, 310.

game n. fun D255.
gan pa. t. as auxil. did C71*, 121*, D543; began to C3*.
gesse pr. 1 sg. guess D626; pr. 3 pl. C99*.
gete v. get C49*, D795; get pr. 3 sg. gets D117*.
gibet n. gallows D130*.
gye pr. 1 sg. me ~ conduct myself, behave C139*.
gilt n. guilt, sin C349*, D76*, 91*, D665, 685, 808; pl. C403*, D717.
gilty adj. guilty D129*.
gyn n. trick D141*.
gynneth pr. 3 sg. begins to D273, 319; gynne pr. 3 sg. subj. D228*.
glade v. gladden D548.
Gloucestre Gloucester D534.
go v. go, walk C228*; goon C290*, D612; pass current D125*; goost pr. 2 sg. D495; gooth pr. 3 sg. D639; goon pp. C207*, D799.
good n. possessions C38*.
goon see go.
goost n. spirit D692.
gouernance n. conduct C385*, 406*; command D718.
gouerne v. ~ hem conduct themselves D606.
grace n. grace, favour D90*, D679, 686; pl. D688, 716, 753.
greable adj. gratifying D690.
gredith pr. 3 sg. cries out D173*.

greef n. grief C29*, 287*, D167*.
greet adj. great C63*, 185*, 345*, D607, 667, 682; grete pl. D151*, D284, 498; gretter(e) compar. C250*, 330*, 345*. as n. grete greater part D314; pl. grete great ones D266.
greeue v. vex D419, 750; greeued pp. D112*, D328.
greuance n. distress D719.
greuous adj. grievous, injurious C234*, 353*.
grype v. get C265*.
grope v. probe, examine D220*.
grownde v. ground; hem ~ base an opinion C211*.
grucche imp. sg. complain C363*; grucchyng pr. p. C384*

haaste n. hurry C375*.
haaste v. hurry D646; haastith pr. 3 sg. D247*.
hachet n. small axe; hange vp his ~ let him give up D736.
halke n. corner C133*.
halpeny n. halfpenny D122*.
han v. have C107*, 143*, 383*, D536, 561, 586; ha(a)st pr. 2 sg. D23*, 34*, D295, 515, 518, 539; with pron. hastow hast thou D404; haath pr. 3 sg. D557; han pr. pl. C59*, 168*, 268*, D321, 322, 323; had(de) pa. t. C28*, 66*, 144*, D382, 430; had pp. C177*, D536.
happith pr. 3 sg. happens C105*.
hard adj. difficult D296, 486, 496; dangerous D227*, D746, 750.
harde adv. severely C215*.
hastow see han.
heed n. head C76*, 122*, 126*, D724, 728; on ~ impetuously D630.
heede n. heed C116*, 396*, D43*, D605.
heedlynge adv. precipitately D647
heelden see holde.
heep n. heap, mass D360.
heere v. hear D304, 740; pr. 1 sg. D48*.
heere adv. here C128*, 136*, 262*, D434, 466.
heeron adv. about this C348*.
heerto adv. to this D448.
heewe n. colour D270.
hele n. health D93*.
hele v. heal C112*.
hem pron. them C5*, 48*, 49*, D495, 586, 588.

hennes *adv.* hence D208*; hens C138*; ~
foorth henceforth C387*; ~ *forward*
C404*.
Henri Henry Duke of Lancaster D573.
herkne *imp. sg.* hear D369.
herte *n.* heart C135*, 263*, 297*, D319,
342, 548; herte *gen.* C7*; hertes *gen.*
C81*, 287*.
herth *n.* hearth D309, 311.
hertly *adv.* earnestly D491.
heruest *n.* autumn C1*.
hete *n.* heat C92*, 184*, D500.
heuy *adj.* miserable C146*, 285*, 316*,
D253; ~ *of* sorry for D665.
heuyere *adv. compar.* more heavily D417.
heuieth *pr. 3 sg.* oppresses D176*.
heuily *adv.* gloomily D45*.
heuynesse *n.* misery C188*, 351*, 408*;
pl. C342*.
hy *adj.* high C261*, D340, 577, 595; hye
wk. C53*, D183*.
hid *pp.* hidden D181*.
hie *v.* hurry C138*.
hye *adv.* high C122*, D264.
highte *pa. t.* vowed C47*.
hildid *pa. t.* poured C26*.
hyndre *v.* hinder D531; do harm D509.
hyndrynge *vbl. n.* hindrance D231*.
hir *pron.* her C260*, D290, 315; hire
D289.
hir *pron.* their C3*, 95*, 293*, D494, 671,
678; hire C76*, 170*, D179*, D676,
746, 768.
his *pron.* its D105*, 106*.
ho *interj.* stop D26*.
Hoccleue Hoccleve D3*.
hokir *n.* scorn D741.
hold *n.* possession D120*; handhold D354;
stronghold D568.
holde *v.* hold D106*; consider D501; *pr. 1
sg.* C378*, D661; holdist *pr. 2 sg.* D449;
holde *pr. 3 sg. subj.* D116*; *imp. sg.*
D353; heelden *pa. t. pl.* C300*;
holde(n) *pp.* considered C143*, D327;
obliged (to) D81*, 94*, D549.
holsum *adj.* salutory C385*, D289, 622.
hond *n.* hand C196*, D713; ho(o)nde *dat.
take on* ~ undertake D235*, D520
honestee *n.* decency D627, 705.
honure *v.* honour C397*.
hool *adj.* healthy C289*; whole, unda-
maged D113*.

hoom *n.* home C155*, 233*. *adv.* back
home C64*, 278*.
hoomly *adj.* familiar, everyday C221*.
hoot *adj.* hot C154*, D356.
hore *v.* become hoary, grow old C33*.
how *adv.* however C11*, 16*, D267; ~ *so*
C246*, D54*, D345, 785.
how *interj.* hey D3*.
humble *imp. sg.* make humble D692.
Humfrey Humphrey Duke of Gloucester
D589, 596.

y *pron.* I D422, 428, 451, 516.
yblowe *see* blowe.
ybroght *pp.* brought D200*.
ybroken *see* breke.
ye *n.* eye C20*, D640; yen *pl.* C133*.
yfalle *see* falle.
yknowe *see* knowe.
yle *n.* isle, peninsula D576.
ymaginacioun *n.* speculation C380*.
ymagyne *pr. pl.* speculate D489.
ymagynynge *vbl. n.* speculation C307*.
yment *see* meene.
in *adv.* ~ *and out* indoors and out C187*.
infect *pp.* infected D194*.
inned *pp.* brought in C1*.
innocent *adj.* unaware D180*.
ynow *adj.* enough D430. *as n.* D602.
ynow *adv.* enough C153*, D101*, D488,
788.
inpacience *n.* impatience C177*.
ywis *adv.* certainly, indeed D204*.

Ihesu Jesus D61*, D368; ~ Cryst C256*;
gen. D517.
ioie *n.* joy C350*, 356*, D404, 695.
ioielees *adj.* joyless C262*
iourneyynge *n.* campaigning D575.
iugement *n.* judgement C244*, 393*,
D482.
iugeth *imp. pl.* judge D511.
iust *adj.* just D393*, D230*.
iustice *n.* justice D133*.

kaght *see* cacche.
keepe *v.* keep D341, 789; *pr. 1 sg.* wish
D31*; wish to make D435.
keye *n.* key C144*.
kerue *pr. 3 sg. subj.* cut D350.
keuerchiefs *n. pl.* women's headcloths,
kerchiefs D826.
kid *pp.* known C214*.

kyn *n.* kindred D759.

kynde *n.* nature; position D33*.

knyghthode *n.* knightly qualities D563, 600.

knytte *pa. t.* tied D338.

knowe *v.* know D478, 481, 807; kneew *pa. t.* C41*, 141*, 292*, D430, 525; knowe(n) *pp.* C43*, 200*, 203*; yknowe D64*.

konnynge *n.* knowledge, ability C161*, 220*.

kowde *pa. t.* could C289*, D360.

kowth *pp.* known C43*.

kut *n.* D789 *(see note).*

laborous *adj.* laboursome D381*.

laboure *v.* ~ *me* exert myself D443.

lak *n.* lack D650; blame D667.

lakke *pr. 1 sg.* lack C324*; lakkith *pr. 3 sg.* lacks D107*; lakke *pr. pl.* D86*; *pr. 3 sg. subj.* D105*.

langour *n.* affliction C26*.

lappe *n.* loose-hanging piece of clothing D490.

largeliche *adv.* intemperately D755.

late *adv.* late D362; recently D309; *now ~* just recently D821.

lattere *adj. compar.* later, last D407.

laude *n.* praise C407*, D577.

leche *n.* physician, healer C236*, D85*.

lede *pr. 3 sg. subj.* lead D146*; ledith *pr. 3 sg.* leads D172*.

lees *n.* falsehood C193*, 300*.

leese *pr. 3 sg. subj.* lose D125*.

leeue *n. by* ~ with permission D420.

leeueth *pr. 3 sg.* believes D330; leeue *pr. pl. subj.* D329.

leye *v.* lay; wager D187*; *pr. 1 sg.* D418; *imp. sg.* lay D713; leide *pa. t.* lent C134*; ~ *vpon* struck D11*; leid *pp.* laid D29*.

leyne *v.* conceal D16*.

lene *adj.* lean, scanty C220*, D214*.

lene *v.* grant D212*; lent *pp* lent D282; supplied D114* *(see note).*

lenger *adv. compar.* longer C271*, 372*, D441; lengere D508.

Lente *n.* Lent D662.

lerned *pp.* informed D465.

lesse *adj. compar.* smaller D110*. *as n.* lesser amount D495.

lete *v.* let C389*; let *imp. sg.* C239*, 308*, D410, 434, 501; lat D199*; ~ *be* let it

alone D32*, D384; ~ *see* let us see D416, 711.

lette *v.* confine C33*; hinder D531; prevent C197*, D171*, D438; let *pp.* D131*.

lettrid *pp.* lettered; *wel* ~ well read C251*.

leue *v.* leave undone, let it alone D448, 653; *pr. 3 sg. subj.* D117*; *imp. sg.* D714.

leuer *adj. compar.* preferable; ~ *is me* I would rather D817

lewde *adj.* ignorant C219*, D36*.

lewdenesse *n.* foolishness C101*.

lieutenant *n.* regent D533.

lige *adj.* liege D163*, 180*, D554.

light *adj.* easy D728.

lightly *adv.* easily C361*, D502; lightlyere *compar.* D709.

lyk *prep.* like D268, 697.

lykith *pr. 3 sg. impers.* it pleases C36*; lyke *pr. 3 sg. subj.* it may please C390*, D226*.

likne *v.* compare C242*; *pp.* C82*.

lymes *n. pl.* limbs D248*.

list *pr. 2 sg.* wish to D455; *pr. 3 sg.* D212*, 287; *pa. t.* C69*. *impers. pr. 3 sg.* it pleases C198*, 308*, D115*, D414, 465, 524; liste *pr. 3 sg. subj.* it may please C108*; list *pa. t.* it pleased D358.

lyte *adv.* little C105*, 106*, D331. *as n.* D506.

lyth *pr. 3 sg.* lies D480; is required D682.

liueree *n.* retinue, following C271*.

lo *interj.* lo; ~ *heere* see here D805.

logged *pa. t.* lodged; ~ *him* encamped D615.

lok *n.* lock C388*.

Londoun London C73*.

long *adj.* long D198*, D426; longe *pl.* D275.

longe *adv.* long C113*, 302*, 306*, D362, 496, 545.

looth *adj.* unwilling C270*; ~ *me were* I would not wish D21*, D794; ~ *is him* he is unwilling D403.

lore *n.* teaching D322.

lowly *adv.* humbly D813.

lurkid *pp.* lain low D545.

lust *n.* desire D242*, D505, 507, 703; pleasure C28*, D701.

lusty *adj.* vigorous C4*, 16*.

maad *see* make.

mafey *interj.* my faith D41*.

maintenaunce *n.* abetting of wrong D150*.

maintenour *n.* ~ *of causes* unscrupulous supporter of one party in a lawsuit D68*; *pl.* those who abet wrongdoing D158*, 175*.

maistrie *n.* mastery D732; *for the* ~ completely D565.

make *v.* make; compose D524, 541, 553, 618; ~ *of* write about D626; made *pa. t.* made C27*, 54*, 70*, D318, 337, 544; maad *pp.* C278*, 389*, D23*, D486, 683, 685.

makynge *vbl. n.* composition D645.

man *n.* a person D225*, D280, 497.

maneere *n.* manner C163*, 243*, D1*, D467, 737; *in al* ~ *way* in every way D493; manere C322*.

maners *n. pl.* estates D284.

Marie Mary C223*.

Mars Mars D592.

martire *n.* anguish C63*.

mateere *n.* matter, subject C119*, D26*, D302, 358, 464; matire D351; matires *pl.* D498.

maugree *n.* ill-will D795.

medle *pr. 1 sg.* ~ *of* dabble in D498.

meene *pr. 1 sg.* mean C218*, D313; meeneth *pr. 3 sg.* C337*; mente *pa. t.* D24*; ment *pp.* intended D539, 641; yment D515.

meeueth *pr. 3 sg.* moves D57*; *pp.* D807.

meynee *n.* company D178*.

mencioun *n.* mention D43*.

mene *n.* intermediary D709; *pl.* third parties D184*, 188*.

mene *adj.* ordinary C218*.

merciable *adj.* merciful D368.

meruaille *n.* wonder D39*.

mescheef *n.* wrong D168*; trouble D172*.

messager *n.* messenger D290; messageer (*in rhyme*) D293.

me-ward *pron.* + *suffix to* ~ towards me D469.

Mighelmesse *n.* Michaelmas C2*.

might *n.* power D86*, D274, 377, 480.

mynde *n.* mind; *made* ~ recalled D318.

mynge *v.* draw attention to, recall D52*; *imp. sg.* D429; *pp.* D70*.

mynystreth *imp. pl.* impart to D623.

mirour *n.* mirror C157*, 162*; example, model D409, 608, 646.

mirthe *n.* entertainment D705.

mis *n.* fault D455.

mis *adv.* amiss, wrongly C283*, 401*.

misauysed *pp.* misguided D771.

misberynge *vbl. n.* misconduct D675.

mischaunce *n.* unfortunate state of affairs D148*.

mischeese *pr. 3 sg. subj.* choose wrongly D75*.

mistyden *pr. pl.* go wrong D644.

myte *n.* coin of small value D334, 509.

mo *adj.* more D19*, D537. *as n.* more people D102*.

mo *adv.* more; *euere* ~ evermore C226*, D87*.

moche *adj.* great C258*. *as n.* much D125*, 194*.

mochil *adj.* much; ~ *thyng* many things D671. *adv. ouer* ~ too much D419.

moneyours *n. pl. false* ~ makers of false coin D174*.

monicioun *n.* urging D234*.

moot *pr. 1 sg.* must C367*, D361, 790, 822; *pr. 3 sg.* D126*, D298, 765.

mortified *pp.* dead D243*.

morwe *n.* morrow, following day C35*.

mourne *v.* feel sorrow C305*.

mournynge *vbl. n.* sorrow C258*.

muse *v.* ponder D404, 496.

muste *pa. t. 1 sg.* had to C31*.

naght *adv.* not C373*.

nay *adv.* no. *as n. (it) is no* ~ it cannot be denied D572, 779.

name *n.* reputation D56*, 87*.

namely *adv.* especially D398, 631; namly C88*.

narw *adj.* narrow D123*.

nas *pa. t. 1 sg.* was not D761.

nat *adv.* not.

nathelees *adv.* nevertheless C221*, D813.

natiuite *n.* birth C326*; horoscope D592.

ne *adv.* not D121*; *nat* ~ C289*, 307*, D31*, D523.

ne *conj.* nor C28*, 44*, 56*, D429, 531, 556.

neede *adv.* of necessity D298; needes C31*, D790; needis D822.

needith *pr. 3 sg.* it is necessary C118*; requires D633; *what* ~ *it* why is it necessary C277*.

neewe *adj.* new D320, 322; *of* ~ recently D165*.

nere *pa. t. 3 sg. subj.* were not D130*.

next *adj. superl.* next to D554.

ny *adv.* near D342, 612; nearly C257*, D243*; *wel* ~ very nearly C229*, 269*.

nycetee *n.* folly D70*.

noble *n.* gold coin (value 6s. 8d.) D122*.

noblesse *n.* nobility D624, 635.

noght *adv.* not D198*.

nolde *pa. t. 1 sg.* would not C32*.

noon *pron.* none C9*, 205*, 324*, D555, 702.

noon *adj.* not any C20*, 44*, 247*, D346; no C95*, 129*, 164*, D729, 760.

noot *pr. 1 sg.* do not know D619, 781.

nothyng *adv.* not at all D108*, D691.

notice *n.* knowledge D181*.

now *adv.* ~ and ~ now and again D506.

o *num.* one, a single D33*, D526.

offense *n.* offence C179*, D664, 675; displeasure D746.

oghte *pr. 3 sg.* ought to D55*, D409; ought to be C159*; oghten *pr. pl.* D157*, D471, 777.

oghte *pa. t. 3 sg.* owned C374*.

ones *adv.* once C183*, 215*, 225*, D353, 393, 400.

oon *pron.* someone D2*; *many* ~ many a one C85*, 208*, D160*, D557; *swich* ~ such a one D466.

oon *num.* one C288*, D100*, D457.

or *conj.* before C60*, D290, 299, 363; ~ *that* D443, 793.

or *prep.* before D34*, 127*, 209*, D255, 367, 459.

ore *n.* mercy D5*.

othir *pron.* other; an alternative D118*.

ouris *possess. pron.* ours D282.

out *adv.* outdoors C187*.

oute *v.* utter, make known D81*.

oute *adv.* out; ~ *therwithal* come out with it C31*.

outhir *adv.* either D347.

outrers *n. pl.* utterers, circulators of false coin D175*.

ouer *adv.* too D170*, D385, 419.

oueral *adv.* everywhere C257*, D124*.

ouergrowe *v.* grow all over D196*.

ouersee *v.* look over D796.

ourshake *pp.* passed away C68*.

paas *n.* pace, way of walking C127*.

pay *n.* pleasure C402*.

payndemayn *n.* loaf of bread D383.

parcas *adv.* perchance, maybe D122*, D297, 720.

parchaunce *adv.* perchance, maybe D587; parchance D707.

pardee *interj.* by God C94*, D446, 509, 620.

parfourme *v.* perform D237*, D296.

parlement *n.* parliament D140*.

partie *n. make* ~ do battle D691.

passynge *ppl. adj.* extreme C92*.

past *pp.* passed C87*, 96*, D314.

pauyment *n.* paved road C186*.

peere *n.* peer, equal C242*.

pees *n.* peace C301*.

peyne *n.* pain D19*, 231*; punishment D156*; *do* ~ take pains D348, 802.

peynte *v.* paint, alter C149*.

peys *n.* weight C360*; official weight of a coin D105*, 106*.

peise *v.* weigh D417; *pr. 3 sg. subj.* D54*.

pertinent *adj.* appropriate D154*.

pynche *pr. 3 sg. subj.* pinch, squeeze C346*.

pyne *n.* (*in rhyme*) suffering C238*.

pitous *adj.* piteous D817.

planed *pp.* smoothed away C268*.

plate *n.* precious metal, gold or silver coin D186*, 188*; iron fireback D311.

pleye *v.* take a break C51*; act the part of D742.

pleisir *n.* pleasure D701.

plentee *n.* plenty C324*.

plesance *n.* pleasure C330*, 405*, D618, 690, 821.

plese *v.* please D682, 745.

plyt *n.* plight C172*, 285*, D303, 393, 712; condition D487.

port *n.* demeanour D769.

portreye *v.* adorn, embellish D804.

poure *v.* pore D405.

pourge *v.* purge D825; *pp.* C358*.

pray *n.* spoils of war D571.

praunce *v.* prance D824.

precedent *adj.* previous D251*.

preef *n.* practical test C200*, 205*, 245*.

prees *n.* crowd C73*, 139*, 191*.

preeue *v.* prove, demonstrate C34*, 224*; test C361*, D444; *pr. 3 sg. subj.* prove D133*; *pp.* D566.

preye *pr. 1 sg.* pray D415, 428, 493; preide *pa. t.* C297*.

preysynge *n.* praise D577, 673.

preiudice *n.* detriment D162*.
prest *adj.* ready D553.
prike *v.* spur, ride fast D824.
priuee *adj.* privy C296*.
probacioun *n. in* ~ when put to the proof C383*, D735.
profre *pr. pl.* offer D113*.
prolle *imp. sg.* ~ *after* look for D744.
promesse *v.* promise D594.
prudence *n.* prudent act D449.
purchace *v.* purchase, obtain C188*, D145*, D678.
purchas *n.* obtaining C276*; purchase D147*.
purpos *n.* plan, project D201*, D301, 306, 439.
purpose *v.* plan; *me* ~ *pr. 1 sg.* D503; **purposist** *pr. 2 sg.* D527; **purposid** *pp.* D211*, D363, 641; **purposed** D515.
purs *n.* purse D89*.
purueance *n.* provision D292.
purueide *pa. t.* provided C97*; **purueied** *pp.* C356*.
putte *v.* put; ~ *vpon* impute to D696; **putte** *pa. t.* ~ *in* imputed to C288*; **put** *pp.* ~ *on* imputed to D668.

quarter *n.* quarter of the year D6*. *as adj.* eight-bushel D669.
quod *pa. t. 1 sg.* said D13*, D740; *pa. t. pl.* C92*.
qweeme *v.* please C397*.
qweynte *adj. make it* ~ make an issue of it D15*.
qwyt *adj.* quit, free C284*, D305.
qwyten *pr. pl.* repay D578; **qwit** *pp.* paid back D668.
qwook *pa. t. 1 sg.* quaked, shook C151*.

rakil *adj.* rash D655.
raue *pr. 1 sg.* am raving C264*.
recche *pr. 1 sg.* care C307*.
receit *n. hir* ~ what they receive D189*.
reconsiliacioun *n.* restoration to favour C58*.
rede(n) *v.* advise D719; read D226*; **rede** *pr. 1 sg.* advise D32*, D300, 389, 395; read D157*; *pr. pl.* advise D50*; **redde** *pa. t.* advised D801; read D17*, 41*, D317; **red** *pp.* advised D460; read C314*, 372*, D783.
reed *n.* counsel, advice C125*, 340*, D237*, D386, 450, 452.

reewe *v.* regret D166*; take pity D414, 415; *pr. 2 sg. subj.* regret D385.
refeere *v.* recur D49*.
reft *pp.* taken C229*.
refuse *v.* renounce D403.
regne *pr. 3 sg. subj.* reign D133*.
reherce *v.* report D76*, D582, 764; *imp. sg.* D27*; *pa. t.* mentioned D100*.
reioisynge *n.* cause for celebration C281*.
rekenynge *n.* reckoning D230*.
rekke *pr. 3 sg. subj.* care D625.
rekne *v.* ~ *of* reckon up D221*.
releef *n.* relief D62*.
releeued *pp.* relieved D63*, D329.
remembre *pr. 1 sg. me* ~ call to mind D526.
remissioun *n.* forgiveness D689.
renne *v.* run D630; ~ *in* incur D746.
renoun *n.* renown D580, 602.
rente *n.* income D281.
repeire *v.* return C278*.
repente *v.* repent C136*, 403*, D721; *him* ~ D663; *pr. 1 sg.* C371*; *thee* ~ *pr. 2 sg. subj.* D385.
replicacioun *n.* rejoinder D435.
reportour *n.* reporter D761.
repreef *n.* reproof D55*, D357, 671, 730.
repreeuable *adj.* objectionable C167*.
resonable *adj.* reasonable C168*, D442.
resorte *v.* return C88*, 391*.
resoun *n.* reason C221*, 312*, 315*; **reson** D732; a reasonable thing D472.
resounlees *adj.* irrational C125*, 222*.
respyt *n. putte in* ~ set aside D306.
restelees *adj.* restless C194*.
restreynt *n.* restraining influence D207*.
retenance *n.* retinue C272*.
reuers *n.* opposite C258*, D735.
rial *adj.* royal D274.
richesse *n.* wealth D281.
riotous *adj.* troublesome, unruly C67*.
ripnesse *n.* ripeness D808; ~ *of* readiness for D247*.
ro *n.* roe deer C128*.
rogh *adj.* rough D286.
Romayn *adj.* Roman D820.
Roon Rouen D610.
roop *n.* rope D401.
roote *n.* root C7*,
routhe *n.* pity D151*.
rowe *n.* row, company C124*.
rowned *pp.* whispered D185*.

GLOSSARY

rule *v.* ~ *him* govern himself D654; *pr. 3 sg. subj.* D394.

sad *adj.* settled D366, 558.
sadnesse *n.* stability C126*.
say *see* sy.
sak *n.* sack D669.
Salomon Solomon D351, 391, 457; **Salomons** *gen.* D451.
salue *n.* salve, soothing remedy C328*, 408*.
sanz *prep.* ~ *faille* without fail D461.
satisfaccion *n.* satisfaction, penance D666.
sauf *prep.* save; subject to D661.
saut *n.* leap C162*.
sauuacioun *n.* salvation C61*.
sauage *adj.* cruel C86*.
sawe *n.* words D764.
scant *adj.* sparing D469.
science *n.* knowledge D86*.
sclendre *adj.* slender, slight D366.
scourgid *pp.* scourged C23*, 362*.
scripture *n.* writing D699.
secree *n.* secret C100*.
secte *n.* crew D191*.
seeche *imp. sg.* seek D658; **soghte** *pa. t. 1 sg.* sought C195*; **soghte(n)** *pa. t. pl.* undertook C48*; searched out C133*.
seege *n.* siege D569, 610.
seek *adj.* sick D88*; **seeke** *pl.* C213*. *as n.* the seeke the sick person C237*.
seeknesse *n.* sickness C22*, 38*, 86*, D290, 314, 376.
seel *n.* seal; *priuee* ~ privy seal C296*.
seelden *adv.* seldom D374.
seeme *v.* seem D144*; **seemeth** *pr. 3 sg.* C240*, D510, 590, 728.
seende *pr. 3 sg. subj.* send D791.
seene *adj.* evident D312, 812.
seye, seyn *v.* say C78*, 171*, 181*, D619, 714, 765; *is to* ~ is to be interpreted as D597; **seye** *pr. 1 sg.* D412, 413; **seith** *pr. 3 sg.* D330, 344, 378; **seye, seyn** *pr. pl.* D37*, 150*, 186*, D747; **seide** *pa. t.* C98*, 120*, 122*, D365, 451, 724; **seid** *pp.* C78*, D37*, D387, 472, 518; said (*in rhyme*) C377*, D755.
selue *adj. wk.* *þat* ~ *same* the selfsame D731.
sent *n.* smelling C325*.
sentement *n.* feeling D252*.
sentence *n.* opinion D47*; maxim D451.

sepulture *n.* burial C266*.
serchynge *vbl. n.* searching; ~ *of* investigation into D431.
sese *pr. 3 sg. subj.* seize C346*.
sete *n.* seat, place D145*, D265.
sette *v.* set; ~ *by* pay regard to D169*; *pr. 3 sg. subj.* ~ *him adoun* submit D736; **set** *pp.* ~ *the lesse by* paid less regard to C379*.
seur *adj.* sure C166*, 370*, D519.
shadwe *n.* shadow C321*, D276.
shal *pr. 1 & 3 sg.* shall C12*, 13*, 173*, D286, 288, 343; **shalt** *pr. 2 sg.* D371, 626, 649; **shuln** *pr. pl.* D188*, 233*, D320, 710; **shul** D285; **shole** D283; **sholde** *pa. t.* C132*, 327*, D87*, D536, 564, 588; **sholdest** *pa. t. 2. sg.* C365*, D721, 794.
sheelde *pr. 3 sg. subj.* forbid C216*.
shent *pp.* ruined D642.
shewen *v.* show D707; **shewid** *pp.* D95*, 185*.
shoon *pa. t. 3 sg.* shone C24*.
shoop *pa. t. 3 sg.* turned out C98*, 373*; ~ *me pa. t. 1 sg.* prepared to D802; **shapen** *pp.* shaped D824.
shour *n.* shower C25*.
shoue *v.* drive away D343; *imp. sg.* push D617.
shrewes *n. pl.* villains D141*.
shrifte *n.* confession D83*.
sy *pa. t. 1 sg.* saw C22*, 74*, 310*, D821; **say** (*in rhyme*) D781; **sy** *pa. t. 3 sg.* C401*; *pa. t. pl.* C77*, 79*, 290*.
syke *v.* sigh C389*.
sikir *adv.* certainly D512, 540, 723.
sikirnesse *n.* certainty, security C110*.
syn *adv.* since C57*.
syn *conj.* since C22*, 96*, 176*, D382, 662, 677; ~ *þat* D58*, 140*, D288, 396, 492.
sythe *n.* time D177*; *ofte* ~ oftentimes C295*.
sythen *adv.* since C379*.
sitte *v.* sit; be appropriate D815; **sit** *pr. 3 sg. it* ~ it is appropriate (for) D663, 704.
skile *n.* device, method C340*.
sleeth *pr. 3 sg.* kills C354*.
slipir *adj.* slippery, unsafe D354.
slouthe *n.* sloth, slackness D152*.
smal *adj.* thin D123*; little C147*, D432. *as n.* little C264*.
smal *adv.* little D118*, 169*, D758.
smert *n.* pain D409.

smerte v. suffer C367*, D693; smertith
pr. 3 sg. D650; smerted pp. hurt D651.
smit pr. 3 sg. smites C113*.
so conj. ~ þat provided that D627.
sodeyn adj. sudden D439.
softe adv. softly C178*.
soghte(n) see seeche.
soiourne v. remain C306*.
soleyn adj. as n. morose or sullen person
D742.
someres n. pl. summers C96*.
sonne n. sun C25*.
sonner adv. compar. sooner D283.
soonde n. Goddes ~ what God has sent
D522.
soote adj. sweet D271.
sooth adj. true D279, 365, 656.
soothe adj. as n. truth C199*, 212*, 253*,
D465; for ~ indeed 473.
soothfastnesse n. truth D427.
soothly adv. truly D78*, D535, 616, 633.
sope n. soap D826.
sore adv. bitterly, painfully C18*, 30*,
71*, 367*, D385; severely, exceedingly
C46*, 62*, D326, 328, 336; vigorously
D2*.
sory adj. wretched D403.
sorwe n. sorrow C386*, D262; pl. C332*.
souffyse pr. 1 sg. suffice, am adequate
D613.
souffrable adj. long-suffering, patient
C354*, D369.
souffrance n. long-suffering, patience
C349*, 384*.
sour adj. sour, bitter D285.
souerain adj. sovereign C236*.
sowe pp. sown, widespred D423.
sownde adj. pl. healthy C213*.
sowneth pr. 3 sg. ~ to tends towards D758.
space n. period of time C51*.
spak see speke.
special adj. as n. in ~ in particular D159*,
D582.
specialtee n. of verray ~ as a mark of
special favour D593.
spectacle n. eye-glass D96*.
speke pr. 3 sg. subj. D333, 652; spak,
speek pa. t. 1 sg. D9*, D772; spak pa.
t. 3 sg. C85*, 130*, 337*; speke pa. t. pl.
C150*, D44*.
spilt pp. ruined, lost C368*.
spredith pr. 3 sg. spreads D170*; spred
pp. spoken of D58*.

stablisshid pp. established, settled D307.
stande, stonde v. stand D294, 679, 686;
pr. 1 sg. C189*; standith, stant pr. 3 sg.
D318, 468, 478; stood pa. t. 3 sg. C45*,
298*, D29*, D659; standen, stonde pp.
D34*, D468.
statut n. statute D136*.
steer n. young ox C120*.
stikith pr. 3 sg. sticks D775.
style n. reputation, name D579.
stille adv. quietly C291*.
stynte(n) v. cease D361, 434, 508; pr. 1 sg.
C336*.
stired pa. t. stirred, prompted D232*.
stirynge vbl. n. prompting D437.
stirte v. fall D303; pa. t. forth ~ jumped
about C128*.
stirtes n. pl. by ~ by fits and starts D505.
stithie n. anvil D440.
stonde see stande.
stoon n. stone D558.
straunge adj. distant C70*.
strecche v. stretch D499, 595; streighte
pa. t. 1 sg. ~ vnto reached for C157*.
streight adv. immediately C119*, D14*.
strook n. stroke C328*, 355*, D54*, 79*,
D350.
studie n. study D302, 379, 398; in a ~
pondering D659.
sturdy adj. refractory, obstinate D692.
sue v. follow C321*.
suffre v. endure C280*; imp. sg. permit
D20*.
sum indef. pron. some D315, 623.
sum indef. adj. some C243*, D547.
sumdel adv. somewhat C281*, D248*,
D675.
sumtyme adv. formerly C106*, D254.
sumwhat n. a certain amount D107*,
D757; something D673. as adv. some-
what D216*.
suspectly adv. in suspect fashion C292*.
susteene v. bear D475; pr. 1 sg. C363*.
swal pa. t. 3 sg. swelled C29*.
swart adv. black; ~ wrooth full of black
anger D756.
swerd n. sword D583.
swete v. sweat C187*; pr. 3 pl. D144*.
swetnesse n. sweetness C328*, D258.
swich adj. such C59*, 88*, 253*, D299,
302, 375; swiche pl. C257*.
swynke v. labour D241*; pr. 3 pl. D144*.

swythe *adv.* quickly; *as* ~ straightaway C274*.

swoot *n.* sweat C153*

taast *n.* tasting C204*, 325*.

taaste *v.* taste, test C210*; taastith *pr. 3 sg.* savours, takes pleasure D250*; taastid *pp.*tested C241*, D485.

tables *n. pl.* writing tablets C268*.

taght *pp.* taught C376*, D399.

take(n) *v.* take C65*, D520, 605; ~ *vpon him* undertake D447; ~ *on thee* accept D718; *pr. 1 sg.* understand C394*; takist *pr. 2 sg. thee* ~ *amis* misunderstand C364*; take *pr. 3 subj.* ~ *on him* undertake D480; token, took *pa. pl.* ~ *hem (a)mis* misunderstood C94*, 283*; take(n) *pp.* C384*, D598.

tale *n.* discourse D198*; *pl.* D762.

tamende *prep. + v.* to amend C406*.

tendreliche *adv.* attentively, scrupulously D220*.

thank *n.* thanks, gratitude C407*, 411*, D82*, D791; *his* ~ thanks due to him D587; ~ *of* thanks for C409*, 410*.

thanne *adv.* then C89*, D136*, 209*, D308, 628; than D539.

þat *pron.* that which D22*, D412, 525, 631; ~ *þat* D801.

theffect *def. art. + n.* the effecting D502.

thende *def. art. + n.* the end C17*, D200*.

thens *adv.* thence D570.

thepistle *def. art. + n.* the epistle D754.

there *adv.* there; ~ *as þat* where D313.

therfore *adv.* of that D749.

therfrom *adv.* from that D131*.

therin *adv.* in that D501, 609, 757.

therto *adv.* to that D132*, 212*, 231*, D297, 308, 392.

therwith *adv.* with that D195*, D647; in addition D202*.

therwithal *adv.* with that C31*, D630; furthermore C169*.

theschaunge *def. art. + n.* the exchange D124*.

thexcitynge *def. art. + n.* the inducement D234*.

thidir *adv.* thither D146*.

thyng *n.* thing; *any* ~ at all D52*; *no* ~ not at all C167*, D564.

thynke(n) *v.* think C365*, D55*, D729; *pr. 1 sg.* intend (to) C280*, 387*, D83*, D792; thoghte *pa. t.* thought C32*, 169*, 185*, D443; intended (to) C372*, D15*, D561, 773.

thynkith *pr. 3 sg. impers.* it seems D4*, D490, 702; thoghte *pa. t.* it seemed C147*, 158*; *pers.* seemed D255.

tho *pron. demons. pl.* those C356*, D71*, 72*.

tho *adj. demons. pl.* those C91*, D188*, D767.

tho *adv.* then D59*.

thoght *n.* anxiety C19*.

thoghtful *adj.* anxious, full of anxiety C21*, 184*, 388*, D398.

Thomas D10*, 20*, 25*, 199*, 203*, 295, 369, 415, 449, 473, 484, 512, 539, 620, 624, 628, 649, 661, 698, 703, 721, 739, 743, 749, 754, 781, 782, 785, 797.

threew *pa. t. 3 sg.* threw C42*; throwe *pp.* D195*.

thridde *adj. as n.* third C124*.

thriste *v.* strike C13*.

throwe *n.* time D649.

throwe *see* threew.

thurgh *prep.* through C393*, D215*, D260, 588, 725.

tyde *v.* turn out D644.

title *n.* claim D132*.

titled *pa. t.* entitled D594.

to *adv.* too C122*, 302*; ~ *and* ~ more and more C30*.

toffende *prep. + v.* to offend D21*.

torne *v.* turn C140*; tourne (*in rhyme*) C303*; *pr. 3 sg.* D259.

touche *v.* touch; ~ *of* allude to D52*; *pr. 2 sg. subj.* D31*.

trauaille *n. do* ~ make an effort D348.

trauaille *v.* labour D527.

trees *n. pl.* gallows D402.

treewe *adj.* true D163*, 179*, 230*, D540, 598, 798.

treewely *adv.* truly D433.

trespace *pr. 1 sg.* commit an offence D816.

trete *v.* treat, D547; tretith *pr. 3 sg.* D562; trete *imp. sg.* D441.

tretice *n.* treatise D205*, 225*.

triacle *n.* remedy D93*.

tryce *v.* snatch D208*; *pp.* D265.

troubly *adj.* full of trouble C302*.

trouthe *n.* honesty D119*, 195*; truth D767.

trowe *v.* believe C123*, D486; *pr. 1 sg.* C206*, D528, 646, 782; trowest *pr. 2 sg.*

D624; **trowe(n)** *pr. pl.* D148*, D421, 809.

trussid *pa. t.* packed; ~ *me my weye* packed myself off C145*.

Tullius Marcus Tullius Cicero D344.

tweyne *num.* two D18*.

twixt *prep.* between C247*, D739.

vndirnome *pp.* rebuked D455.

vndirstande *pp.* understood D774.

vndirtake *pr. 1 sg.* guarantee D788.

vnfeyned *ppl. adj.* truthful, frank C297*.

vnhad *pp.* not having been obtained D135*.

vnhappy *adj.* unfortunate C327*.

vnkonnynge *n.* lack of skill D588.

vnlust *n.* disinclination D537.

vnpyke *v.* pick (a lock) C387*.

vnreke *pp.* displayed D197*.

vnsadde *adj. pl.* unsettled C255*.

vnto *prep.* to; until D224*, D356.

vntrouthe *n.* dishonesty D149*.

vntrust *n.* distrust D335, 336.

vnwaar *adj.* unaware C91*, 375*.

vnwasshen *pp.* unwashed D182*.

vnweeldy *adj.* weak, feeble D248*.

vpbreide *pr. pl. subj.* reproach D787.

vsage *n.* practice D606.

variance *n.* changefulness C10*, D371.

varie *v.* vary D765.

Vegece Vegetius D561.

venym *n.* poison C234*, D170*.

verray *adj.* very C151*; real, true C333*, D328, 332, 344.

vertu *n.* power C52*.

vexid *pp.* afflicted C184*, D336.

vilenye *n.* dishonour D730.

visitacioun *n.* visitation C382*, D96*.

visyte *v.* visit D792; afflict C104*; *pr. 3 sg.* C37*.

voide *imp. sg.* discharge C339*; **voidid** *pa. t.* C234*.

waar *adj.* aware D652; *be* ~ beware D158*, D668, 749.

waar *imp. sg.* beware (of) D25*, 210*.

waastith *pr. 3 sg.* decays D249*.

wan *pa. t. 3 sg.* won D572, 576.

wasshe *v.* wash D182*; *pp.* washed D106*.

wasshynge *vbl. n.* washing D116*.

weel *adv.* well C298*, D261, 797; **wel** C313*, D279, 298, 307.

weende *v.* go D790.

weene *v.* suppose D476; *pr. pl.* C105*, D811; **wende** *pa. t.* C106*, D521, 784.

weet *adj.* wet C153*.

weye *n.* way D51*.

weye *v.* weigh D137*, D417, 600; *pr. pl.* hoist D402; *pr. subj.* weigh D54*, 103*; **weyed** *pa. t.* weighed D135*.

weyue *v.* avoid C15*; reject D105*, D450.

wele *n.* prosperity C267*.

welthe *n.* well-being, prosperity C338*, 396*, 409*, D275.

wende *see* weene.

werkers *n. pl.* performers D156*.

werre *n.* war D818.

werre *adj. compar. as n.* worse; *me putte atte* ~ get the better of me D819.

werreyour *n.* warrior D67*.

wers(e) *adj. compar.* worse C193*, D141*, D408.

Westmynstre Westminster C72*, 183*.

wexe *v.* grow D355.

whan *conj.* when C72*, 105*, 108*, D258, 277, 287; ~ *þat* C114*, 155*, D208*, D505, 507.

whanne *adv.* when C104*, D210*.

what *pron. indef.* whatever C279*; ~ *is yow* whatever is the matter with you D316.

what *adj. indef.* whatever C319*, D524.

what *exclam.* what, why D5*, D322, 454, 616.

whatso *pron. indef.* whatever C142*, D333, 489, 747; **what . . .so** C99*.

whens *conj.* whence C55*.

wherthurgh *adv.* as a result of which C258*, D471, 795.

whethir *conj.* whether C213*, 298*, D611, 678.

why *adv. as n.* why; *doon* ~ given cause D752.

whidir *adv.* whithersoever C319*.

whyle *n.* time C314*, D578.

whyt *adj. as n.* white D670.

who *pron. indef.* whoever D638, 653.

whoso *pron. indef.* whoever D330, 600, 629; ~ *þat* C116*, D764, 768.

wight *n.* person C69*, 83*, D336, 343, 375; *gen.* C14*.

wyldenesse *n.* disturbed state C107*.

wyldhede *n.* disturbed state D52*.

wyldid *pp.* driven wild C235*.

wirke *v.* work D647; act D450; **wroghte**

pa. t. acted C156*; **wroght** *pp.* performed D222*, D642.

wys *adj.* wise C240*, 252*, 385*, D261, 511, 640; **wyse** *pl.* D279, 681.

wyse *n.* fashion C118*, 156*, 275*, D512, 614; *othir* ~ otherwise D427.

wisly *adv.* surely D413, 806.

wist(e) *see* wite.

wit *n.* mind C59*, 64*, 207*, D406, 497; intelligence, judgement D223*, D366, 382, 450; prudent course C115*, 340*; **wittes** *gen.* mind's D440; *pl.* mental powers C213*, 229*, 255*, D494.

wyte *n.* blame D667*.

wite *v.* know C204*; **woot** *pr. 1 & 3 sg.* C100*, 206*, D7*, D261, 463, 488; **woost** *pr. 2 sg.* D298, 638, 667; **woot** *pr. pl.* D456; **wiste** *pa. t. subj.* knew C175*, D552; **wist** *pp.* C200*, 214*, 303*, D525.

withdrawe(n) *pp.* withdrawn C87*, D80*, D310.

withynne *adv.* indoors C293*.

withoute *adv.* outdoors C293*.

withoute(n) *prep.* without D619, 639.

witnesse *n.* ~ *vpon* witness C40*; *to* ~ as witness D567.

witnesse *v.* witness, vouch for D49*; *pr. subj.* D733.

wole *pr. 1 & 3 sg.* will C88*, 93*, 119*, D297, 308, 326; **wilt** *pr. 2 sg.* C360*, D492, 646, 686; **wole** *pr. pl.* C192*, D104*, 105*, D737; **wolde** *pa. t. 1 & 3 sg.* C160*, D89*, D340, 355, 390; **woldest** *pa. t. 2 sg.* D380, 476; **wolde(n)** *pa. t. pl.* C65*, 143*, 181*, D669; **wold** *pp.* wished D570.

wondir *adv.* amazingly, very D257.

wondirly *adv.* amazingly, very C325*.

wondrynge *n.* distress C188*, 305*.

wondryngly *adv.* with wonderment C150*.

wont *adj.* accustomed C75*.

woonde *imp. sg.* hesitate D523.

woost, woot *see* wite.

worthy *adj.* noble, honourable D568, 573, 579; *am* ~ deserve C368*.

wowndith *pr. 3 sg.* wounds C356*.

wrastle *imp. sg.* wrestle C342*.

wrecche *n.* miserable creature D815.

wreke *v. me* ~ take vengeance C280*.

wryte *v.* write D508, 524, 636; *pr. subj.* D333, 652; **wroot** *pa. t. 1 & 3 sg.* D134*, D583, 762; **write(n)** *pp.* C203*, D671, 698.

wroght(e) *see* wirke.

wroot *see* wryte.

wrooth *adj.* angry D20*, D756.

yaf *see* yeue.

yate *n.* gate D213*.

yee *pron. 2 pl. nom.* you C268*, 272*, D39*, D322, 323, 329.

yee *adv.* yea, yes (*in response to open questions*) D24*, 203*, D540.

yeeme *n.* notice C396*.

yeer *n. pl.* years C56*, D192*, D446.

yeue *v.* give C126*, D324, 629; *pr. 1 sg.* D516; **yeueth** *pr. 3 sg.* C237*, D332; **yeue** *pr. sg. subj.* D291; **yaf** *pa. t. 3 sg.* gave C312*, 395*, 398*; **yeue(n)** *pp.* given D73*, 149*, D269.

yifte *n.* gift D84*; *pl.* C412*.

yilde *pr. sg. subj.* ~ *it* reward for it C49*, D558; ~ *thee imp. sg.* submit D698; **yildynge** *pr. p.* ~ *thee* confessing yourself D688.

yis *adv.* yes (*in response to negative questions or statements*) D81*, D295, 473, 535.

yit *adv.* yet C52*, 94*, 221*, D311, 315, 369; still C208*; hereafter D410.

yore *adv.* long ago D4*, D321.